Black and Brown
Education in America

Culture, Humanity, and Urban Life

Series Editors: Jessica Bodoh-Creed (California State University) and Melissa King (San Bernardino Valley College)

Mission Statement

How are urban processes entangled with human experiences? In the *Culture, Humanity, and Urban Life* series, scholarly monographs and edited volumes explore this question and illuminate diverse forms of such entanglement through empirically-based research. This series emphasizes anthropological approaches to the study of human life in relation to the urban. It seeks to illuminate experiences and effects of urban cultures and situate specific cases in a comparative set. By exploring the intricacies of human-urban relations, this series contributes to better understanding of the ways that humans particularly conceive of and experience nature, personhood, ethics, culture, and social life.

Books in Series

Black and Brown Education in America: Integration in Schools, Neighborhoods, and Communities, by Samina Hadi-Tabassum and Persis Driver

Metropolitan Intimacies: An Ethnography on the Poetics of Daily Life, by Francisco Cruces

The Belfast Imaginary: Artists and Urban Reinvention, by Katherine Keenan

The Everyday Life of Urban Inequality: Ethnographic Case Studies of Global Cities, edited by Angela D. Storey, Megan Sheehan, and Jessica Bodoh-Creed

Urban Mountain Beings: History, Indigeneity, and Geographies of Time in Quito, Ecuador, by Kathleen S. Fine-Dare

Black and Brown Education in America

Integration in Schools, Neighborhoods, and Communities

Samina Hadi-Tabassum and Persis Driver

LEXINGTON BOOKS
Lanham • Boulder • New York • London

Published by Lexington Books
An imprint of The Rowman & Littlefield Publishing Group, Inc.
4501 Forbes Boulevard, Suite 200, Lanham, Maryland 20706
www.rowman.com

86-90 Paul Street, London EC2A 4NE

British Library Cataloguing in Publication Information Available

Library of Congress Cataloging-in-Publication Data

Names: Hadi-Tabassum, Samina, 1971- author. | Driver, Persis, 1980- author.
Title: Black and brown education in America : integration in schools, neighborhoods, and communities / Samina Hadi-Tabassum and Persis Driver.
Description: Lanham, Maryland : Lexington Books, 2023. | Series: Culture, humanity, and urban life | Includes bibliographical references and index.
Identifiers: LCCN 2022054166 (print) | LCCN 2022054167 (ebook) |
    ISBN 9781666900767 (cloth) | ISBN 9781666900774 (ebook)
Subjects: LCSH: African American children—Education—Illinois—Maywood. | Hispanic American children—Education—Illinois—Maywood. | Racism in education—Illinois—Maywood. | Discrimination in education—Illinois—Maywood. | School integration—Illinois—Maywood. | Community and school—Illinois—Maywood.
Classification: LCC LC2803.M38 H34 2023 (print) | LCC LC2803.M38 (ebook) |
    DDC 371.829/009773—dc23/eng/20221207
LC record available at https://lccn.loc.gov/2022054166
LC ebook record available at https://lccn.loc.gov/2022054167

I want to thank my family for supporting me on this second book that took time away from them as they sat patiently for me to close the laptop: my children Najda, Salma, and Yusef, and my husband, Bartholomew. I want to thank the Maywood teachers who were in my graduate classes for their insights and opportunities to observe them teach and get to know their students over time.
Samina Hadi-Tabassum

Thank you to my unconditionally supportive family, my husband, Tushad, and my children, Rayhan and Anahita for encouraging my involvement and effort in this integral project. Most importantly, thank you to my coauthor, Samina, for being an inspirational force and a catalyst in my professional life.
Persis Driver

Contents

List of Figures

List of Tables

Preface

According to the literary theorist Mikhail Bakhtin (1982), we spend our entire lives trying to answer the question "Who am I?" and how we define ourselves and our multiple and competing voices and images. Both authors identify themselves as South Asian American but have different journeys and identity markers while being heavily influenced by race, culture, and language on a personal and professional level. Samina Hadi-Tabassum was born in Hyderabad, India, to a Muslim family and lived in the old city with her intergenerational household and without electricity and running water. Her father was an engineer and had first migrated to Iran for work and then to Chicago as a part of the post-1965 Asian immigration policy that opened doors to South Asian immigrants with backgrounds in math, science, medicine, and engineering.

Upon arrival, Samina's family moved to a white, working-class, inner-ring suburb outside of Chicago where they lived in Section-8 housing composed of hundreds of townhouses that eventually were torn down. Her father worked for the city as an engineer on an H1-Visa status and her mother worked the night shift in a perfume factory, barely making $26,000 a year combined and with four children. Samina became racialized on the first day of school when the white students called her siblings and her the N-word, bullied them, and often physically assaulted them in the hallways, gym lockers, and classrooms, often with their white teachers and administrators watching. By the time she was in high school, there were full-fledged race riots as the number of South Asian and Mexican American families grew in the 1980s and clashed with the white majority. Throughout her life, Samina identified with the minoritized community and the oppressed and still struggles with acceptance into white mainstream society.

After graduating from Northwestern University on a full scholarship, her career began as a middle school, bilingual science teacher in an under-resourced school in Houston, Texas, where she worked with first-generation immigrant students for four years. Then, while pursuing her doctorate at Teachers College, Columbia University, Samina worked as a literacy special-ist with the Newark, New Jersey school district, and mentored and coached first-year teachers in schools that were racially diverse but segregated. After receiving her doctorate, Samina returned to Chicago and became a professor at a Catholic university located near Maywood, Illinois, where the study takes place, a historically Black suburb located west of Chicago. There she devel-oped cohorts with the school district and taught hundreds of teachers in the district as they pursued their master's degree. Over time, she began noticing the changing demographics in the schools and the community as more Latinx families moved into Maywood. In turn, Samina collaborated with her then-graduate students and now colleague at the same university, Persis Driver, on this study.

Persis Driver identifies as an Asian Indian immigrant and naturalized citi-zen of the United States, a teacher, and an educational psychologist. Persis Driver merged an outsider researcher position with an emic ontological per-spective to the data in this book. Through her own experiences of obstacles and affordances within an overwhelmed immigration system that initially restricted work and other basic rights such as driving or owning property despite her legal status, she was able to bring an insider understanding of how and why immigrants in a new land might gravitate toward creating smaller, more intimate, and safe communities. Her professional journey from a teacher-in-training to an assistant professor is also one that has at times seemed propelled by social and political forces beyond her control. The chal-lenges of transcending cultural, social, and political spaces in a new land were real and intimate. Additionally, Persis brought a unique worldview as a member of a small, almost extinct, Zoroastrian community that originated in ancient Persia but was forced to seek refuge in India.

While the Zoroastrian community has thrived in India and made invalu-able contributions to the country's progress in all sectors, its members have also worked hard to retain their cultural identity, often consciously or uncon-sciously creating exclusive spaces that few outsiders are allowed to enter. Yet the impetus for these spaces has not just been self-preservation but also history as many of these spaces were created in response to a promise made to the very people providing refuge to the community, a promise to not dilute their culture. Persis' identity palimpsest, which has compelled her to navigate complex global relations between fitting in and standing out, drew her to this study first as a graduate research assistant and then as a psychology professor. As an instructor working with racially and socio-economically diverse and minoritized students in a large public university and then in a small, Hispanic Serving Institution, she is constantly learning about her students' local, lived experiences that both mirror and diverge from her own global experiences. Consequently, rather than a participant observer, she brought a historical, social, and educational lens to understanding the complex relations of race, space, and place to the large volume of qualitative data in this project.

Acknowledgments

The last decade in America has seen radical changes in its political and social landscape. Racial demographics are shifting, and our country is becoming a majority-minority nation, even though Black and Brown children still attend schools taught mostly by white middle-class female teachers. The privileged elite class moved the pendulum with all its powers so that we are now a nation of haves and have-nots with a depleting middle class and an economic infrastructure that does not serve the needs of the most vulnerable populations. Ongoing violence against Black and Brown communities led to the pivotal Black Lives Matter (BLM) Movement which changed our world and the perspectives in this book. The COVID pandemic highlighted the inequities in our country and who does and does not have access to health care, housing, food, and job security. Of course, the presidential elections highlighted the divisiveness in our country, the culture wars, and the polarizing politics that are destroying our communal identity and exasperating racial tensions. Against the backdrop of these macro and exo-level changes to our national landscape, our study took place in Maywood—a Black and Latinx suburban community outside of Chicago, which mirrored these changes at the micro level.

We want to acknowledge all the people who live and work in Maywood for sitting down with us and sharing their stories and childhood memories. We want to acknowledge all the teachers, students, parents, principals, and school administrators who agreed to this study and allowed us to enter their hallways, classrooms, and communal spaces. We want to thank the parents who informed us about their children's needs when we attended school board meetings and made sure we captured their voices, as well as the voices of the school and community leaders whom they wanted to hold accountable. We want to thank the faith-based organizations that are striving to connect Black and Brown communities in Maywood and bring coalitions together. We want to thank Michael Romain, a newspaper reporter and the director of the Village Free Press, whose writing and reporting make up much of this book. And, finally we want to thank the scholars and thinkers whose seminal work has paved the way for such meaningful dialogue and discourse.

We want to thank Dominican University, located in neighboring River Forest, our employer and supporter of faculty research. Dominican University is also trying to be a better neighbor by engaging with the faith-based communities in nearby Maywood and Melrose Park. In the end, we hope this book inspires us to reflect on who we are as a nation, as a community, as a neighbor, and on the ways in which we can provide love and nurture, security and stability, and address the needs of Black and Latinx children growing up in integrated suburbs and who will become the future leaders of our country.

Introduction

While scrolling through the social media pages on Facebook for the "I Love Maywood" site, where our study takes place, we noticed many posts from middle-aged residents, both Black and white, waxing nostalgic for the places in their childhood memories:

"You were the envy of your city cousins because you lived in the suburbs, and they always wanted to spend the night."

"Your Thanksgiving or Emancipation Proclamation service was more than 3 hours long because you were either a member of 1st or 2nd Baptist, Canaan, ROA, or MRC and their annual get together!!"

"You ever received medical treatment or had your ears pierced at Joslyn Clinic on St. Charles Rd and 20th Ave.?"

"You remember we didn't have to go out of the neighborhood to shop because the A&P was on St. Chas & 4th ave. and the Jewel was where Miracle Revival sits."

"You bought 45's, LP's and incense from either Reimer's or Bop City on 5th."

"Your parents got S&H green stamps and those flower decals from what used to be a full-service gas station on the corner of 19th & Madison."

"You remember the KFC on the corner of St. Charles & 5th with the big rotating bucket that later became Chicken Unlimited?"

"Your father got his hair cut at Baker's Barber Shop on 19th before the tracks and if it was a Friday, went next door to the fish market to get fresh catfish or buffalo."

"You partied at the rec center and saw someone's mother come up in rollers and a housecoat looking for their child who didn't have permission to be there!!"

"You'd go to the store across from the library on 5th to get penny candy and those little cookies with the pink glaze to bring back to the library to 'help you study'."

These Facebook posts were sometimes accompanied by grainy pictures of Maywood in its heyday from the 1930s through the 1960s of places and sites no longer there: art deco movie theaters, soda fountain shops, the Bataan Day parades commemorating WWII soldiers, brand new bungalows, and streetcars with overhead power lines. Bruce Zimmerman's family moved to Maywood from rural Indiana in 1956 and stayed until 1969 when white flight shifted the racial demographics of Maywood. His father, Robert L. Zimmerman, took this photo below of him at the Bataan Day Parade in Maywood on September 22, 1963.

After a few dozen posts, the nostalgia waned, and now there were posts about the demise of Maywood and how there is so much crime and gun

Figure 0.1   The Bataan Day Parade on September 22, 1963, on Fifth Avenue. *Source*: Robert L. Zimmerman.

Figure 0.2   The American Can Company Photograph, 1911. *Source*: Maywood Public Library.

violence, no grocery stores to buy fresh produce, and children who no longer have use for imagination. One person posted about the smell on the morning that the American Can Factory was destroyed by a fire—a company that had produced most of the world's beer and soda cans and set up a factory site in Maywood in 1901, employing thousands of men and women. The factory shut down in 1975, laid off close to 8,000 workers, and started the economic decline that led to white flight and the imminent loss of good-paying jobs for Black middle-class residents (Sjostrom, 2005).

There were also posts about unsolved murders from the death of a nine-year-old Black child inside her own home on St. Charles Avenue in the 1980s to a white police officer sitting in his parked car on a notorious drug corner at night also near St. Charles Avenue in 2006. Some posts complained about rising taxes, awful potholes, garbage pickup delays, and fallen trees left on the streets from a storm. But there were always positive posts about high school graduates selected into top colleges, remembering beloved community members who recently passed away, celebrating native sons like singer John Prine and basketball coach Doc Rivers, and where to get the best food in Maywood from BBQ to tacos.

Sharing these stories of Maywood brought comfort to many of the online members who grew up in Maywood while also reflecting the racial politics from the 1970s to the 1980s that shifted Maywood from a predominantly white suburb to a predominantly Black suburb. The history of segregation and the fundamental contradiction of post-WWII suburbs like Maywood point to the persistence of racism and political fragmentation, while also showing growth in terms of opportunity and economic mobility for Black and Brown communities (King, 2017). Now, in 2022, Maywood is shifting again in its composition to becoming a predominantly Latinx community, reflecting the changing landscape of our country, and leading to shifts in school and community demographics and identities. On the Maywood Unido page on Facebook, there are not any posts waxing nostalgic for the Maywood of yesteryears; rather, the bilingual posts of recent Latinx arrivals highlight instead upcoming community events, job prospects, and local politics.

THE SHIFTING DEMOGRAPHICS

The Latinx population makes up 18.5% of the US population and constitutes the largest racial minority group, outnumbering the Black population at 13.4% of the US population (US Census Bureau, 2019). The national growth in the Latinx population has been accompanied by a growth in the Latinx student population. From 1996 to 2016, the number of Latinx students enrolled in schools, colleges, and universities in the United States doubled from 8.8 million to 17.9 million. Latinx students now make up 22.7% of all individuals enrolled in school. The percentage of Latinx students in elementary schools (Grades 1–8) went from 14.1% to 25.0%, high school went from 13.2% to 23.7%, and college and university students went from 8.0% to 19.1% (US Census Bureau, 2019).

According to the National Center for Education Statistics (2017), close to 48% of white students were enrolled in public schools that were composed of students of their own race (i.e., 75% or more of enrollment was white), while only 6% of white students were enrolled in schools in which less than a quarter of the students were white. About 25% of Black students were enrolled in public schools that were predominantly Black, while 32% of Black students were enrolled in schools in which less than a quarter of the students were Black. Similarly, 32% of Latinx students were enrolled in public schools that were predominantly Latinx, while 21% were enrolled in schools in which less than a quarter of the students were Latinx. Over half of Black and Latinx students attended public schools in which the combined enrollment of minoritized students was at least 75% of total enrollment, leading to the phenomenon of majority-minority schools.

There are no studies that show that Latinx schoolchildren are fleeing their communities due to integration with Black students, and there is no extensive documentation of a "Latino flight" phenomenon; however, there is some evidence that Latinx students enroll in private schools in response to larger concentrations of Black students in low-performing neighborhood schools (Fairlie, 2002). The Latinx community may have different racial attitudes than whites in relation to school integration and may differ in personal prejudice toward Black school children and their families. Furthermore, the majority of Latinx school mobility is based on economic reasons and families moving closer to job prospects rather than the racial composition of a new community and school and changing demographics (Fairlie, 2002).

There has also been a decrease in segregation between the white and Black population due to attitudinal change, the growth of the Black middle-class, regional population shifts, and the growth of multiethnic metropolises like Houston and Phoenix, places in the West and South where there is less segregation. There were no court rulings or laws that led to less residential segregation between white and Black populations, and white neighbors are still rated much higher than any other racial group (Logan, Stults, & Farley, 2004). The absence of Black residents in a neighborhood often prevents future Black residents from seeking housing in that neighborhood and therefore there is no pressing demand from Black individuals in all-white communities for further integration. Black middle-class families did tend to move to the suburbs outside major cities like Chicago and live in suburban neighborhoods with white families. Latinx families are also moving to live in suburbs outside of major cities and therefore helping to reduce segregation.

In addition, segregation between the white and Latinx populations increased while the proportion of Latinx residents in historically Black communities rose more rapidly. White people's perceptions of living alongside other races depend on the size of the minoritized population, and as the group becomes larger in size, the negative attitude toward that group increases as well—as the composition of the country changes so does the racist attitudes (Alba, Rumbaut, & Marotz, 2005). We can also refer to the "tipping point" phenomena in racial segregation and how Thomas Schelling's (1971) famous mathematical model showed white families leaving when the minoritized population ranges from 5% to 20% in the neighborhood, along with the speculation and belief of increasing racial integration. Yet, white residents often misperceive the sizes of racial minority groups, inflating their numbers to implausible measures and lack enough interracial contacts that this exaggeration or "innumeracy" often leads to a heightened degree of threat such as a loss of white power and representation in all social spheres (Nadeau, Niemi, & Levine, 1993).

In turn, Orfield (2003, 2016) states that the largest percentage of racial integration in the last decades includes Black and Latinx integration, while the smallest increase has been in white and Latinx integration: "The share of Blacks living in Black/Latino neighborhoods rose from 18 percent to 28 percent" (p. 5). Latinx school children have a greater likelihood of interacting with Black school children than they do with white school children due to geographic segregation, with lower levels of segregation between Black and Latinx children than between Black and white children. Majority-minority schools also show a rise in double segregation by race and poverty for Black and Latinx students who are concentrated in schools that face impoverishment and opportunity gaps, unlike predominantly middle-class schools with largely white and Asian student populations. Yet, when we think of racial integration, we think of integration between Black and white students rather than integration between Black and Latinx students.

Historically, significant struggles have occurred between the Black and Latinx populations over several national concerns in areas of political rights, economic means, social identity, and housing rights. Within the field of education, contentious arguments have occurred over political, cultural, and linguistic issues along with failing to recognize each minoritized group's own hidden racism against each other: whether we should support bilingual instruction in public schools and resentment over funds set aside for the linguistic needs of the Latinx student population; undocumented migrant students may not be supported by certain school districts; persistent attempts by both sides to break into the corridors of power within school boards; deciding who gets to preside over the Civil Rights Agenda in public schooling; the demands of inclusion into the school district's political and economic structures; a lack of race-based representation in terms of teachers, administrators, school board members; the degree of integration with each other; and curricular issues such as whether Black History and Culture should be mandated in public schools along with Latinx History and Culture.

The extant research on Black/Latinx race relations can be categorized into two frameworks: (a) the *shared interest perspective* framework is grounded in the ideology that both racial groups have shared interests and needs by virtue of their similar histories and minoritized status (Kauffman, 2003) while (b) the *heterogeneity principle* framework states that the Black and Latinx students' academic, cultural, psychological, and social experiences are unique and therefore demand heterogeneous approaches toward understanding their educational needs (Arias, 2005; Carter, 2006; Contreras, 2004). In the field of education, the shared interest perspective provides a powerful argument for Black/Latinx solidarity because both communities face the challenge of intense hypersegregation within public schools (Orfield, 2006), systemic inequities and opportunity gaps in relation to the white majority (Lee, 2008; Magnuson & Waldfogel, 2008), higher dropout rates (Konstantopoulos, 2006), disproportionate representation in Special Education and lower tracked courses (Oakes, 1995, 2008), inadequate funding, and poor teacher quality (Darling-Hammond et al., 2008).

The shared interest perspective has the potential for positive intergroup race relations between the two populations because of the stress of similar circumstances experienced by both groups as oppressed racial minorities within the white majority landscape. Common goals include higher educational opportunities, higher wages, better standard of living, better health care, and residential integration—all of which provide a seemingly logical foundation for interracial coalitions between Black and Latinx communities (Kauffman, 2003). Furthermore, Ladson-Billings (2007) states that an *education debt* has been accumulated by the school systems in this country toward students of disadvantaged minorities due to centuries of neglect, underfunded schooling, the denial of education, and the exclusion of entire groups of people from political decision making. Thus, the shared histories of oppression, exploitation, and discrimination within the American educational system could provide a form of solidarity in challenging hegemonic racial and economic disparities for both groups.

On January 15, 2007, for example, a collective solidarity march of Black and Latinx community members took place in Chicago after recent violence broke out between Black-Brown youth near the Little Village Lawndale High School. Train tracks and viaducts between the Latinx population in Little Village and the Black population in North Lawndale divided both communities but tensions rose in the 1990s when to relieve overcrowding, the Chicago public school district sent Latinx kids to a predominantly Black school. The Latinx parents protested that the solution is not that simple and that their children's culture, language, education, and safety are at stake (Cholo, 2004). There were no bilingual staff in the predominantly Black school. Other members of the Latinx community argued for racial integration and that this issue was not about racial divide but about ignorance. Meanwhile, the parents at the predominantly Black school welcomed the new students and had hurt feelings when they heard that the Latinx parents were not eager for this transition. There were much imagined and unfounded fears, even though both the Latinx school and the Black school were on academic watch and had the same academic standing:

The march and rally in 2007 were healing and focused on bringing together the two Lawndale neighborhoods: North Lawndale is predominately Black and is known for its history of political activism while South Lawndale, or Little Village, is a predominantly Mexican American community also known for its history of political activism.

The rally was followed by a "Solidarity March" through both communities to create unity around common goals and struggles, and to proactively respond to negative and divisive forces. "It doesn't make sense that we don't work more together. We all need affordable housing, jobs," he said. "There are things that we can learn from each other—strong cultural values in each group." Lisa Pugh, a North Lawndale resident and mother of a student at the high school, concurred. "We all have the same issues—not having enough money and getting our lights turned off. We all bleed red, eat the same food—it's prepared different, but it's the same. Even our children are dating one another, dancing together. They're together; they're united. It's not the children [who remain separated], it's the parents. King started the dream; it's up to us to keep the dream alive." (New Communities Program, 2007).

In 2016, a Chicago nonprofit organization, My Block * My Hood * My City, started youth-led tours in North Lawndale and Little Village that support the Black-Brown communities. Latinx teens in Little Village and Black teens in North Lawndale lead tourists around their respective communities where they live and provide a historical overview from an emic, insider perspective (Bauer, 2016). In La Villita, tourists can purchase T-shirts in Spanish that say "Mi Calle * Mi Barrio * Mi Cuidad"—a form of cultural commodification that has gained a bit of criticism from outside the community. However, we often hear just about the violence in communities like North Lawndale and Little Village, but the youth-led tours are designed to challenge stereotypes and to allow outsiders to see the complexities from within (Daniels, 2021).

On the other hand, some scholars have accurately pointed out that the experiences of Black and Latinx students in American public schools are heterogeneous because of the unique needs of both racial groups within the United States (Contreras, 2004; Hutchinson, 2007; Vaca, 2004). John Ogbu (2008) classified students in American public schools as autonomous, voluntary immigrant students like the Latinx students in Maywood who may have been discriminated against but are not oppressed like the involuntary migrant Black students in Maywood whose ancestors were enslaved against their will by whites, leading to the social inequities today. Thus, to bind both groups on the basis of ideological similarities or objective circumstances simply because of their shared status or shared histories overlooks the individual educational needs and interests of each group such as the need for language education or the need for a culturally congruent curriculum.

One area of contention has been the discourse of desegregation. The fight for equal educational opportunities and the subsequent focus on desegregation formed a major part of the Black struggle for Civil Rights. The 1954 *Brown v. Board of Education* decision that overturned the "separate but equal ruling" has traditionally been heralded as a victory and a major impetus for equal education legislation in the mid-twentieth century. More recently, scholars have argued that the Latinx American narrative within the struggle for school desegregation has been sidelined, marginalized, or completely ignored by society at large, often with an intense detrimental impact on Latinx student achievement.

The federal courts had ignored Latinx segregation from 1954 to 1973, even when it had clearly persisted, and instead concentrated on the segregation of Black students. According to Arias (2005), during the most prolific period of empirical research on the effects of desegregation on student outcomes, this indifference is due to Latinx students not being seen as the primary target of desegregation policy even though the majority were being educated in Mexican-only schools. In fact, in places like Kansas, Mexican Americans were classified by the federal government as "Caucasian" (even though the majority of Mexican Americans claim mestizo heritage composed of Spanish and indigenous ancestry) but local school districts and white parents used the decision-making power of school boards to force all Mexican American children to attend schools separate from white students (Donato & Hanson, 2017). When the Mexican Consulate protested this de facto segregation, the chief of police told the Mexican consul that Black establishments were open to Mexicans but not white establishments. Thus, Mexican Americans faced de facto segregation while their Black peers faced de jure segregation that was a federal law. The white population in the 1900s regarded the Latinx and Black students as one monolithic racial group and thus different from the newly arrived European immigrants who were seen as white, like them, even though there were cultural and linguistic differences.

Legal activism for desegregation by the Latinx community has nonetheless persisted throughout the twentieth century. Although the *Brown* decision provided much impetus for Latinx activism, it failed to provide any definitive steps to address the individual needs of Latinx school children and focused instead on Black school children. The famous 1947 *Mendez v. Westminster* case set a precedent for later court cases, such as *Brown v. Board of Education,* when the Mendez family in Westminster, California, claimed de facto segregation when the school district would not allow their daughter to attend school in the white majority area where they lived as a wealthy business family (Arriola, 1995; Moll, 2010). Thurgood Marshall legally represented nine-year-old Sylvia Mendez and the case went to the California Supreme Court when Earl Warren was the governor and who later became Chief Justice of the Supreme Court during the 1954 *Brown* case. The Mendez legal approach was to present social science research stating that segregation led to feelings of inferiority among Mexican American children, which was the same approach in the *Brown* case. Here the Mexican American community came together as a collective and won the case, thus heralding desegregation, but the *Mendez* case did not end up going all the way to the Supreme Court.

By 1970, the *Cisneros v. Corpus Christi* circuit court case found that Mexican Americans were an identifiable ethnic minority for desegregation on the basis of their physical characteristics, their Spanish language, their Catholic religion, their distinct culture, and their Spanish surnames, and thus the 1954 *Brown* decision applied to them as well (Contreras & Valverde, 1994). Prior to the *Cisneros* case, Mexican Americans were seen as white and therefore desegregation did not apply to them as racial minorities. In 1973, the US Supreme Court ruled in the *Keyes* case in Denver that Mexican Americans were victims of discrimination and that although they were a distinct class, they had much in common with the Black community by virtue of their objective disadvantage suffered and thus these disadvantages needed to be remedied through school desegregation (Horn & Kurlaender, 2006). The *Keyes* case also stated that schools with only Black and Latinx students, which we today call majority-minority schools, are not considered a form of desegregation. At the same time, the mere extension of school desegregation law to the Latinx community has often created unsatisfactory results for Latinx students whose diverse cultural and linguistic needs were often left out of the remedies designed to help them succeed academically. Consequently, Latinx activism for equal education has emphasized the implementation of bilingual instruction rather than the mere elimination of racial isolation (Arias, 2005; Contreras, 2004; Hutchinson, 2007; Vaca, 2004).

Bilingual education is another area of contention between the Black and Latinx communities. Black Americans are often portrayed as being opposed to bilingual education mainly because of the misperception that funding bilingual programs creates a strain on already limited financial resources—given the inequalities that exist in school funding, the vicious cycle of poverty, failing schools, and high taxation (Vaca, 2004). A second reason for opposition lies in the potential of bilingual programs to displace monolingual Black teachers in favor of those who have bilingual skills. Reactions of Black parents and community members in places where resistance to bilingual programs has manifested led to overt Black-Latinx political conflicts. Black voting behavior on restrictive propositions like the "English-only" movement has lent anecdotal and quantitative evidence of Black resistance to bilingual education (Bowler et al., 2006).

The "English-only" movement in the 1990s claimed that bilingual education is wasteful, costly, and ineffectual, and thus it effectively cut down any funding available for such programs through political initiatives like Proposition 187 in California. Public schools, teachers, and administrators who continued to defy the law were fined and sued. Although heavily supported by the divisive interests of politicians, elite agendas to establish and maintain white dominance and sentiments of resistance toward the Latinx minority-majority in California, the English-only movement received reasonable support from the Black community in California: In Miami, the birthplace of the English-only movement in 1980, 44% of Blacks supported this proposition, and in California, Proposition 187 was supported by 42% of Blacks (Franklin & Seltzer, 2002). Hutchinson (2003) goes so far as to state that Blacks were among the most vehement in protesting bilingual instruction because they felt it hurt their children the most.

In a 1997 *Time* magazine article, the volatile relationship between Latinx parents in the working-class town of East Palo Alto in California and its predominantly Black school board members captured the contentious debate surrounding bilingual education in which the Latinx parents were told to go back to Mexico, even though the school district was 70% Latinx (Ratnesar, 1997). The Latinx parents were also protesting the mediocre academic performance and the cronyism and graft evident in the district leadership. A similar situation in 1995 at Cooke Elementary School in Washington, DC, where neighborhood demographics transitioned from a predominantly Black neighborhood to one with an increasing number of Central American immigrants, led to discontent and friction over the matter of bilingual education. The issue was exacerbated when the urban school, which was in a working-class, low-income neighborhood, received a $1 million federal grant to enhance bilingual instruction. In the end, the politics of exclusion, practiced by both racial groups, appeared to have a stranglehold on any potential for intergroup cooperation during the 1990s when the demographics were shifting in major urban areas (Camarillo, 2007).

While there has always been a backlash against bilingual education, there has been equal resistance over the use of the Black dialect in schools due to the Oakland, California, ruling on the Ebonics case as well as judicial arguments during the 1954 *Brown v. Board of Education* trial. Several desegregation cases mentioned the distinctiveness of the Black dialect because Black children who have been segregated from the mainstream community will inevitably acquire "habits of speech, conduct, and attitudes reflecting their cultural isolation" just as Mexican American children in segregated Los Angeles communities (Alim, 2005, p. 26). Although there is plenty of research examining white negativity toward the use of the Black dialect (Billings, 2005), there is little research focusing on what the Latinx population thinks of the use of the Black dialect in school settings; however, the Pew Research Center did survey both populations as to how they perceive each other and where the differences lie in other matters (2008):

> While blacks and Hispanics hold broadly favorable views of each other, Hispanics are less likely to say the two groups get along well. At the same time, blacks are far more likely than Hispanics to say blacks are frequently the victims of racial discrimination...Hispanics and blacks living in counties with relatively

high concentrations of blacks are somewhat more likely to say that blacks and Hispanics get along well (65% Hispanics, 72% blacks) than are Hispanics and blacks living in low-density black counties (50% and 57% respectively), suggesting proximity is associated with greater acceptance.

The role of the US mainstream media, news shows, and articles has often been criticized as fueling competitive relations between the two minoritized groups. Mainstream media articles often emphasize intergroup conflict and antagonism because of the demographic change without providing any social context to notions of competition, historical analysis of ethnic relations, or in-depth critique of census reporting methods. Shah and Thornton (1994) used a quantitative and textual analysis of 21 articles in US mainstream magazines between 1980 and 1992 that talked about the interactions between the two groups and concluded that the coverage in these articles usually stereotyped Black-Latinx interaction as primordial, homogenized racial and cultural characteristics, and differentially valued the temperament and lifestyles of both minoritized groups.

In addition, Black-Latinx interaction was presented in an ahistorical manner, and structural conditions and causes for racial conflict were ignored. Although both minoritized groups were predominantly portrayed with unflattering characteristics, Latinx Americans were placed higher on the racial hierarchy than Black Americans because their values and morals are depicted as being closer to those of whites and therefore superior within the mainstream media (Shah & Thornton, 1994). More recently, Rodriguez (2007) offers a critique of the press coverage of the 2003 US Census Bureau reporting of Latinx Americans when they became the nation's largest racial minority in 2002. A frame analysis of 20 mainstream, 9 Latinx, and 10 Black publications was done through the lens of Critical Race Theory and found that from the headlines and lead paragraphs readers learned that the Latinx population had "*surpassed, replaced, outnumbered, challenged* or *eclipsed*" Black Americans to "*lead, arrive* or *win*" the status of the largest ethnic group. Census statistics thus entered public dialogue on demographic trends as part of a larger narrative of Black-Latinx competition and continues to do so.

A second strong influence for the contention that has not been given due importance is the influence of white attitudes and intentions in influencing relations between the two groups, especially from the standpoint of creating sustainable political coalitions. Meir, McClain, Polinard, and Wrinkle (2004) point out that most racial coalitions between Black and Latinx communities suffer from an inherent fallacy in assuming a passive role of white politicians when confronted with a potential racial coalition. Instead, they emphasize that whites have the power and option to create coalitions with either the Latinx or Black population to safeguard their own interests against a minoritized-led racial coalition. However, since social distance is often perceived to be less between white and Latinx communities than between white and Black communities, white-Latinx coalitions are more likely than Black-Latinx coalitions.

An empirical analysis of 118 multiracial school districts with at least 5000 students lent greater support to the power thesis in their study by showing that as the Black population increases, the Latinx population gains political representation while as the Latinx population increases, the Black population loses political representation. This is because as Black voters increase, whites would be more supportive of Latinx candidates. However, as Latinx voters increase, the white population would still not vote for Black candidates since they consider Latinx candidates to be more like themselves. On the other hand, Rocha's (2001) analysis of data from the National Latino Education Study (NLES), a national sample of 1,831 school districts across 49 states, revealed no evidence for the formation of white-Latinx coalitions. Instead, white-Black coalitions have the potential to form when an area becomes populated by Latinx noncitizens, possibly due to the increased social distance this causes between the Latinx community and other racial/ethnic communities because of divisive issues around language and citizenship. Undoubtedly, the actions of powerful white individuals often influence Latinx perceptions of social distance from both the white and Black racial groups.

Competition for jobs and educational resources, affordable housing, and political power as well as extreme cases of violence, gang warfare, and race riots are more commonly seen as examples of the "divide and conquer" rule in which the white establishment remains in power and creates divisions between the largest two minoritized groups in the country. The Black community may resent the economic leapfrogging on the socioeconomic ladder afforded to the Latinx community, especially from older Black men, as well as the skin-color prejudice from the Latinx community against Blacks. The Latinx community may also feel singled out for an assumed undocumented status by the Black community and resentment that the Black community does not feel that the 14th Amendment can apply to the undocumented.

The past three decades have seen a dramatic increase in the number of violent incidents between Black and Latinx communities from Miami to Houston to Chicago and especially California. Jails, county prisons, streets, and schools have provided unfortunate backgrounds for such flare-ups (Buchanan, 2005). These hostilities have been in direct contrast to the cooperative intergroup relations of the 1960s when both groups led by minoritized leaderships joined into a common struggle against oppression and disenfranchisement and were united to oppose the "white establishment." Nonetheless, racial tensions have dominated national and local news and painted a grim picture for the future of relations between the two groups, which is the basis for this book. Los Angeles county jails and the New York City jails were most affected by intense and bloody violence between Black and Latinx prisoners leading to numerous deaths and injuries.

Outside the prison system, the real eye-openers for the general public have been the number of innocent deaths in both racial groups and in places like Los Angeles, Florida, Maryland, and New Jersey—these racially motivated robberies, beatings, and deaths present a feeling of vulnerability (Cave, 2004). However, the violence that hits home directly is the kind seen on school and college campuses. Once again Los Angeles took the lead when in 2005 Jefferson High School in South Los Angeles was shaken by three racial fights in three weeks that involved hundreds of students (Shields & Lin II, 2005). Racial transition due to demographic changes in the neighborhood led to a dramatic decrease in the number of Black Americans as the population of Mexican immigrants continued to soar. As the L.A. *Times* article states, the tension outside gets carried onto the school campus. In the months prior to and after the incident, racial violence in schools struck campuses from South Bay to the Inland Empire and Antelope Valley as well as high schools in Reno, Nevada; Monroe, Washington; and in Chicago, Oakland, Rialto, and San Jacinto, California (Hutchinson, 2007).

More recently, during the riots that took place in Chicago after the murder of George Floyd by a white police officer in Minneapolis, stores in Little Village were looted just like many other businesses. However, racial tensions escalated when news reports came out that the looters were mostly Black, and subsequently, the Latinx gangs in Little Village began racial profiling cars with Black passengers by shooting at them and beating up Black residents who lived in Little Village (Perez, 2020). Social media posts warned Black residents to avoid Mexican neighborhoods due to racial profiling and retaliation. Community activists within both racial groups came out soon after and led a peace solidarity march to stop the racial tensions and divisions between Black and Latinx communities in Chicago. These activists are known as "violence interrupters" and come from many grassroots social service organizations whose goal is to prevent crime from spiraling and to end conflicts at the bargaining table (Sabino, 2020). Claiming that a few individuals cannot speak for an entire community, hundreds of people came out to clean the looted neighborhoods after the riots and stood on guard as well (Perez, 2020):

> Protesters held signs that read 'Brown people for Black power' and some carried Mexican flags as they marched from Pilsen's Plaza Tenochtitlán down Cermak Road. A protester said he wanted to show the black community that Latinos stand in solidarity and want to continue to fight against racism and police brutality. The 2020 riots brought to the surface how both racial groups sometimes feel slighted by the other, and in truth, really don't know much about each other, which makes

them feel even more threatened. Others argue that the Black and Latinx communities have completed a painful period of adjustment and are now truly ready to build Black-Brown unity to address solidarity issues such as environmental racism, racial discrimination, systematic inequities, and centuries of exclusion.

THE AFRO-LATINX IDENTITY

Henry Louis Gates Jr, a renown historian and public intellectual, called it an "identity crisis" since for two hundred years the topic of race was defined by white-Black relations and now the term "Latino" was going to challenge and disrupt the dynamic and perhaps even change the privileged status of the Black community at the leadership table (Lee, 2003). Others argued that scholars need to define Blackness more broadly and include the "Afro-Hispanic" narrative with a greater focus on the Black diaspora and the history of places like Cuba and the Dominican Republic. Historically, Black and Latinx populations tended to reside in the same clustered, low-income communities in places like New York and Tampa and WPA records described Black and Latinx men eating in the same restaurants, socializing in theaters and nightclubs in the 1930s, and intermarrying (Opie, 2008). They shared the same class status and racial group identity and shared common passions and employers, along with a patois of English, the Black dialect, Spanish, and Spanglish. Yet, the curriculum today in a Chicano Studies program in California is inherently different from the curriculum in a Black Studies program. Universities need to decide how not to be divisive in terms of funding and support and build alliances instead across Black, Latinx, and Afro-Latinx communities.

The Latinx community is not a monolith of uniformity either and nor is the Black community; there are cultural ties that bind but there are also separate interests, histories, and racial references (Amoruso, 2005). In Chicago, there is an Afro-Latinx community composed of people from Puerto Rico, Cuba, and the Dominican Republic who are Spanish speakers, as well as an Afro-Latinx population from Mexico and from port cities like Veracruz and Central America. They have an Africanized culture with distinct non-Western customs and religious practices, and in the Dominican Republic 85% of the people have African blood lines. At the same time, there is also an identification of white culture within the Latinx community, and the label of "white Hispanic" is seen in government documents, a population with no genetic ties to the African slave population in Latin America and ties only to the white Spanish slave owners.

African slaves helped build the country of Mexico by toiling in silver mines, cutting sugar cane in the fields, fighting alongside Zapata's guerillas

Figure 0.3   Casta Painting, Eighteenth Century, Oil on Canvas, 148 cm × 104 cm.
Source: Museo Nacional del Virreinato, Mexico.

during the 1910 Revolution, and shaping cultural traditions such as Carnaval, along with being lynched by Spaniards (Avila, 2006). Yet, Afro-Mexicans also faced racism from their own country people both north and south of the border, leading to the modern-day divide between the Black and Latinx communities in the Southwest. Castas or caste paintings from the colonial era depict the many different skin colors and shades that make up the racial taxonomy and racial order in Latin America, as well as the terms and labels for mixed-race categories between Native Americans, African slaves, and Spaniards. Even though Mexico did not have de jure segregation, the darker-skinned population was at the bottom of the social order and mostly invisible. At the same time, slaves in America followed the Underground Railroad to Mexico to seek freedom from American slavery.

There is colorism in the Latinx community which favors light-skinned, blonde-haired television stars, suppressing indigenous communities and their languages and cultures, while adopting Sambo-like caricatures in children's books like Memín Pinguín and Juan Bobo, and on national stamps. African slaves were brought into the New World by the Spanish Empire. The first slave was a servant to Cortés and came to the Americas in 1519; the population of African slaves in Mexico reached 20,000 by 1570 and mostly in places like Veracruz, Oaxaca, and Guerrero. Mexico was also the first country to free African slaves in the Americas, and a man named Yanga in 1609 founded the first settlement of freed slaves in Veracruz (Avila, 2006). At the same time, the terms in Spanish for Black Americans have a pejorative connotation such as "moyo," "moreno," and "negrito," and people have called out the Latinx community for its anti-Black culture that is considered politically incorrect in the United States. These complexities of race, culture, and language are explored in great depth in this book as we look at a mixed-race community that is still plagued by the vestiges of slavery, colonialism, and Empire building.

OUR ETHNOGRAPHIC STUDY

The backdrop for this book is the raciology between the Black and Latinx communities and how this raciology is signified and re-signified, even transcending "race" and its structured hierarchies, in the United States. We have seen above how race relations and racial dynamics can divide these two communities, as well as bring them together, and how racial identity matters so much more in our contentious world (Gilroy, 2000). Our book delves into this Black-Latinx community outside of Chicago and explores how racialized conflicts can be understood as a commentary on the incompatible identities that mark our postmodern selves.

The book also describes the interplay between Black and Latinx subjective experiences within a specific cultural and historical setting in which those meaningful subjectivities are formed. There is a critical interest here in the history and culture of Black-Latinx sub/urban communities and attention to race, belonging, and identity. We are living in a profound time when the idea of "race" is at the forefront of our human existence and when the concept of race is being transformed at a rapid speed. Within the predominantly Black community of Maywood, Illinois, there have been mixed statements regarding the shifting demographics and an increase in Latinx neighbors who are culturally and linguistically different from their own Black community. Our book delves into these tensions as well as the empathy and goodwill from the Black community in Maywood toward the Latinx newcomers.

Our book is an ethnographic study focusing on a school district outside of Chicago composed of two neighboring suburbs: (a) a historically Black community known as Maywood that is slowly becoming more Latinx and is the focus of this book and (b) a historically Italian neighboring community known as Melrose Park that has become predominantly Latinx (75%) but with a governing Italian power structure (US Census Bureau, 2019). In terms of the Latinx student population, the majority is of Mexican American descent, and there is a smaller Puerto Rican presence. In this study, the racial and cultural world within the selected suburban school district embodies an in-between, liminal racial space (Bhaba, 1994): it brings together a nearly 61.5% white female teaching staff (mostly Italian American and Irish American), a predominantly Black administration and school board, an aging Italian political power base and an increasing Latinx student population that is nearing half of the student body.

In such racially charged borderlands between whiteness and Blackness, the Latinx community has historically transgressed the racialized boundaries by rupturing the white-Black polarity and producing a *tri-racial geography* constituted by complex and overlapping sites of racial power and difference (Foley, 1999). As the population of Black students slowly continues to decline within this school district (42%) and the population of Latinx students continues to increase (45%), public schools that once were predominantly segregated Black schools are slowly becoming "integrated" as more and more Latinx families are moving into middle-to-low-income neighborhoods that once were all-Black such as those in Maywood, Illinois—a historic suburb located outside of Chicago.

The integration of Latinx students into Black neighborhoods within urban districts has been documented in places like Oakland and Los Angeles; however, our study focuses on the post-WWII, inner-ring suburbs of Chicago—a new racial frontier. Recent sociopolitical changes in the racial geography of the Chicagoland area have led to the outward migration of racial minority groups, such as Mexican Americans, from urban core areas and into the "inner-ring" suburbs on the fringes of Chicago where our research study is set—an in-between geographic space between the inner city and outer-ring suburbs (Garza, 1994; Koval, 2010). After WWII, the boom years for inner-ring suburbs began, and they became a haven for the young white families swept up in the great outward movement from the inner city. Oftentimes, descendants of Southern and Eastern European immigrants, such as the Italians and the Czech, moved away from the squalid urban tenements of their ancestors and into small towns carefully laid out along the railroad. Today, inner-ring suburbs are slowly deteriorating and decaying due to the bull's eye phenomenon in which white, middle-class families continue to move farther and farther away from urban areas in what is now known as the suburban sprawl (Jackson, 1987).

Inner-ring suburbs today struggle to create good jobs, provide affordable housing, and meet the social needs that arise with concentrated poverty. Caught uncomfortably between the gentrification of Chicago's older ethnic neighborhoods such as Logan Square and the economically booming outer suburbs, inner-ring suburbs are collapsing in post-industrial America and are facing the same issues that affected major cities in the 1970s: rising taxes, declining populations, deindustrialization, older housing, rising crime, loss of political clout, declining incomes, over-reliance on property taxes, a highly fragmented corrupt government, and so on (Neikirk, 1985). Maywood slowly became predominantly Black during the 1970s, even though it was one of the rare suburbs that had early signs of integration starting from its Underground Railroad roots. From the 1960s to the 1980s, it became close to 85% Black but remained at 15% white. Now, as the Black population continues to decrease, the Latinx population has risen since it has shifted toward the postwar inner-ring suburbs where now there are more Latinx students within its school districts than in all the Chicago Public Schools. In turn, more and more Latinx families are choosing to migrate outward as well toward the inner-ring suburbs and away from urban areas for the very same reasons chosen by earlier white middle-class families.

Mendell and Little (2006) state that in between sprawling outer suburbs and changing city neighborhoods, the inner-ring suburbs of Chicago like Maywood and Melrose Park face major challenges to their middle-class stability due to the influx of residents from a lower SES background, crumbling infrastructure, depreciating tax base, overall neglect, the dispersal of Chicago Housing Authority residents outside of the city and into places like Maywood, and new immigrants from Mexico—creating a bull's eye pattern on the state map. Blue Island, one of the larger inner-ring suburbs, lost 4,400 white residents from 1990 to 2000 and gained 3,600 Latinx residents and 2,700 Black residents, leading to similar changes in nearby smaller suburbs. The geographic morphology of the Chicagoland area has become the backdrop for this study as a full range of interracial tensions and interracial unity come to the surface in an ethnoracial borderland in which Latinx Americans are filling up that in-between, liminal racial space between Blackness and whiteness in the inner-ring postwar suburbs of Chicago (Foley, 1997).

In terms of schooling, more poor children attend high-poverty schools in the inner-ring suburbs than in the entire city of Chicago where poverty levels are now declining along with enrollment numbers (Cooke & Marchant, 2006; Zielinski, 1996). According to the Brookings Institution, the "tipping point" occurred during the 2000s and led to a new geography of the nation's poor where for the first time the suburbs had more poor residents than the cities and most of the poor are native-born Americans as opposed to immigrants living in the suburbs (Kneebone, 2017): "In 2015, 16 million poor people lived in the suburbs, outnumbering the poor population in cities by more than 3 million, small metro areas by more than 6 million, and rural areas by more than 8 million." More than a third of the poor in the suburbs are children and come from working families who are moving to the suburbs for low-wage jobs and industrial work, affordable housing in the post-recession landscape of foreclosures and housing vouchers, but without the safety nets that come from philanthropic nonprofit organizations in Chicago, along with a bigger city government where transportation is more accessible.

Due to the economic downturns in the past decades, close to 43% of the student population in this school district (4,839 students in Grades PreK-8th) is classified as low-income, which is double the amount from a decade ago. The district expenditure per pupil for instructional services was $6,408 in 2019 and $12,622 for operational spending—almost four thousand dollars lower than the average instructional expenditure in the nearby Chicago Public Schools (Illinois Report Card, 2019–2020). The children in this PreK-8 school district then move onto three possible high schools in their township in which children from multiple inner-ring suburbs attend schools based on an application process. Most children in our school district attend the local and nearby high school that is a majority-minority secondary school, East High School, and has 1,660 students in Grades 9–12. The total operational spending per pupil at the local high school is $17,338 and 46% are low-income students.

Even though there is a 65.4% Latinx population in the school district, we examined three K-8 schools located in Maywood that used to have an

Table 0.1   Student Demographics of the School District

Student Demographics of the School District	Black	Latinx	White	Asian	Two or More Races	Native American
	29.9%	65.4%	1.2%	0.3%	2.7%	0.0%

80% Black student population a decade ago and a small Latinx population (20%) that has now grown to 45–50% today in these three specific Maywood schools (Illinois State Report Card, 2019–2020). The entire school district is composed of the historically Black suburb of Maywood, along with Melrose Park, which is the neighboring Italian suburb, now predominantly Latinx. The third suburb is Bellwood which is a smaller, Black suburb and has one elementary school in this district's borders. These three inner-ring suburbs are combined into one school district.

In terms of the academic background of the school district, here is the breakdown of student performance in the Reading section of the standardized Illinois Assessment of Readiness test in 2019, prior to the pandemic (Illinois Report Card, 2019–2020): (a) 2% exceeded expectations, (b) 19% met expectations, (c) 27% approached expectations, (d) 28% partially met expectations, and (e) 25% did not meet expectations. In the Math assessment, we see a similar pattern: (a) 1% exceeded expectations, (b) 27% met expectations, (c) 27% approached expectations, (d) 25% partially met expectations, and (e) 16% did not meet expectations. In terms of academic gaps, there is a 10% academic achievement gap between the higher-performing Latinx student population and the Black student population.

In terms of school accountability, six elementary schools were noted as commendable in the Illinois State Report Card: a school that has no under-performing student group, a graduation rate of greater than 67%, and whose performance is not in the top 10% of schools statewide. Both middle schools for Grades 6–8 were targeted for school improvement along with one elementary school with the largest student population size and that is predominantly Latinx with mainly non-English speakers: a school in which one or more student groups are performing at or below the level of the "all students" group in the lowest performing 5% of schools.

Research Methodology

During our ethnographic study, we began by studying the schools first and foremost in 2011 but then decided we needed to branch out from the micro-systems of individual actors engaged in everyday interactions, their roles and identities, within these schools. We then examined the meso systems and structures of school boards, municipal offices like the Maywood police, government offices like the mayor's office, Black and Latinx churches, and the community at large by the time the study ended in 2022. Educational research needs to go beyond the brick-mortar walls of the schools and into the complex spaces and places within the neighborhoods and communities that provide context for the schools (Tate, 2012). Education falls under the civic realm and therefore neighborhood inequality, violence, social infrastructure,

Maywood, IL
(pop. 23,158; $22,570 per capita)

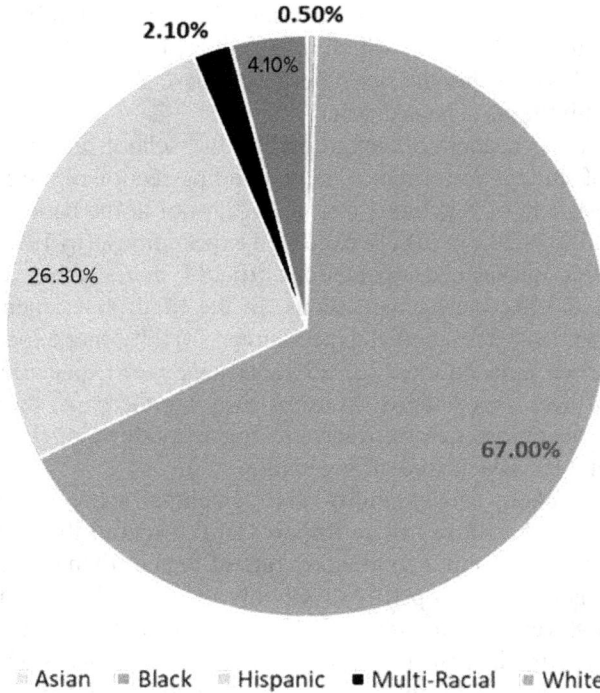

Figure 0.4   US Census Demographics for Maywood, Illinois. *Source*: United States Census, https://www.census.gov/quickfacts/maywoodvillageillinois.

social mobility, racial polarization, and many other issues inevitably affect the ecology of a school community. We hope to provide that ecological framework in this book as well as lend and add to the macro-level, large-scale patterns of majority-minority schools.

We began our work in the three Maywood schools and wrote thick descriptions of how the students, teachers, parents, and administrators interacted socially to construct and negotiate the meaning of race, language, and culture in their local classrooms and schools. We kept extensive field journals and observed mostly middle-school classrooms where the discourse was most relevant by sitting in the back of the classrooms with the students a few days a week from 9:00 a.m. to 3:00 p.m. in each classroom. We noted what teachers and students were saying and doing in both the formal and informal spaces found within and outside the classrooms—hallways, lunchrooms, bathrooms, playgrounds, bus lines, and so on. We attended district-wide meetings, school board sessions, as well as professional development workshops. We sat in the teacher's lounge, waited in the main office, walked around the neighborhood, chaperoned dances, and attended school-wide events. We also audio-taped formal interviews with key research participants—from students to teachers to parents to administrators to local community members—based on our initial coding of the field journals. Although we have conducted an extensive study of this majority-minority school district and the changing community of Maywood, our book provides a limited scope and perspective and there needs to be many more voices added to the narrative.

The larger goals for our study included analyzing the social dynamics between the two minoritized groups within school settings and across multiple social groups such as school board members and local politicians. We cataloged how larger social structures change as demographics change such as language education programs offered in the schools or increased Black/Latinx coalition-building in the local churches. Through extensive ethnographic research, the study met many of the following objectives:

- Examining Race—To analyze how two racial groups interact with each other in terms of the following concepts: power dynamics and the quest for greater political power through an increased number of race-based representation at all levels of leadership; the notion of "becoming Latinx" and "becoming Black" and the intersections of race and identity such as the development of postmodern, hybrid identities like the "Blaxican" identity; and citing how a predominantly white power structure reconfigures itself within these changing racial borderlands.
- Examining Language—To examine how two cultural groups understand and empathize with each other's language needs and language histories: the degree to which the Spanish language is tolerated and accepted within the formal curriculum as well as the hidden curriculum within schools and in school board meetings and other public discourse; how both cultural groups' use of language is closely tied to their personal identity within a Black/Brown setting; and the role of the Black dialect versus Standard English and the use of Spanish and Spanglish for both the Black students and the Latinx students.
- Examining Culture—To examine how two historically marginalized groups come to terms with each other and how they define the oppressor/oppressed relationship with each other as well as with the white majority: the degree of cultural alienation from the white mainstream for both groups; Black and Latinx gang culture and the marking of new turf and territory as well as a larger culture of racial violence; white teacher reaction to a strong racial

identity within students; how the colonial rule of divide and conquer plays itself out in a Black/Brown school district.

To examine the intersection of race, language, and culture, we used a critical ethnography methodology, which is influenced by neo-Marxist theory. Critical ethnography places human participants at the center of analysis and examines their interpretive and negotiating abilities in social settings (Holston, 1989). Critical ethnography has borrowed its focus on thick descriptions of human participants interpreting and negotiating among themselves from interpretivist ethnography. In this decade-long research study, we studied the social reality of three majority-minority schools and wrote thick descriptions of how the students, teachers, parents, and administrators interacted socially to construct and negotiate the meaning of race, language, and culture in their local classrooms and schools. Critical ethnography interrogates specific and local meanings in a social setting and presents multiple and perhaps incompatible perspectives of that lived social reality through a heterogeneous recording of differences between and among the negotiated meanings such as the heated school board meetings we attended where there was contention and debate about race, language, and culture. Critical ethnography also seeks to identify contradictions, gaps, inconsistencies, slippages, and other paradoxes between actual and perceived social realities to initiate empowering change in existing asymmetrical power networks (LeCompte & Priessle, 1984).

Furthermore, the human participants in a critical ethnography are seen as empowered agents who can change the structure of their social realities through acts of resistance (Gore, 1992). In our study, the complexities of race, language, and culture were documented through critical discourse analysis to provide an understanding of the contradictions, conflicts, and cooperation between the Black and Latinx populations in Maywood and how they went about negotiating and mediating these conflicts. Critical ethnography also calls for giving voice to the viewpoints of informants who are marginalized or silenced in research such as middle-school students who often feel invisible. We did not take the archetypal approach from the previous centuries of anthropological research that tended to see people not as participants but as objects through a racist and paternalistic lens. However, we are unsure of whether our study truly benefits the community we researched and whether we have engendered community shame, especially since both of us are cultural outsiders who do not live or work in Maywood.

Critical ethnography also stresses the need for asking questions that have never been formulated before and addressing them through unconventional methods. Our extensive interviews of people living in the community attempt to allow the participants to retain cultural authority and negate what we have to say. Simultaneously, within critical ethnography, the researcher is given permission to interpret the research results through new theoretical lenses and present them in novel ways that portray the multiple viewpoints and perspectives that can constitute the social reality of schools and communities. To increase the validity of these theoretical assumptions, the critical researcher must consult and collaborate with the researched subjects and co-define the data together by seeking the informant's perception of these sites of resistance and the theoretical construct of the in-between, liminal racial space. In the end, we did consult with the participants and tried to gain their approval of the content and analysis in this book. Checkpoints throughout the data collection process did allow us to check for understanding and to make sure the story we are telling is accurate and honest.

Thus, as critical ethnographers, our terrain was the landscape of resistance, opposition, tension, and negotiation—where the racial, linguistic, and cultural borders and boundaries between the Black and Latinx populations became heightened and in which perhaps the transgression or maintenance of borders and boundaries was magnified (Soja, 1996). Here are some of the questions that guided our research:

1) Do the majority of Black schools make accommodations and curricular changes for a bilingual student population and its predominantly Spanish-speaking parent population?
2) What types of peer networks and dynamics occur between and among the Black and Latinx student populations?
3) Does the Black student population undergo a significant transformation in its ethnoracial status and identity as the racial demographics shift toward equal numbers of Latinx students?
4) Does the discussion of race, language, and culture manifest itself in the classroom discourse? If so, why and how?
5) What types of school spaces allow for the racial integration of student populations versus segregation, displacement, and isolation?
6) How do schools handle conflicts and contention around the minority-majority dynamic?
7) How do the racial dynamics within the schools get mirrored in the larger community?
8) How do different social institutions and organizations accommodate the changing demographics?
9) Who are the political actors in the community who can create a unifying identity to build racial solidarity between the Black and Latinx communities?
10) Where, when, and how do racialized conflicts manifest, and what are the political processes that ensue?

In essence, we are telling stories about schools and communities and creating "story constellations" trying to pair interlocking stories from both the Black and Latinx members of Maywood that make visible the complexities that shape racial landscapes. There are multiple clusters of stories, many versions of stories narrated by multiple individuals and collective story tellers, and competing/conflicting plot lines (Craig, 2000). The different knowledge, perceptions, and experiences of various community members are highlighted across different eras and contexts in Maywood, giving rise to different metaphors and analogies that capture the broad-grained shifts in changing landscapes. In the field of education, our book tells the stories of struggling schools, communities coming together, the impact of the economy on the lives of working-class families, the increasing violence that tears us apart, and the political machinery looming in the background. These stories inform our book, but we also know that we are biased as we interpret and reinterpret these shared stories through our own positionality.

Theoretical Framework

The tendency to either homogenize the experiences of both minoritized groups or highlight the heterogeneous needs of both groups tends to create a false binary and therefore fails to capture the complex and contradictory interactions between the Black and Latinx communities. Binary thinking found in modernist thought often produces an "either/or" dichotomy that has been debunked toward the later end of the twentieth century as our world became more complex and less absolute. Black/Latinx race relations should not be solely narrated from the shared interest perspective or the heterogeneity principle binary; one racial group should not perpetually be pitted against another nor bound to each other infinitely. Collaboration between and within both positions of heterogeneity and homogeneity is necessary for a holistic understanding of Black/Latinx race relations via a "both/and" framework that advocates for pluralism, that rejects generalizations, and that casts doubts on grand narratives with a healthy skepticism. It is no longer a discourse about Black versus Latinx communities; rather, the discourse must center on authentic, meaningful experiences that delve beyond the surface level and that capture how the social actors' identities and attitudes toward each other are shaped in a multifarious, pluralistic, and contradictory fashion.

The expansion beyond binary thinking has led to diverse typologies such as the more recent race-space-place theoretical framework that allows researchers to generate rich, valid, and detailed data from the perspective of the research participants and from within their geography (Yull, 2014). In matters of race relations in America, the race-space-place framework strongly states that geography influences opportunity as it is inextricably linked to differential access to employment, education, and other forms of human and social capital (Pastor, 2000; Lewis, 2003; Tate, 2008). The disparities we see within school systems are based on geographical locations and that racialized social processes are always spatialized—whether rural, suburban, or urban. At the same time, racialized social structures, such as schools, shape racial experiences in varied and complex ways. Individual social actors such as teachers and students become involved in negotiating and contesting racial boundaries in these multidimensional social and cultural ecologies, and in the process, reproducing and challenging such borders and boundaries at the local level, during the everyday life of a school and in real time (Pollack, 2005). Our study, for example, examines Latinx adolescents in Black spaces and how their identity shifts and changes, as well as spaces where Black and Latinx students together feel race-less. Or when Black students from Mississippi who migrated to suburban Maywood identify differently from Black students who migrated to suburban Maywood from urban neighborhoods in Chicago—the argument that Black identity development is based on the spaces and places in which students live and grow.

In addition to the race-space-place theoretical framework, we are also using Critical Race Theory to understand how race and racism are actualized and the important thresholds in thinking about race. Critical Race Theory (CRT) states that race is an important context that affects the lives of those who are oppressed in social structures and systems like schools and segregated neighborhoods. In fact, CRT puts race, racialization, and racism as central forces of oppression that contribute to the widening gaps in areas such as poverty, unemployment, and education (Bell, 1980; Delgado & Stefancic, 2001). Our book is grounded in CRT and examines how racism is endemic in our school structures, customs, and experiences; how majority-minority schools come to construct differential racialization between the Black and Latinx communities; and how the interest of dominant power groups, from local politicians to school board members, can confer material and psychological benefits for the power-wielding agents.

Lastly, our study uses a historical methodology to understand the schooling experiences of Black and Latinx children in Maywood and therefore relies on primary and secondary sources of information (Donato & Hanson, 2017). Our primary sources included interviews with children and adults who lived in Maywood and grew up in Maywood, along with archival work from newspapers and historical records at the Maywood Public Library. Our secondary sources included textbooks on Maywood as well as online sources such as Facebook pages and posts, a master's thesis on Maywood, journal articles, and extensive newspaper articles from Michael Romain, a Black reporter covering the western suburbs of Chicago and whose brilliant writing forms a strong foundation in this book.

Researcher Positionality

In studies addressing race, language, and culture, the positionality of the researchers matters immensely. In relation to our roles and responsibilities as researchers, it is important to ask how much bias went into our analysis as well as the degree of authenticity as individuals who do not live within the Black-Brown community we were researching. Both researchers here identify as South Asian American and our positionality as neither Black nor Latinx influenced how participants connected with us, how the data were collected and analyzed, and how we interpreted the data. Teaching at the local Catholic university and working closely with the neighboring Maywood-Melrose Park school district provided ease of access to the participants in this study and to the community when completing the IRB approval process. Most participants were familiar with us and all the teachers we interviewed were former graduate students of ours, which helped facilitate dialogue and discussion around the controversial subject matter.

At the same time, the participants had high levels of trust with us, and it may have helped that we were neither Black nor Latinx since it allowed for more sharing and transparency: we were seen as people of color who they could confide in during the one-on-one, in-depth, ethnographic interviews. There was also "own-group face recognition bias" in which we were mistaken for being Black and Latinx due to the salience of our phenotype and could "pass" for being non-white like our participants (Meissner & Brigham, 2001).

Our interviews were a cross-section of teachers, students, parents, school administrators, community members, public officials, and former residents, all of whom were interdependent and nested with each other in this community. To promote trustworthiness and credibility, we debriefed with each interviewee and made sure we reviewed what was captured in the interview and assessed its accuracy. In addition, we reached out to academic peers of color who work in this field to provide critical feedback on the study's development and data analysis. During our sessions with academic peers, we probed to see if there are alternative findings and/or alternative explanations and themes to our conclusions (Lawson & Alameda-Lawson, 2012).

We wanted to probe and challenge one racial group's perception of another as well as within-group variations. To continue addressing positionality and researcher bias, we conducted "member checking" with those participants we interviewed by reviewing the transcripts and codes as well as reading the sections of the books where excerpts of their interviews were inserted to align with the chapter's themes. If our interpretations diverged, we went back to the transcript so we could enhance our response as well as ensure an emic perspective is at the forefront of analysis. However, in the end, there will be inevitable researcher bias and framing of the research from an etic perspective since we do not identify as Black or Latinx. Even though measures were in place to address positionality, we recognize there could be errors and misconceptions in the coded data and invite readers to question the conclusions and challenge the underlying assumptions in this book.

We also want to pay respect and homage to the Black and Latinx scholars who greatly influenced the content and ideas in this book. We are strengthened by the generations of Black and Latinx writers and community activists who spoke on the behalf of the oppressed and pushed for self-determination to strengthen freedoms in the United States. It is indeed misery and disenfranchisement that make us people of color the same, and our histories are linked in colonialism and slavery. Against the country's narrative of steady progress, middle-class norms, and modernization, we instead challenge this narrative by examining the inequalities and contradictions that have persisted in our homes, schools, and communities. So, we owe a debt to the Black and Latinx scholars who have taught us to be critical of historical narratives and make scholarship accessible to the broader audience.

CONCLUSION

Black and Brown Education in America: Integration in Schools, Neighborhoods, and Communities is a book concerned with the changing racial demographics of our country and our schools. Historian James Anderson (2017) points to the year 2014 when the nation's school population became majority-minority due to when the "overall number of Latino, African American, Asian American and Native American students in public K-12 classrooms surpassed the number of non-Hispanic Whites" (p. 76S). Our book addresses majority-minority schools with critical understandings related to race and identity, power and authority, and whether the intersections of our rooted history can lead to greater inclusivity.

We are living in a profound period in history when these constructs of race and identity are shifting in seismic waves. How race is viewed and seen today is radically different from even a few years ago, and these constructs are continuing to shift and will transform quickly in a few years from now. The historic conditions that led to the Black Lives Matter movement as well as the DACA Movement and DREAM Act are disrupting the discourse around the rights of minoritized groups and leading to positive changes and shifts from these moments of crises. Yet, the enduring effects of slavery, genocide, colonialism, and white supremacy are still with us today and continue to challenge the power of critical theory and continue to challenge the prospect of ever "transcending" race.

At the same time, in a place like Maywood, it is difficult to determine whether there are any beneficiaries of a racial hierarchy and racial privilege. Have the Black and Latinx populations in Maywood been subordinated by race-thinking and its color-coded social structures to reproduce racial hierarchy among themselves? For the racialized populations in places like Maywood, are hard-won oppositional identities in relation to white power not to be lightly or prematurely given up regardless of the demographic shift? Or are places like Maywood "affording protection and reversing the polarities of insult, brutality and contempt" and instead becoming places of "solidarity, joy and collective strength" in which race-thinking is denounced for the sake of belonging to one another as a community? (Gilroy, 2000, p. 12). Our book attempts to answer the above questions and bear witness to how race is understood in Black-Latinx communities and mark the spaces in which race—along with language and culture—comes to life.

There are four chapters in between the book's Introduction and Conclusion. Chapter 1, "Race and Place: A History of Maywood," investigates the history of a suburb that lies outside of a major Midwestern city and how it shifted in identity over three centuries. We trace its history from rural farmland to an Underground Railroad site founded by Lutheran churches to an industrial site in WWII that brought Black workers to live in a restricted area and then to a sleepy bedroom community along the railroad line in which white men who worked in downtown Chicago came home to Victorian homes with grand front porches. It was when the "work disappeared" in post-industrial America and racial tensions heated up in the 1960s and 1970s that led to a major shift in racial demographics from Maywood being a predominantly white Lutheran suburb with a Black area of town to then an all-Black, suburban middle-class community (Wilson, 1997). The current iteration of Maywood becoming more Latinx will be addressed in the remaining chapters that focus on the present state of Maywood. In the end, Chapter 1 makes "the spatialization of identity problematic and interrupts the ontologization of place" by examining the history of one suburban community on so many different allegorical levels: racial, religious, national, and local (Gilroy, 2000, p. 122).

Chapter 2, "Sub/Urban Schools: White Teachers, Black and Latinx Students, and Systemic Racism," takes us into the schools. Here we meet teachers, students, and administrators and hear them talk about the racial, cultural, and linguistic intersections and affinity between the Black and Latinx students, their ways of speaking and connecting with each other, the dynamic of identity and belonging constituted between them, as well as their Othering of each other that begins in middle school and gets heightened when they enter the local high school where racial tensions splinter along gang lines. We look at the implicit racism toward Black-Brown students and their families from a predominantly white teaching body and how it creates divisions and inequities between the two racial groups. The chapter ends by examining the community's collective actions to start a dual language school that still today brings together Black and Latinx students in a PreK-8 setting to learn each other's languages and cultures, creating a protective pod of closed kinship and integration within the school district.

Chapter 3, "Divide and Conquer: Division and Unrest over Power and Representation," expands beyond the schools and into the larger Maywood community. It examines the new progressive and leftist leaders and activists who brought immense political change in 2020 to the Maywood community, mirroring the national trend. The Democratic Party is being reimagined by progressive politicians who want to shift policies toward the left through civic engagement in order to advocate for the truly marginalized and to do so by changing local election outcomes (Wickenden, 2021). The progressive actors highlighted in this chapter include Norma Hernandez, a young Latinx candidate who became an elected Trustee for the local community college and now an elected state representative to the Illinois legislature, as well as Mayor Nathaniel Booker who overthrew the moderate and elder mayor of Maywood, Edwenna Perkins, who had been a part of the Democratic machine over several generations of Black leaders—both epical moves led by scrappy young people of color. Their progressive campaigns focused on the social justice movement and a pushback against the racist systems that continue to oppress Black and Brown communities such as the food desert in Maywood and action on the streets to stop violence. The grassroots movement has national figureheads like Senator Bernie Sanders and Senator Alexandria Ocasio-Cortez whose moral certainty guides and helps us feel better in these times of crises by offering clear answers and solutions to get us where we need to go with specific strategies and goals, which the Democratic machine cannot guarantee due to years of graft and corruption in Maywood. Nathaniel Booker and Norma Hernandez saw that things were shifting in their community, remained open to the political debate, and decided to become stewards of change in this new ideological landscape.

Chapter 3 also addresses the role of school boards, elected officials, the Italian power structure, the mayor's office, the Maywood police, and the journalists who draw attention to the political dynamics between and among these constituents. It examines racialized conflicts among the various groups competing for power and comments on the incompatible identities that mark these deep conflicts. We examine the political conflicts in Maywood and Melrose Park and how identity is bounded in marking divisions in our lives and our uneven, local attempts to make sense of a brave new world. The participants highlighted in this chapter talk about who they are and what they want in Maywood as a collective "we" and as an individual "I" and how the we/I dynamic can create patterns of inclusion and exclusion.

Chapter 4, "People of the Dream: Tearing Ourselves Apart while Building Spiritual Connections to Belong," focuses on community-based organizations in Maywood also setting out to bring change such as the Coalition for Spiritual and Public Leadership (CSPL), which is affiliated with our university. CSPL trains and develops faith leaders and their respective congregations and institutions to address racial, social, economic, and environmental injustice by building power that is rooted in the vision of the Gospel of Jesus Christ. Religion and faith bring the Black and Latinx communities together in Maywood and our chapter ends by examining these possibilities for racial solidarity, rooted in a history of ineffable suffering, and tied together by biblical narratives.

We end the book with a Conclusion, "Leading with Equity and Justice in the Birthplace of Fred Hampton," in which we examine the life of Maywood's native son, Fred Hampton, his legacy and recent revival. Fred Hampton, a prominent member of the Illinois Black Panther Party who rose to become its national chairman, was raised in Maywood and attended Triton College for one year before leaving to start the movement and eventually being assassinated by the Chicago machine and the FBI (Brody, 2021). Maywood today is at a crossroad and recently recognized the legacy of its native son with a Fred Hampton Center to commemorate a part of Black history that it hopes to instill in the next generation of Black and Latinx leaders who will carry on that same vision for social justice.[i]

NOTE

[i] 1. We primarily use the term *Black* but do use *Black* and *African American* interchangeably, selecting the term of a selected author whenever possible.
2. We use the term *people of color* throughout to reference African Americans, Asian Americans, Pacific Islanders, Latinxs, and Native Americans to identify their shared racialization in the United States.
3. We use the term *Latinx* to reference all people of Latin American descent in the United States but adopt the term used by specific authors when appropriate. This term is increasingly being used to address the gender norming implicit in other ethnic labels derived from Spanish.

Chapter 1

Race and Place

A History of Maywood

"Being part of Proviso Township is knowing that our community is a product of white flight, the racial wealth gap and self-organized segregation. It's us being the product of an underfunded education system operated by property taxes and knowing people of color inhabit our most impoverished communities." These are not the words of a politician or community organizer but those of a teenage girl spoken at a Y2020 solidarity rally of Black and Brown community members in Maywood, Illinois, protesting generations of racism, implicit and overt (Romain, 2020). While it paints an honest yet grim picture of the community in and surrounding Maywood, it does not capture the rich and varied history of this town that has not only borne witness to but also participated in shaping some of the most influential societal changes nationally and in the Chicagoland area.

"A good place to live," "An industrial town," "An at-risk segregated suburb," and "A distressed but resilient community" are some of the paradoxical phrases that have been used to describe the village of Maywood by historians, scholars, geographers, and government officials. The history of this Chicago fringe suburb, from its ambitious industrial beginnings to its current goals for future survival and progress, can be learned by tracking its sequential evolution from each of the above-mentioned phrases to the next. Recounting the history of this remarkably resilient village warrants digging much deeper than mere statistical census data. Maywood has been an integral part of several national and local moments that have characterized the history of the United States of America. In doing so, Maywood has had to oscillate between the roles of an obedient conformer of and a stubborn rebel against the changing national and local trends. Therefore, the history of Maywood at the micro (city) level cannot be viewed in isolation from some of the greatest macro-level changes occurring in this country like the Civil War, The Great

Migration, immigration, and The World Wars. However, the most important national movement that has forged the character of Maywood was probably the movement toward Black suburbanization and home ownership.

This chapter uses a developmental lens to chart the geopolitical and socio-economic changes experienced by the Maywood community in four important metrics: industry and economy, racial diversity, poverty and crime, and education. In doing so, it uses a chronological lens to document how Maywood and its community has changed in character and development from the late nineteenth century when the Civil War instilled hope for a better and dignified future for enslaved individuals, to the early 2000s as it continues to fight for equity and justice for all marginalized and minoritized people. Yet the overlapping themes of race and place within each of these sections are a constant reminder of the

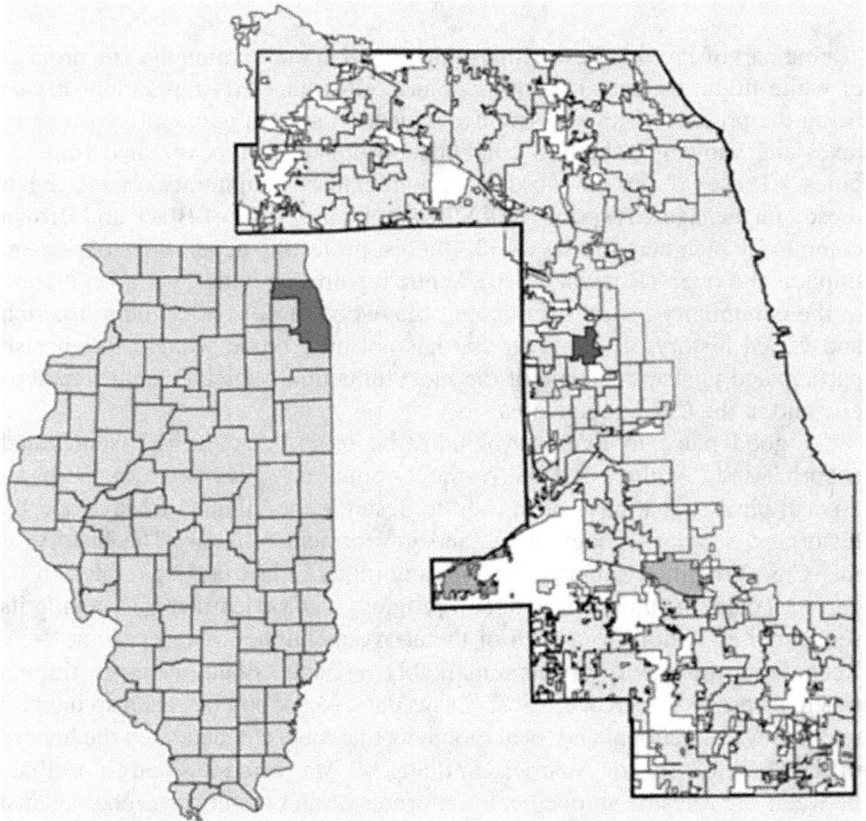

Figure 1.1   A Map of Illinois and Where Maywood (Highlighted) Is Situated as an Inner-Ring Suburb Directly West of Chicago. *Source*: Mapsof.net, https://www.mapsof.net/maywood-il.

complex yet fragile ecosystems within the ever-evolving, liminal spaces such as an inner-ring suburb like Maywood, located directly west of Chicago.

MAYWOOD: A BOURGEOIS UTOPIA?

Maywood is a village in Proviso Township, Cook County in Illinois. Often characterized as an "inner-ring" suburb, it is located 11.6 miles west of the city of Chicago. The Chicago area is located on ancestral lands of indigenous tribes, such as the Council of the Three Fires—comprised of the Ojibwe, Odawa, and Potawatomi Nations—as well as the Miami, Ho-Chunk, Menominee, Sac, Fox, Kickapoo, and Illinois Nations. These tribes had thriving trade networks in the Great Lakes area prior to European contact. Post-European contact, the tribes maintained trade arrangements with both the French and British, leading to the historical role of famous explorers like Jean Baptiste Point du Sable, the first non-Indigenous settler of Chicago, born in present-day Haiti to a French father and Black African slave mother, and recognized as the "Founder of Chicago" (Gates, 2013). However,

> On May 28, 1830, President Andrew Jackson signed the Indian Removal Act proposing to relocate indigenous tribes west of the Mississippi River. This would mean the relocation of tens of thousands of indigenous people still living east of the river. The tribes in what is now Chicago, and the Great Lakes area would feel the brunt of many land cessations and several relocation efforts over the coming years after this (American Library Association, 2022).

Chartered in 1869 on the site of two Native American trails and several large farms, Maywood was "founded" by Colonel William T. Nichols and six other Vermont-based businessmen who formed the Maywood Land Company. Its geography was a typical efficiency model laid out on a grid with a park in the center, similar to towns in Europe. Col. Nichols created the name Maywood in honor of his deceased daughter May, and to celebrate the 20,000 trees that he had planted in the village. In the book, *Chicago and Its Suburbs* (1874), Everett Chamberlain described Maywood as the youngest but one of the most prosperous suburbs of Chicago and attributed the rare success of the town to the financial strength and practical common sense of the founding company's vision in creating facilities for drainage and ease of transit to and from the central business district. This was an accurate analysis since right from the outset, the Chicago and Northwestern Railroad became the catalyst for Maywood's early boom period. By 1875, there were 16 trains stopping daily in Maywood, which still causes traffic delays for today's residents.

Demographically, a growth spurt occurred after the Chicago Fire of 1871 when prosperous Chicagoans began moving toward a vision of a pleasant, wide-open suburb and away from the ruins of a city. Maywood with its original plan for only four houses per block seemed to be a perfect choice. By 1874, a hotel, a post office, a school, a barber's shop, and various stores were established, all within walking distance from the tracks. The Maywood Hotel built at a then astronomical price of $30,000 boasted a guest list of some of the most famous personalities of the time. In addition, grand houses built in "French style," a Social Hall, and a 16-acre park with an open-air dance floor, band facilities, and a 124-foot-high observatory made Maywood an ideal place for many prosperous and fashionable white families to live in the 1870s and 1880s (Maywood Chamber of Commerce, 2021).

Schools and churches also played an important role in making Maywood an attractive proposition for white prosperous families. In the first two decades, it was known for its "fine up-to-date schools with progressive curriculums" even though memorization of facts, noble thoughts, and "Practical Penmanship" were paramount (Chamberlain, 1974). Churches were some of the first buildings to be constructed in Maywood and for many denominations: Congressional, Episcopalian, Baptist, Methodist, and Presbyterian. The denominations all had organizations and maintained services in Maywood along with a Union Sabbath school with 135 Christian scholars. By 2004, there were almost 30 places of worship in Maywood. Churches have always strived not only to provide spiritual support but to also serve as key settings for socializing, which we will discuss in later chapters (Deuchler, 2004). Despite the picture of prosperity and comfort, categorizing Maywood as a "bourgeois utopia" would be a fallacy.

Industry as the Backbone of Economic Stability

Light industry has always been the backbone of Maywood's economy. It was in the early 1880s starting with Chicago Scraper and Ditcher, a manufacturer of agricultural machinery, and after the Norton Brothers opened their metal can factory (later called the American Can Co.) that marked the boom period for the village and laid the roots of its industrial history. By 1890, Maywood was one of the leading can manufacturing centers of the world and helped supply metal soda cans for Canfields and Canada Dry. Other industries were subsequently attracted to the area located primarily within the factory district along the north side of the railroad tracks. Maywood gained a major institution in 1920 when Edward Hines Jr. Memorial Hospital was established for the care of war veterans. These businesses and their workers were served by excellent transportation, including the Chicago and Northwestern train (1870), electric street railways (1893), and Chicago's rapid transit system.

During the 1920s, Checkerboard Field (now Miller Meadow, a prairie walking trail) provided air service for the area such as air mail delivery (Young & Callahan, 1981).

In providing a topology of the kinds of suburbs African Americans settled in the first part of the twentieth century, Wiese (2004) defined Maywood as an industrial suburb. As Harris (1994, p. 28) stated, "The existence of blue-collar districts on the suburban fringe early in the twentieth century might seem odd. The pattern does not fit the image of Chicago, in which *suburbs* were described as places from which the affluent commuted to jobs in the central-business district (CBD)." Several scholars like Harris and Wiese have also confirmed that blue-collar suburbs were prevalent all throughout the country right from the beginning of the twentieth century and many, like Maywood and Pullman, had their roots in the late nineteenth century. Decentralization of industry, homeownership, and open spaces to raise a family were the predominant motives for most blue-collar workers to move into suburbs like Maywood.

Entrepreneurs in Chicago were among the first in the United States to plan and service entire districts that were intended exclusively for industrial use, or what today is called an industrial park. Companies like Western Electric, with its site in the western suburb of Cicero and in which several Maywood residents worked, built factories that were sizable enough to justify their own sites. If not already available, labor was sure to follow, and spur lines could readily be laid (Harris, 1994). The heavy presence of industry would lead one to believe that Maywood was a predominantly working-class suburb. The reality however was that Maywood had a unique mixture of both the "new middle class" of salaried professionals who commuted daily to Chicago's Loop via the train and the blue-collar workers, toiling in the city's factories (Deuchler, 2004).

Through a study of the Maywood City Directory from 1929 to 1930, Nyquist (2000) showed that almost half of Maywood's population could be categorized as middle class (professional, semi-professional, managers/proprietors/officials, and clerical/sales) and the remaining as working class (crafts/foreman, laborers, operatives, service workers, those in Public Emergency Work, and domestic service employees). Thus, on the eve of the Great Depression, Maywood was a mixed suburb, occupationally and economically. This would be in direct conflict with the often-accepted stereotype of a white affluent suburb. As Wiese (2004) states, Maywood was not a rich suburb like its neighbor, Oak Park, but it was a comfortable suburb with movie theaters, soda shops and diners, public services, and parks for children.

Maywood's population meanwhile increased exponentially since its inception. From a little over 1,000 in 1874, it had jumped to 4,532 in 1900, 8,033

Figure 1.2   Postcard of the Post Office in Maywood, Illinois, ca. 1930–1945. *Source*: Boston Public Library, The Tichnor Collection, https://www.digitalcommonwealth.org/search/commonwealth:wh246v457.

in 1910, and 12,072 in 1920 (Deuchler, 2004). Like most of the Chicagoland area, the 1920s were a period of immense growth, and the population of Maywood exploded to 25,829 in 1930. Industry continued to provide the biggest boost for this population growth. Thirty years later, Maywood's population reached a total of 27,330 in 1960 and then touched 30,036 in 1970. Even in the years of the Great Depression, the American Can Company continued to be the largest employer in Maywood with a payroll of over 2,500 employees in 1938.

The Great Depression hit the Maywood community extremely hard. Maywood State Bank was one of the thousands that failed, taking depositors' life savings along with it. Residents often found jobs in various federal projects like the W.P.A. (Works Progress Administration) and the C.C.C. (Civilian Conservation Corps). Some of the projects included building a stadium at the high school which has seen many thrilling matches through the years and was recently renovated in 2021: "During the 1930s, the W.P.A. constructed a new storm sewer system with 480 manholes. This provided steady employment for hundreds of out of work Maywood men during the depths of Depression. They also repaired and repaved many sections of the brick streets" (Duechler, 2004, p. 67). Perhaps the most innovative project was the Maywood Community Garden that became a Great Depression model throughout the region. Conceived by civic-minded businessmen, it utilized several vacant prairies and motivated villagers to raise their own crops. Nearly 200 unemployed people tilled the ground that produced a large crop of foodstuffs for the needy. There is a current resurgence in urban farming such as the Real Food Collective as Maywood became a food desert with no grocery stores in its current boundaries.

In the 1970s, several of Maywood's industries transferred out of the region, including the village's major employer, the American Can Company. In the year 1973, the American Can Company laid off 900 people at its plant, and this was the beginning of Maywood's plunge into poverty as white flight began to increase right away and impoverished Chicagoans began to move into the village. In 1975, the American Can Company closed its doors forever which led to the economic decline in Maywood due to a massive job loss via deindustrialization (Keating, 1988; Stillgoe, 1988). In the next few years, more manufacturing companies in the industrial strip closed their doors, leading to a cascade effect of job loss. The loss of wages drained the retail strip along 5th Avenue and caused those retail businesses to close their doors, turning Maywood into an economically depressed area with many residents living below the poverty line. Those who had lived in the village for years began packing up and moving out in the late 1970s and early 1980s, especially the white middle-class families who moved to the outer suburbs. Some sought employment in other regions of the state, but many residents, especially the Black working-class residents, did not have the savings or equity in their homes to leave Maywood. At the same time, by 1975, drugs and crime rose in Maywood as burglaries and drug-related crime began to spike, leading to the flight of the Black middle class.

The village's retail base also declined, as Montgomery Ward and Sears, Roebuck department stores left the main shopping street, Fifth Avenue. The impact on the community was devastating as a large proportion of the population found themselves unemployed (Village of Maywood, 2021). The number of people below the poverty line in Maywood increased from 13.5 in 1979 to 15.2 in 1989 and then decreased to 13.4% in 2000. In citing the predictions for 1990 to 2000 of the real-estate advising company, Robert Charles Lesser & Company (RCL & Co.), Myron Orfield (1998) states that the Cook County western suburbs were predicted to have the worst growth rate in the Chicagoland six-county region. In addition, while office space was being absorbed in northern Lake County at more than three times the average rate, office space was being abandoned in western Cook County and parts of Chicago.

In his analysis of employment subcenters in Chicago (subcenter being defined as a concentration of firms large enough to have a significant effect on the overall spatial distribution of population, employment, and land prices but outside of the central business district), McMillen (2003) provides an accurate picture of the changes in employment opportunities in Maywood in the last three decades of the twentieth century. Described as a subcenter along with Broadview and Oak Park in 1980, Maywood's employment composition in manufacturing was only 7.23% as opposed to 10.42% in retail, 36.21% in services, 12.62% in TCU (transportation, communication, and utilities), and 5.75% in FIRE (finance, insurance, real estate). However, this cluster specialized in government services (27.18%) with Maywood having a significant county governmental facility (federal, state, and local) such as the present-day Maywood courthouse used for the prosecution of crime in suburban Cook County.

Along with the continued decentralization of manufacturing away from the central city and the western suburbs into the Northwestern suburbs, the Bellwood-Broadview-Maywood cluster of Black inner-ring suburbs specialized in the service employment in 1990 (48.78%). By 2000, Maywood no longer qualified anywhere on the list of 32 employment subcenters in Chicago. According to the SOCDS data, the share of people employed in manufacturing in Maywood had fallen from 35.8% in 1970 to 17.1% in 2000, while professional services had increased from 18.6% to 22.8%. In 2000, the largest category of workers by occupation in place of work was Healthcare Practitioners and Technicians Occupations (25.1%) followed by Education, Training, and Library (7.1%). A change in the basic structure of an economy from manufacturing to service usually necessitates a different set of skills, knowledge, and education, all of which may not be readily present within the current labor force. This could lead to increased unemployment and poverty within the community as evident in Maywood during the final years of the twentieth century.

The leaders and residents of Maywood today seem to have understood and embraced the idea to "think and link" their economic progress with that of other regions through efforts like the IWA (Illinois Workforce Advantage) and MFAA (Maywood Fine Arts Association). In doing so, they have not only strengthened the "within group" bond of their social capital but also bridged "across group" social capital to maximize opportunities outside their immediate reach. The IWA is a place-based community development initiative that links state agencies and local communities to buttress local economic, communications, and human services infrastructure. IWA aims to add value to community initiatives. According to their website, the MFAA was formed to help combat escalating rates of drug activity, gang involvement, and teen pregnancies by providing enrichment through arts education and community outreach programs. Through grass-roots efforts within the community, as well as support from state officials and business and civic leaders, MFAA purchased and transformed a previously abandoned and boarded up bank building into a vibrant center of arts activity in downtown Maywood. From this initiative, MFAA now serves as an anchor site for the redevelopment of several other businesses around the area. The picture below showcases the students in MFAA at a recent parade in the village of Maywood.

Most recently, The Twin Cities Covenant, a vow made in 2020 by the boards of Maywood and its more affluent neighbor, River Forest, signed in the aftermath of George Floyd's murder, is establishing a meaningful working relationship to support commerce and youth development. Fueled by the Women's Chamber of Commerce Affinity groups, the collaboration addresses issues of systemic racism, advocates for the rights of marginalized individuals, and protects the interests of small businesses owned by marginalized groups (Romain, 2021). In many ways, the history of Maywood's changing economic character is like that of many fringe suburbs across the United States that saw a population boom coupled with increased opportunities for economic mobility brought about by industry—only to be left in the lurch when the manufacturing base disappeared, prosperous families fled, and unemployment and crime rose. When attempting to provide a brief history of a complex physical place such as Maywood, it is easy to emphasize these deficit lenses. Yet the purpose of this chapter is to think about the history of Maywood through the lens of its flexible and resilient character that has allowed it to leverage the affordances of changing times. As it looks into the twenty-first century, Maywood is investing in its youth, its culture, and its ability to not just weather the changes but shape them.

Figure 1.3   The Annual Maywood Fine Arts Walk for Equity and Opportunity in the Arts in 2021. *Source*: Paul Goyette.

Racial Diversity and Segregation

Racial diversity is in Maywood's DNA. The Maywood Company founded by Vermont businessmen to establish the township of Maywood may seem like an important player in shaping the structural inception of the town. Yet, it also hints at the demographic dynamics playing out during the early years. In these years and by 1900, 95.5% of the population in Maywood was white with 25.1% being native born, and 38.5% being white, native born but with foreign-born parents, indicating the heavy influence of the immigrant communities, mostly European, in shaping this suburb (Encyclopedia of Chicago, 2021). This view can be affirmed by looking at the pictures in Douglass Deuchler's book (2004) on Maywood in which large, close-knit family and friend groups of white European immigrants like Italians, Germans, Swedes, and Jews were the majority. Elegant homes with prosperous and fashionable, multigenerational, mostly white families resided in Maywood in the 1870s and 1880s. And, as the twentieth century began, Maywood was firmly a town that embraced recent immigrants such as those from Norway and Ireland but also hosted a small minority of Black families as they migrated North in search of a better, more dignified life along the Underground Railroad.

Contrary to the major trend in suburbanization, it was not surprising that Blacks had a nominal presence in Maywood right from the beginning. Diving into the history of the Vermont founders, we also learn that Zebina Eastman, who purchased several blocks of land in Maywood, was a staunch abolitionist, operated as a "conductor" on the Underground Railroad, served as a friend and confidant to President Abraham Lincoln and wrote for the Western Citizen, which became part of the Chicago Tribune (DePaul Newsroom Archive, 2011). Additionally, founded just after the Civil War by an abolitionist, Colonel Nichols, Maywood seemed to reflect the sentiments of that era. Prior to the Civil War, the Ten Mile House in Maywood served as a rest stop on the Underground Railroad for abolitionists to shelter escaped slaves along their route North. Maywood was ten miles or a day's ride from Chicago (Hill, 1998). During the last decade, it has been well established by scholars that Black Americans have played an important role in the development and growth of various suburbs all over the country. According to Wiese (2004), few Black Americans lived on the fringes of northern and western cities before WWI, and most of those who lived in older, densely settled suburbs were linked to decentralizing employment in manufacturing or domestic service. Maywood would be a case in the former.

By 1930, as the population grew exponentially, Maywood's foreign born and native population with foreign origins had declined to 15.5% and 13.6%, respectively. This led to an overall decrease in the white population from

99.5% to 97%. Although marginal, the Black population constituted almost 3% of the city's population in 1930, an increase from 0.4% in 1900. This change was in line with the larger local trend during the Great Migration that saw one in every six Black migrants moving into the Chicago suburbs, such that by 1940, there were around 25,000 Blacks living in the Chicago suburbs including Maywood (Wiese, 2004). Like most Chicago suburbanites, Blacks in Maywood shared neighborhoods with working-class whites, mostly European immigrants.

In the years of the early twentieth century, the interplay between the two major historical events could be held responsible for the major move of Black Americans into the suburbs: WWI with its restrictions on the new arrival of immigrants that subsequently increased the demand for labor in factories; and the Great Migration of a large number of Black Americans from the South who looked to urban life and the industrial economy for the social and economic foundation of full citizenship and its prerequisites (Jones & Holli, 1995). In Maywood, at the American Can Company, most Blacks and whites worked together, receiving equal pay for comparable jobs.

Another important feature that has been emphasized by scholars for the establishment of both blue-collar suburbs and the movement of Blacks into these suburbs is homeownership. According to Wiese (2005), in a town like Maywood, Black Americans sank their roots in relatively new neighborhoods and found opportunities to own homes of their own. In a typical suburb like Maywood, homeownership could range from 17% in East Chicago to 52% in nearby Berkeley. This allowed Black residents to share in the dream of steady wages, better integration into a consumerist society, and a relatively safer suburban family and social life. Higher taxes on industries helped maintain a high level of services, schools, and teacher salaries. The ownership of buildings played a vital role in the settlement of many thousands of workers on the urban fringe (Harris, 1994). Deuchler (2004) provides an example of Iva Hurst, a cook in the Chicago Loop who purchased two lots and built a three-room home in Maywood as early as the 1880s.

Social networks were at the core of most migration and settlement patterns of Blacks from the South. Ties of family and acquaintance provided bonds that made suburbs into specific destinations. No account of the migration is complete without the documentation of innumerous letters written by Black Americans in the North to their relatives in the South attesting to the world of opportunities available in Northern cities and suburbs. Historians have used these cultural artifacts, such as posts in the Black newspaper *The Chicago Defender*, to emphasize the importance of social networks in determining settlement patterns of Blacks migrating to the North (Michaeli, 2016).

Maywood's already extant Black community provided the impetus for its future settlers. In addition, two of Maywood's churches—the Second Baptist

Church and Canaan African Methodist Episcopal (A.M.E.)—were Black at the time of the Great Migration. Some Black residents worshiped at the local, racially integrated Episcopal Church but did not feel wholly included in the life of the church and started a mission church, named St. Simon's, for Black residents (Nyquist, 2000). In addition, Washington School, now a dual language academy, had 375 students in 1931, 175 of which were Black. Many students at the school attest to the high quality of education they received in an integrated setting just as they do today. The student body was a mix of Jewish and Black children since both minority populations lived in the same parts of Maywood.

In some ways, Maywood was progressive at that time due to racial integration, and in other ways, it was not since it relegated certain sections of town to Blacks and Jews (Nyquist, 2000). However, perfect conditions for the complete integration of Blacks and whites in Maywood have never existed. Initially, although Black Americans could buy property in Maywood, they could not live outside the tightly delineated "colored neighborhood" between Ninth Avenue on the East and Fourteenth Avenue on the West. Restrictive covenant real-estate policies made certain that property in adjacent zones could not be sold to people of Black descent. According to Wiese (2005), it is this kind of concentration of Blacks in low-rent sections of suburbs that has been a predecessor to the larger segregation movement of the later 1900s.

As observed by Deuchler (2004) through his archival work, in the very early twentieth century, it was also possible to tell the race of a villager by their address since the code "col" (for colored) followed their names in the Maywood directories. In addition, during the 1930s, only a handful of photographs of Black residents appeared on the pages of the *Maywood Herald*, the local newspaper. In each case, the picture featured a photograph of a high-school athletic team, in which Black students were often featured. Over time, famous athletes, such as Doc Rivers, a professional basketball coach and former player who was the head coach for the Philadelphia 76ers of the National Basketball Association, made their way into the national sports teams through high-school athletics in Maywood.

In 1938, Maywood celebrated its seventieth anniversary. The town's leaders produced a well-crafted booklet about the town's organizations, schools, churches, police, and fire departments, and governing bodies. If one knew nothing else about Maywood, one would assume the town was all-white since not one Black resident is featured in any of the photographs. Similarly, glancing through the high-school yearbooks at the Maywood Public Library, one is struck by seeing virtually no Black faces in any of the pictures or the clubs and organizations sponsored by the schools during this first migration period. However, the period of 1940–1970, often labeled the Second Great Migration, saw an exponential rise in the Black population of Maywood which increased from 2.8% in 1930 to 19.1% in 1960 after which it doubled to 41.3% in 1970. Early suburbanization of the Black population was a national phenomenon mirrored in Chicago as overflow from the urbanized Black belts with squalid, overcrowded living conditions led to Black migrants moving into the Chicagoland suburbs. In the city of Chicago, three-fourths of the growth of 53,000 Black Americans between 1940 and 1960 was absorbed by only seven suburban localities, including Maywood.

Wiese (2005) and Connolly (1973), through an analysis of 24 suburbs that demonstrated similar growth during this period, provide interesting insights into the reasons and the conditions of the Black population in Maywood. Both authors agree that the already extant Black community formed an important social network for the new arrivals. This pipeline coupled with the existence of traditional housing restrictions ensured that most Black migrants settled in segregated nodes in or contiguous to existing Black suburbs. In Maywood, there were 1,200 Blacks in 1940—all of whom lived in what the authors above called the old and shabby neighborhood located in the shadow of the American Can factory. Most Black homeownership in Maywood resulted from the new arrivals moving into older homes of the whites who had left the city to move away from the soot and noise of the factories. Thus, although Black migrants moved into older housing units of frame bungalows and two-story houses, the spatial consequence continued to be the same as before and virtually all of Maywood's Blacks remained confined to a segregated and sharply bounded neighborhood in the middle of town.

A more interesting trend that was occurring all over the country was that the new wave of Black suburbanites was predominantly white-collar workers and industrial workers with a relatively high stable income, what Wiese (1999) calls the growing Black bourgeoisie. Connolly (1973) confirms this view by using the variables of income, home ownership, and the proportion of Blacks employed in white-collar jobs. Concentrating on Maywood, his analysis of the census bureau statistics of the 1970s reveals that in comparison to Chicago, Black median family incomes in Maywood were 133% greater. Yet, income inequality with white counterparts in Maywood stubbornly persisted. Compared to white median family incomes, the Black median income was only 84.4% (Connolly, 1973).

While race and place are the predominant lenses used to describe the evolution of social identities in this book, their intersectionality with gender in shaping Maywood's history and future cannot be disregarded. Both Wiese (2005) and Connolly (1973) have emphasized the contribution of married, working Black women in raising the overall family status during the late twentieth century. Although industrial suburbs were traditionally male dominated with the male population between 55% and 60% in 1920 in a suburb like Maywood, Black women formed families and continued to be active participants in the workforce. With the opening of opportunities for Blacks during WWII period, Black women found greater opportunities in occupations like teachers, nurses, and retail services. In Maywood, almost 67% of Black married women were in the workforce in 1970 as opposed to only 42% of white married women. Extended family and social networks helped Black women work without having to worry about the care of their children (Asher & Branch-Smith, 2005). This could also explain the sizable racial differential between white and Black working women with children under six years of age (Connolly, 1973). The impact of this was that while Black family incomes were higher the cumulative wealth of the household was much lower than the white counterparts.

There also existed a general correlation between family incomes and home ownership, and like most communities with their median family incomes higher than 10,000 (10,552 for Maywood in 1972), Black homeownership reached 55.9% (66.3% for whites) in Maywood (Connolly, 1973). Yet, Maywood had only 29.6% of its Black workforce working in white-collar jobs (54.2% for whites) and was an exception to most communities with a median income higher than 10,000 that had almost 40% of the workforce in white-collar jobs. Ironically, at the age of the Civil Rights Movement, when historical changes were being brought about in education and housing, Maywood was on the threshold of diving into the greatest setback, economic and racial, in its history. While landmark decisions like *Brown v. Board of Education* led to the de jure desegregation of schools and the Fair Housing Act in 1968 swept away de jure residential segregation, Maywood found itself in the chaotic aftermath of a new kind of de facto segregation that grew like fire after the race riots in Chicago when Dr. Martin Luther King, Jr. was assassinated on April 4, 1968. White flight that had begun in the past couple of decades, due to panic peddling and unethical real-estate practices, accelerated to the extent that Maywood's Black population rose to 75.6% in 1980 and to 83.6% in 1990. The school pictures below show the dramatic demographic shift of Maywood schools going from being mostly white (picture taken in 1965) to all Black in 1970.

In "Ending American Apartheid: How Cities Achieve and Maintain Racial Diversity," Lauber (1989) states that over the late twentieth century, suburbs like Maywood have experienced what he calls "block-by-block" segregation driven by harmful biases and misconceptions that produced overt efforts to discriminate against Blacks in the housing market to more covert messages to prime homebuyers that proximity to Blacks would increase criminality and lower property values. While using Maywood as an example, Massey (2001) in an article on residential segregation and neighborhood conditions highlights this national trend by showing that since 1950, although Blacks and whites were becoming more integrated at the state and county levels, municipal and neighborhood segregation seemed to persist and increase.

Figure 1.4   Garfield School Class Photo from 1965. *Source*: Frank Hall.

Figure 1.5   Irving School Basketball Team Photo from 1970 to 1971. *Source*: William Fowkles.

In the fall of 1967, East High School in Maywood erupted with racial tensions which were minutely scrutinized locally but received intense publicity nationally as the first "race riot" in an American high school, which was led by native son Fred Hampton, the future leader of the Chicago Black Panther Party. Following these race riots, two new industries dropped their plans to relocate to Maywood and several projected high-rise developments were canceled. Race relations continued to plague Maywood for the next several years, and this shift coupled with the relocation of industries like the American Can Company and Sears Roebucks Company led to a period of inevitable economic slump, crime, and bad publicity (Deuchler, 2004).

Segregation has been an unfortunate legacy of Maywood's history and continued to persist into the twenty-first century (Duncan & Duncan, 1957). Segregation of the Black community started along spatial (residential) lines in correlation with the decentralization of industry, rapid white flight, and racial tensions that persisted through the end of the twentieth century. In 2003, while making a case to prove that contrary to popular belief most American suburbs are not a monolith, Myron Orfield (2003) provided a topology of the kinds of suburbs that exist around metropolitan areas. In doing so, he characterized Maywood as an "at-risk segregated community": poor and segregated communities have a fraction of the resources of the central cities they surround, low or negative population growth, relatively meager local resources, and struggling commercial districts.

John R. Logan (2001) in a report from the Lewis Mumford Center at the University of Albany (SUNY) showed that the group most segregated from whites in the suburbs is Black Americans, and his findings were based on analysis of 1990 and 2000 census data for 330 metro areas. The persistence of segregation in Maywood fits the claim made in the report that where most minoritized group members live, and where consequently they are a more substantial share of the suburban population, segregation is higher, more unyielding over time, and this minoritized population growth is more likely to be associated with the creation or intensification of racial/ethnic enclaves. Logan analyzed neighborhoods based on income and quality of life, extended the above-mentioned findings, and concluded that the color line for Black Americans still persists and that Black neighborhoods are separate and unequal not because Blacks cannot afford homes in better neighborhoods but because even when they can achieve higher incomes, they are unable to translate these earnings into residential mobility.

While much of Maywood's demographic history through the early and mid-twentieth century has focused on Black-white dynamics, Maywood in the past four decades has welcomed a record number of Latinx individuals who have settled here looking for affordability and solidarity to raise their often-larger families who need bigger homes. Yet, the overall population of Maywood has continued to decline from 1980 (approx. 28,000) to 2019 (approx. 23,000) with the Black population demonstrating a similar trend. Maywood was 82.3% Black in 2000 and 66.4% Black in 2019. As Black families have left Maywood, the loss has been offset by Latinx individuals whose population has increased from 10.5% in 2000 to 27.2% in 2019. Today 12.4% of Maywood residents are foreign born (Census Scope, 2021). This trend can also be found in the city of Chicago where, according to the census report released in August 2021, "Chicago's Black population fell by nearly 10-percent, a loss of 85,000 residents over the last 10 years. At just more than 800,000, Black residents now make up about 29-percent of the city, down from more than 32-percent in 2010" (The Chicago Reporter, 2021). The reasons for the reverse migration of Black residents include the loss of opportunities, rise in brazen crime and surrounding gun violence, lack of economic stability, and policies and systems that have failed the Black population in the last decades such as deaths from police brutality, lack of access to quality healthcare, and underfunded schools.

Within the Latinx population, most of the immigration since 1995 has been intercounty (24.8% out of 40.3%). Proximity to the heavy Latinx population in neighborhood areas like Melrose Park and Cicero helps explain the increased migration of Latinx residents into Maywood, which we will discuss at length in later chapters. Massey (2001) explains the conditions that lead to the concentration of minoritized groups in enclaves and states that when enclaves are filled, group members are forced into adjacent areas, expanding the boundaries of the enclave. Despite the legacy of segregation, Maywood has always strived to be an integrated suburb, and through the turn of the twenty-first century, it is learning to support a new kind of racial integration, one between two minoritized groups, Black and Latinx Americans. Idealistically, it makes sense that when individuals of both racial communities view authentic integration as necessary and beneficial, their combined power could be formidable in addressing the generational injustice and trauma that both communities have faced. Yet, this is challenging especially in a media climate that might consciously and inadvertently stoke implicit biases, which is the heart of our research study and the changing demographics in Maywood.

Examples of harmful rhetoric can be seen when news outlets report on the changing demographics in a place like Maywood. A 2013 *Chicago Sun-Times* newspaper article reported on the changing demographics in Maywood when Latinx students became the biggest ethnic group in the elementary school district:

> Whites lost their No. 1 status to Latinos in 19 suburban districts spread across the six-county area of Cook, DuPage, Will, Lake, Kane and McHenry. Blacks

were displaced by Latinos as the leading group in nine other districts, including
the city of Chicago . . . Enough Latinos have moved into Maywood to push the
elementary school district from 58.2 percent black to 59.1 percent Hispanic over
10 years. (Hinton, Spielman, & Malagon, 2013)

Such divisive rhetoric that perpetuates the stereotypes of Latinx immigrants in competition for resources with other racial groups makes it difficult
for meaningful integration efforts. While racial integration brings with it the
challenges of transcending and learning about each other's unique history
and needs, it also brings the potential to forge formidable alliances and coalitions. This may be what Maywood needs to confront the forces of systemic
and institutional racism that have held it back from realizing its true potential
all these years.

Poverty and Crime

Maywood's median household income at $50,176 is lower than that of its
neighbor's, Chicago, and the state with 15.9% of households at or below
the poverty line in 2019 and with the largest group being females within the
age of 25 to 34 (Census Scope, 2021). The largest ethnic group to fall below
the poverty line was Black (60% of families below PL) followed by Latinx
(18%) and white (15%) in Maywood. The economically challenged spaces
of Maywood are evidently racialized and gendered. Unemployment rates
in Maywood between 2015 and 2019 were at 11% higher than the rate in
Chicago or Illinois. Furthermore, a higher concentration of Black and Latinx
children in public schools, coupled with a low tax capacity and slow tax
capacity growth cripples the ability to obtain greater educational resources,
which we discuss at length in later chapters. In 1994, the taxes on a $100,000
house in Maywood were $4,672 (Village of Maywood, 2021). This minimum
level would support the local school spending of $3,350 per pupil. Today, the
average spending per student in the entire elementary school district is around
$13,000 per student with fluctuations within each elementary school, with
spending less per student at the predominantly Black schools in Maywood
compared to Latinx schools in Melrose Park ($16,000), which is closer to its
wealthy neighbor, River Forest (around $17,000).

As one city manager of an at-risk suburb suggested, white homeowners
tend to constantly monitor the schools and test scores, and at the first sign
of decreasing change, they flee and have a sinking ship mentality (Orfield,
2003). Once the middle class begins to leave a community, voter participation, and oversight decline, civic watchfulness disappears, and corruption sets
in. Old housing stock with poverty rates higher than the region and high crime
rates also characterize these communities with a depleting middle class.

According to the 2000 census data, Maywood had a poverty rate of 13.4% as opposed to the 10.3% poverty rate in Illinois and 12.4% in the United States. Almost 40% of the housing units in Maywood were constructed before 1939 and only about 11% of the units were constructed after 1970; however, there is a current revitalization in Maywood of its Victorian, Queen Anne homes with elaborate roofs, porches, and gardens. Yet, Maywood has the 11th highest crime rate in Cook County and, over the years, has acquired the reputation of being a highly crime-ridden place, known as "Murderwoods," which we discuss in chapter 3. Although the rate has been declining in the past years, in 2006, it had a crime rate of 64.1% (crimes per 1000) (City Data, 2021).

In 1975, Maywood stood at a challenging intersection of loss of industry (e.g., American Can Co.), interracial violence, youth unrest, white flight, and a deep plunge into poverty. Crime was an inevitable byproduct. Yet, falling home prices meant that Maywood was now more affordable for Latinx and Black American families escaping higher poverty and crime in the city of Chicago. Gangs such as the Latin Kings also established their first official suburban branch in Maywood in the 1980s (Seidel, 2016). The primary goal was to protect newly arriving Mexican American families and businesses settling in the region, who often faced an unfriendly and racist welcome from their white neighbors. The falling tax base, however, could not support greater investment in anti-gang activity and as newer gangs such as the Black Gangster Disciples and Four Corner Hustlers arrived, conflicts between gangs often ensued.

Despite attempts at forming alliances, inter-gang violence spilled into East High School in Maywood, leading to higher police presence on the campus every school year. The 1980s were a decade of rising crime and economic recession. In a famous study on crime, Zimmerman and Posick (2016) discussed the $54 million dollar research study examining Chicago neighborhoods over 7 years and with 60 research assistants who collectively interviewed 20,000 Chicago residents on videotape and analyzed social networks, crime and violence, collective efficacy, and neighborhood infrastructure. One aspect of the study led to challenging earlier hypotheses about the "broken window" theory and that bleak poverty over large swaths of the neighborhood played the largest role in crime rather than the number of broken windows in a community.

Even when the economic conditions began improving nationally at the later end of the 1980s, there were no signs of economic recovery in Maywood. Manufacturing jobs disappeared completely, and long-time residents fled, leaving no scope for growth and a plunging tax base. Latinx gangs had a particularly hostile relationship with the Maywood police force which was predominantly Black and white. In the 1980s, drug trade, criminal activity, and active recruiting by the gangs kept Maywood in the news for all the wrong reasons, and it had gained negative monikers, which we discuss at length in chapter 3. When allegations of corruption and gang collusion against the police became common, public trust eroded along racial lines, leaving Maywood further vulnerable to criminal activity.

Toward the 1990s and 2000s, Maywood experienced declines in its crime rates across several decades. Although the rate is still higher than most of its neighbors and 1.4 times greater than the US average, the downward trend from 750 acts of crime in 2006 to 380 in 2019 is promising, especially with dramatically lower rates of burglaries and thefts but with the same number of 11 murders per year (City Data, 2021). Yet rising poverty rates especially during the past COVID pandemic bring yet another era of uncertainty, coupled with the fact that the wealth gap between white and Black/Brown families continues to widen. Just this year, Cook County Treasurer Maria Pappas found that Maywood was one of the 12 suburbs in the country that experienced the greatest increase in property taxes for 2020, around $1500, compared to its wealthier neighbors Oak Park ($249 increase) and River Forest ($305 increase), which seems disproportionate. There has been growing resentment regarding the increased tax levies, and the village of Maywood held town hall meetings to address the increase in taxes (Roeder, 2021). Both the population loss and business closures have worsened the situation in suburbs like Maywood, leaving a smaller base to shoulder the tax burden. Business leaders in the region have argued that the county's policy of assessing business property at higher rates than homes puts them at a disadvantage since employers can build in adjoining counties that offer lower taxes. The cost of government also has outpaced what taxpayers can afford in Black and Latinx suburbs due to a lack of commercial property taxes. Meanwhile in Chicago, the homeowner tax bill has not seen an increase in 2021, but the commercial tax bill did go up.

It is ironic that when assessing the prospects of a place for home buying and raising a family people often judge the quality of life as being less than desirable when there are high levels of poverty and crime. Yet, both these measures are often a referendum on the political and socioeconomic forces of the time rather than on individual choices. Suburban homeownership is what propelled Maywood's Black residents into a solid middle class through much of the twentieth century. But segregation in housing due to discriminatory housing practices that restricted access pushed Black families into redlined areas through systemic racism along with white flight—creating a wealth gap so deep that generations of families have been unable to close it. Additionally, the loss of taxes and property values, and acute disinvestment in communities of color due to a self-fulfilling prophecy that Black communities may not be able to sustain businesses, such as the lack of a grocery store, leads to a local community like Maywood having to support the same levels of services as other communities but with a much smaller fiscal base (Husain, Rockett, Johnson, & Brinson, 2020).

Add to this a new frontier of environmental injustice that communities like Maywood are currently experiencing. In 2017, the *Chicago Tribune* newspaper published a deep analysis of the unequal water rates that paradoxically favor the wealthiest communities over those that are the poorest (Gregory, Reyes, O'Connell, & Caputo, 2017). Under little oversight by the state, most local leaders often have the authority to increase rates, and Maywood is one of the two communities that was singled out for fraud and corruption in this regard. Water rates in Maywood were the highest in the Chicagoland regions, and anecdotal stories on social media of water cutoffs and exorbitant rates to restart a basic necessity in an already economically stressed community provide further evidence that poverty and crime may be the byproducts of lack of jobs and lack of skilled workforce but can often be sustained through a complex web of local and national politics, economic trends, systemic inequities, and social injustice.

To address both these concerns, Maywood is making a concerted effort to dismantle power hierarchies in its own local politics and make sure that its representatives truly represent the interests of a changing demographic. In 2014, Maywood's mayor, village clerk, board trustees, and park district commissioner were all Black. In 2021, the board of trustees includes one Latinx member out of six, which does not reflect representational parity since the Latinx population is nearly 30% of Maywood. After media scrutiny, the village board has slashed the water service turn-on fee to half, and the current mayor Nathaniel George Booker is realigning the Community Development and Building and Code department to encourage reinvestment in the community, attract new commerce, and maintain better relations with businesses, especially the new Black and Latinx-owned businesses (Romain, 2021).

Education

Schools can be microcosms of the larger communities of which they are a part of and can provide deep insights into the racial, economic, and social conditions of their communities. They can be primary, early warning signals for several inevitable transformations of larger communities (Orfield, 2003). Maywood schools have historically been frontiers for race relations, mirroring both the complex coexistence of individuals from diverse racial and ethnic groups and the incredible potential of diverse coalitions in affecting societal and justice-related change. Yet, even after landmark desegregation cases such as *Brown v. Board* of Education in 1954 and *Mendez v. Westminster* in 1947, the national ideal of racial integration was hard to realize for many children of color in Northern, suburban communities like Maywood that had witnessed a burgeoning Black population coupled with excessive white flight, leaving barely any white children to be integrated with, except for a small number of Lutheran families whose families had established churches, private schools, and faith communities in Maywood.

H.G. Bissinger in a 1994 article in *The New York Times* wrote on the changing environment in Maywood schools stating that "the change in demographics from white to African-American in a basically blue-collar suburban district can be one of the most unsettling events in American politics." Politics and education were always intertwined in Maywood since native son Fred Hampton, Chairman of the Black Panther Party in Illinois, led the NAACP Youth Group in Maywood during the 1960s and 1970s. The organized and empowered youth under his leadership successfully accomplished many goals of remediating the injustices of covert racism such as the inaccessibility of swimming pools for Black residents (Duffy, 2021). Through the years, Black students continued to protest marginalization that was obvious in the low number of Black teachers, exclusive dominance of the white ethnocentric canonical literature, a white-washed history of America with no affirmation of the contributions of people of color, racially unfair academic tracking, watered down curricula, and an over-representation of students of color in special education. Spurred by activism in and around Maywood and empowered by the Black Panther ideology, the Black students in Maywood continued to protest.

Then on December 4, 1969, Fred Hampton, the leader of the Chicago Black Panthers, was killed by the police during an apartment raid on the city's West Side. Even though Hampton had been a native of Maywood, white students opposed a Black-student-sponsored memorial assembly in Fred Hampton's honor. Five days later, after 95 police officers were brought in to stop a rock-and-bottle-throwing melee, the school was closed (Bloom & Martin Jr, 2016). In a city like Chicago, which was divided along ethnic lines, the arrival of Black migrants from the South during the Great Migration shifted previously non-white immigrant groups like the Irish and Italian in places like Maywood and Melrose Park to "white" in order to distinguish themselves from the new Black arrivals (Pacyga, 2009). The riots shook Maywood and accelerated white flight, not in the traditional pattern from the city to the suburbs but from the inner-ring suburbs to the outer suburbs, converting Maywood into a solidly Black suburb until the turn of the century which saw a greater influx of Latinx families, children, and youth into the neighborhood public schools, as depicted in our book.

Maywood reflects many communities in America that are changing from being all Black to now mixed with a growing Latinx population. An influx of Latinx immigrants to predominantly Black Southern towns and communities, for example, is changing the old color line and order (Swarms, 2006). For many Black residents, they have always had an uneasy relationship with whites, and now being outnumbered by new Latinx arrivals makes them feel as if they are losing ground. Tensions ran high during the initial years of integration, and Latinx residents talked about being disparaged and discriminated against by Black residents while the Black community felt as if whites favored Latinx immigrants over them.

Mexican American immigrants often come to this country with biased views of Black Americans due to exposure to the biased American media that only portrays an urban population wrought by crime and violence. At other times, there were moments of camaraderie as both populations joined faith-based organizations and often grew up poor, working in the fields: "Lyrical Spanish chatter competes with the sweet Georgia drawl as Blacks and Hispanics share streets, assembly lines and classrooms—and hardships—that could prove to be the basis of community and political alliances" (Swarms, 2006, p. 21). In Black middle-class communities like Maywood, Black residents tend to have higher degrees of education than their new Latinx neighbors and resent the privilege they come with and subsequent success, leading to neighbors keeping their distance and remaining wary of each other. There are also cultural differences that can cause misunderstandings such as when Black residents wave to their neighbors with that Southern hospitality and find that they are often ignored by their new Latinx neighbors. For the most part, current Black Americans have not lived alongside immigrants and still feel uncomfortable socializing with Latinx residents. Perhaps it is also a difference between newcomers and long-timers as well as who adopts the exclusionary barriers of their white neighbors and preserves their own social privileges.

Some Black residents in the South did not support the increase of Latinx residents and suspected that not all of them are citizens and joined the small but fringe group who felt that the greatest threat to Black citizens since slavery is the influx of undocumented migrants with less desirable neighborhood characteristics (Martinez, 2006). They also resented that the Civil Rights Movement language was now being used for other minoritized groups, which some called out as grandstanding. This argument also fails to account for the Afro-Hispanic immigrant population in the United States as well as the slavery and civil rights movements in Latin America.

Rubén Martínez (2002), a professor and writer, follows a Mexican American family that migrates from the Mexican city of Cherán to Warren, Arkansas, a small Southern town, where the young teenage sons live out the "Mexamerican Dream." The patriarch of the family is only one generation away from a monolingual indigenous life in the highlands of Cherán (speaking Purépecha, not Spanish) while the sons speak a hybrid mix of the Black dialect, the Southern twang of Arkansas, Spanish with a slight gringo-accent and English with a slight Mexican accent (Saul, 2002). The family moves into a predominantly Black community and tries to feel their way around their new community, finding similarities with their new neighbors, and wading through the tricky waters of cultural differences, while adopting the dress code, hip-hop style, and lingua franca of urban youth. Black cultural capital is what is valued even in a small Arkansas town, and what it means to be an American is often defined by a Black cultural orientation. This cultural congruence can lead to coalition building and unity if we tap into affinity and ultimately activism: "Because the same wolves are at the puerta as at the door: rage and alienation, drugs, unemployment, the cops, the military, poor school services, gangs, pregnancy" (Martínez, 2002).

Furthermore, more than a decade ago, a study conducted by Loyola University's Center for Urban Research and Learning in Chicago found that the recent wave of gentrification often creates a "us versus them" tension which we found in Maywood as well. The Black residents of Maywood feared displacement by the influx of Latinx residents and saw their neighborhoods and village being remade with new people and new businesses but without a sense of community, leading to misperceptions and fears. Briggs (2006) quoted interviewees from the study who made an analogy of how the new Latinx residents were taking over their community "block by block" and in doing so removing their Black identity "piece by piece."

Subsequently, the mayor of Maywood took the initiatives to create more face to face contacts between Black and Latinx residents in order to create a better sense of community and to break down the damaging narrative of displacement. At the same time, mixed neighborhoods are on the rise and tend to be more stable, especially in multiethnic suburbs (Alba & Logan, 1993). Seeking to build a coalition in the South suburbs of Chicago between Latinx leaders fighting for immigration rights and Black grass-roots activists, the South Suburban Action Conference staged a march and rally to protest regressive immigration laws under former President Trump (Bowean, 2006). Reverend Lawrence Blackful wanted to create a united front for a variety of issues such as more jobs and economic growth for the region as well as homelessness, education funding, and crime and violence, issues that affect both minoritized groups.

Changing Schools

Changing demographic trends are closely mirrored by the changes in school populations in Maywood. In every elementary school, over the past couple of decades, the Latinx student population has consistently increased while the Black population has consistently declined. The white student population, although marginal to begin with, has continued to decline through the 2000s and is now at 2%. Logan (2002) used the standard measures of segregation like the Index of Dissimilarity and Exposure and Isolation indices to analyze segregation among public elementary school children. According to this study, the average level of segregation hardly changed in the 1990s, and in some places, there was a clear rollback of progress made before 1990 with Black children being the most segregated minoritized group by far. In 2003, The Civil Rights Project at Harvard University disseminated a report suggesting that schools were in the midst of a massive resegregation movement that was undoing the legislative achievements of the past century (Frankenburg, Lee & Orfield, 2003). Furthermore, in 2004, John Logan from the Lewis Mumford Center analyzed census data that found that Black exposure to whites decreased during the 1990s. This decrease was not due to growing Black isolation; instead, Blacks were in schools with a higher Latinx and Asian presence, a fact made clear by the changing racial demographics of the Maywood schools.

Maywood elementary schools support this thesis about racial integration between multiple minoritized races in American public schools. Maywood elementary schools have all witnessed a decline in Black students from around 70% in 2016 to 60% in 2020. Meanwhile, the Latinx population has increased from the low 20% to the high 30%. The high schools in Maywood show greater representative parity between racial groups with a Black student population of 40% (a decline from 48% in 2016) and a Latinx population of 58% (an increase from 48% in 2016) since the high schools draw students across the entire township and across five multiracial suburban communities of Maywood, Melrose Park, Forest Park, Hillside, and Westchester.

Today Maywood stands at a point in history where its schools are majority-minority schools, but the racial composition of the schools has consistently changed across the last three decades. While Maywood is often painted as an inner-ring suburb with high levels of crime and poverty, long-time residents are quick to jump to its defense by pointing out the resilient way in which the community has embraced diversity, irrespective of race, and parents and educators are often the first responders. Maywood schools are trying to meet the needs of a burgeoning Latinx student population with bilingual and EL (English Learner) language programs along with cultural congruence. Maywood educators are rising to the challenge of incorporating diverse voices, histories, and perspectives, preparing their students to be successful professionals and social justice advocates.

Youth protests in Maywood have a long history of advocacy. The most recent solidarity marches in June 2020 protesting the unfair policing practices and racial injustice resulted in a large turnout of Black and Brown voices and provided a hopeful glimpse into the future of Maywood as a community that embraces diversity and educates its children and youth to stand up for justice and fairness. The current push by Fred Hampton Jr. to preserve his father's home in Maywood has also drawn multiracial support from Maywood and

Figure 1.6   A Photo from One of Our Research Participants. Mary and Her T-Ball Team in the 1980s. She is in the bottom row, left, making a funny face. The T-ball teams eventually disappeared as the Latinx population increased and soccer replaced T-ball. *Source:* Madilyn Wiley.

beyond its borders. The conditions in Maywood schools are still less than ideal for tri-racial integration given the miniscule proportion of white students. But the changing student demographics position Maywood, like many other inner-ring suburbs, at the frontier of a new kind of inter-group integration between multiple marginalized and minoritized individuals. Teachers, school board members, and families have a unique opportunity to ensure that the mistakes of the past are not repeated but that individuals from both Black and Latinx communities develop a deep and meaningful understanding of their shared and unique histories, cultures, and futures. How Maywood manages this new dynamic might determine its very survival in the coming decades.

CONCLUSION

Understanding the history of a suburb like Maywood means untangling the complex web of place evident in the geopolitical forces that operate in an inner-ring suburb. These forces create affordances of economic stability but can also sustain unequal access to schools, housing, and wealth. Racial dynamics are evident in the changing demographics of the community and school systems that necessitate complex inter- and intra-group solidarity but can also perpetuate competition and interpersonal conflict.

While one can view Maywood's history through the deficit lens of the many challenges it has withstood—loss of industry and job, racial segregation, white flight, poverty and crime, and low-test scores—we use an asset mindset instead to focus on Maywood's resilient character through the years. Maywood has changed its economy to embrace a stronger service sector, acknowledged its painful history of segregation and white flight by embracing a new kind of effort in integrating Black and Latinx populations, actively created collaborative relations with neighboring townships to promote its welfare and economic progress, and is educating a civically engaged and social justice-oriented student population. While it has survived many national and local milestone events in history, its survival in the twenty-first century will depend on its willingness to embrace and empower its Black and Latinx residents.

Chapter 2

Sub/Urban Schools

White Teachers, Black and Latinx Students, and Systemic Racism

Schools are mirrors of their communities and of our country's governance. The dynamics of what occurs in Maywood schools between teachers, students, administrators, and parents are documented here in this chapter including how these participants become aware of the human diversity within their community as well as the social divisions. In this chapter, we interpret the relationships, interactions, and *habitus* embedded in these school-based contexts (Bourdieu, 2020). We extrapolate from interviews and observational data to analyze the complexity of the sociocultural and sociolinguistic phenomena before us. We are not here to talk about how to improve educational practice and student achievement nor discuss the curriculum and standards. Rather, we are here to disclose the meaning of what gets hidden within the curriculum, what the hushed voices in the back of the classroom are saying, the pathos and ethos of teaching in sub/urban schools, and to explore the charged issues of race, language, and culture.

Referring to our Introduction, our study examines three schools in the Maywood school district that were predominantly Black but began shifting toward an increasing Latinx student population in 2008, when the economic recession began and more multigenerational Latinx families were moving into the suburban homes, which we discuss further in chapter 3. As Maywood was coming to terms with shifting demographics and sociocultural change, the schools themselves internalized this changing dynamic and incorporated a tri-racial system with a majority of white teachers, a majority of Black administrators, and a growing Latinx student population in majority Black schools. At the start of our study, there was great discussion of how the Black and Latinx students were being treated by an unequal public school system that is visibly run by the "eyes and actions of a dominant racial/cultural Other," the white teachers and district level administrators, and where students expressed feelings of cultural invisibility and marginalization (Luke, 2017, p. 103S). However, by the end of our study in 2022, the pandemic set by the COVID virus changed the educational landscape profoundly since now the students were engaged in e-learning and were logged into their virtual classrooms from their homes. Here is one Black principal's account of how COVID changed the level of empathy from the white teachers in her Maywood school:

> Because COVID is the one reason why these teachers have a better connection with the kids. Because COVID allowed white teachers to go into the homes of these kids and see what's going on. Teachers actually saw the background. Teachers could actually hear the different languages that were spoken. Some of the profanity that was going on . . . teachers could see kiddos under the floor next to their beds, because that's the only space they have and to me, 'cause it was a blessing in that point of view, because I think teachers are going to be more empathetic when kids come back because it's like I didn't know, right? I didn't know that you come to school like this. Because of what I saw on camera . . . they had a bird's eye view of what some of our kiddos go through on a daily basis. So, I think coming in now, I think they're going to be more empathetic to how they approach kids.

WHITE TEACHERS AND PLANTATION SCHOOLS

At the beginning stages of our study during the early 2000s, many of the white teachers in this district were second- or third-generation Irish and Italian Americans and lived in the predominantly white suburbs west of Maywood in middle-class communities like Elk Grove Village and Palatine—not quite wealthy ex-burbs but middle-class suburbs that were half an hour to an hour away on the highway. As we completed our study, a new superintendent who identified as Afro-Latino brought in a more diverse teaching force of young Black and Brown teachers who often were alums of the school district and had returned to the Maywood of their childhood after college to serve their community. The superintendent also brought a shift toward promoting enhanced cultural knowledge, heightened academic outcomes, research-based best practices, and a strengths-based approach toward children and families in which all children can thrive. At the same time, the teacher union was strong in this district and helped maintain the jobs of white teachers who lived elsewhere but came to teach in Maywood for different reasons—some who came to collect "a paycheck" and others for the love of the community.

There seemed to be a general perception among the Black and Brown community, a kind of "hidden truth," that the white teachers were unlikely to find employment in their own predominantly white home communities and therefore came to Maywood to teach. It did not help the dynamic that the white teachers did not focus on the lived experiences and needs of the families they served; there was no evidence of a reciprocal relationship that involved listening to and sharing stories between the white teachers and the Black and Brown students from our data. Rather, most white teachers came off the highway, drove into the parking lot right before school started, and then drove back home to their white suburbs once school ended, often referring to Maywood as the "ghetto" in our observations, a place where they worked but did not live. In fact, white linguistic and cultural norms often conflate deficit-based words and images such as "disrespectful," "thug," "ghetto," "bad," trouble," "skips school," and "gets bad grades" with Black and Brown school communities (Alim & Smitherman, 2012). Many teachers voiced a deep resentment that they were "stuck" teaching in Maywood and resented being there and subsequently internalized a racist antagonism toward the students and their families, which then perpetuated their dehumanization of "other people's children" for whom they were held accountable by the state government (Delpit, 200). One Black father that we interviewed spoke about this dehumanization process:

> Truth is a lot of teachers and administrators use the district as a training ground same as with the police department. Teachers come there, work a few years, fulfill those obligations of working in low-income areas to get those loans practically wiped out and then go to those great school districts with higher pay with the distinction of having worked in the hood (looked at as heroes). Potential police officers come here because they can't get in anywhere else fulfill those obligations then ride off into the sunset in the suburbs with low crime. Only those with real ties to Maywood stick around. Administrators come here to either build their profile for more attractive positions or they were on their way out at their current positions. They have no real ties to Maywood. We needs a complete reboot to get back to the days where the students were put first. Nowadays it's just political propaganda and our kids are losing.

In Maywood, the ten school buildings all look alike in the district: post-WWII era beige-brown, two-floor brick structures with cinder block walls inside, polished linoleum tiles, fluorescent lights, metal stairs, and thick glass pane windows. There are low-lying bushes in the front of the school buildings; however, in 2008, none of the K-8 buildings had a playground for children minus one due to a state-funded preschool. Instead, there was a cracked, asphalt blacktop where children chased after each other, played with jump ropes and rubber balls, and a few painted games like four squares. There was a security guard at the front of the building where everyone entered minus the teachers who parked in the back and came in from the back of the buildings.

The uniformity across the K-8 buildings and the lack of trees on the school grounds, along with a perimeter of rusty, twisted chain-link fences gave the schools an industrial look that matched the nearby factories where their grandparents may have worked.

Even though the schools were majority-minority schools, there was no discussion of a culture-based curriculum nor a discussion of the students' social and emotional development at the start of our research study; rather, the district functioned as if it was race-neutral even though the racial tensions were palpable. There was no sense of belonging, cultural affiliation, and connection to the Maywood community among most of the white teachers. As schools across the country began placing college-bound paraphernalia on their walls like pendants and mascots to increase academic achievement, the district was slow to make this a requirement, and many teachers mocked the initiative due to their low set of expectations for the Black and Latinx students and held biased assumptions that "these children" will not go to college. The white teachers who received the lowest performance scores often were sent to the schools south of the railroad tracks where the students were majority Black—a practice that no longer exists under the leadership of the new superintendent. During the start of our study, there was a great emphasis on controlling students' behaviors and bodies more so than their academic achievement. This was not initially a school district that allowed Black and Latinx children to thrive; rather, there were deeply rooted issues of social division that needed healing.

W. E. B. DuBois, a prominent American scholar, described the conditions found here in this school district as "caste education" that perpetuated the colonial-plantation era mentality of a domineering white teaching force in which the "public school became a primary place where the racial privilege of the 'white world' and the dehumanizing conditions of the 'dark world' were educated into existence and the old caste codes were dressed in new Jim Crow clothing" (Pierce, 2017, p. 24S). School systems were equated with state/industrial complexes that reproduced racial hierarchies by teaching white workers to internalize racist antagonism toward their non-white working counterparts. The same dynamics of power and control that reigned in slave plantations were carried over into the industrial era and now into the neoliberal ideology of school reform and academic achievement gaps. In the end, it is about social control that maintains unequal systems between white and non-white worlds across systems and structures like public schools, rooted in our history of slavery. Educational tools like the curriculum, teacher recruitment and training, policies around expulsion and suspension, and school funding are all used to reproduce the caste system and promote antagonism between white teachers and administrators and non-white students, parents, and teachers.

In this school district, the students were hyper-policed from the security guards at the entrance to the school to the teachers and administrators in the classrooms and hallways, as well as in the hyper-policed neighborhoods where they lived. It was common to hear teachers blame the students and their parents for the low academic achievement, wrapping their disparaging comments in "discourses of individual responsibility" and often wrongly comparing their own privileged white children to the disenfranchised Black and Latinx children they taught in Maywood. They rarely acknowledged their white privilege and biases, the systemic inequities leading to unequal school systems, a history of oppression and white supremacy, an "epistemic apartheid" of multicultural education and Black history, and the barriers that their students faced outside of school, where the white teachers never ventured (Pierce, 2017, p. 25S).

The Black and Latinx teachers know of this caste education, have grown up in it, and are now prepared to abolish it by challenging the larger legacy of epistemological ignorance. The newly hired Black and Latinx teachers set in motion a progressive public education system for Maywood, along with the leadership of the new Afro-Latino superintendent, that allows people of color to thrive rather than face a social death. The new superintendent began with ameliorations to the physical buildings during and after the 2020 pandemic with new playgrounds, geothermal heating, tuckpointing, new windows, and new interior paint. The teachers noted how he put effort into all the schools and not just the ones north of the railroad tracks and how he is being mindful of the equity among the ten schools.

The hiring of new progressive Black and Latinx teachers brought in a change that addressed the politically charged history of white supremacy and systemic inequities and its accumulation over the years in the Maywood schools. "Either we do this or die" is the opening statement in DuBois' essay on caste education, and it speaks to the need for an alternative form of education that will allow Black and Latinx children to live and to thrive with a focus on their social growth and spiritual renewal (Pierce, 2017). The interview below is with Mary, a young Black teacher who was an alum who returned to teach in her childhood community and no longer tolerated the lack of isomorphism between the world of the white teachers and the students' backgrounds (Luke, 2017). The white teachers were strangers in the land of Maywood and did not know the collective capital of the Black and Latinx students; therefore, the white teacher must learn to look and listen with a "wide awareness" that gives way to understanding the students' cultural backgrounds because the teacher is indeed a cultural worker (Friere, 1998). For Mary, the white teachers were the cultural Other in Maywood while the Black and Latinx teachers provided cultural synchronicity, which research shows can lead to educational benefits for students from the same racial and cultural backgrounds:

Author: It's really about divide and conquer. The white people are in control like the mayor of Melrose Park and the white teachers and administrators in this

school district. And sometimes they pit the Black and Brown communities in
Maywood against each other. What do you think about that statement?

Mary: There are very few white teachers who are not racist here. Those who think
they are not racist are often operating out of the "great white hope" framework
and the savior complex or the "I have a Black friend" game. Or "I adopted Black
kids you know." A lot of my time has been spent coaching these white teachers.
I have to teach them how to be culturally and linguistically competent. Then I
have to inform them about what being trauma-informed means as well. It has
been rough, but we are really pushing the envelope on white teachers. If you
are going to be a racist teacher, then you should not work here. I did professional development on Maywood history with the white teachers like learning
about Fred Hampton and getting to know the truth behind his life. For teacher
appreciation week, I created a video of Black residents, mentors, pastors, and
community members sharing their history. It is important for them to know that
they are here in our community. You are in this building, and this building is on
Maywood land. Your cars are also in Maywood land. Yes, you drive here to get
to Maywood. We do not drive to you. You need to know Maywood and your
place in it.

Mary went on to describe the uphill battle with some white teachers who
were unwilling to put in the effort into truly understanding and leveraging
the strengths of their Black and Brown students. But she also described
alternative solutions where some ineffective white teachers were much more
effective when given the responsibility to work as specialists with smaller
groups of students rather than leading a classroom of Black and Latinx students. According to her, "talking about race" was the greatest "change agent"
in determining which teachers provided the highest quality education for all
the children in the community. Figure 2.1 shows the picture of Mary and her
family who moved to Maywood in the 1980s and are now a bedrock for the
Black community.

However, some of the Black teachers we interviewed also noted other
variables that needed to be addressed for school reform such as the leadership at the top. In another interview with Gina, a Black veteran teacher in
the school district and alum of the school system, she also noted the recent
cultural change but had a different perspective as a newly appointed principal
in the district. Her opinion offered a neutral positioning of white teachers in
the school district. This was evident in her response and acknowledging her
own positionality when we asked Gina the following question to validate or
challenge her observations.

Author: You've had me in class, and I taught the diversity class with the majority
of white teachers in the district. Can you tell me if I am right or wrong here?
The majority of white teachers do not live in Maywood or Melrose Park. The

Figure 2.1 Mary and Her Family before Heading Out to Her Father's (Pastor) Baptist Church. *Source*: Madilyn Wiley.

majority come from suburbs like Elk Grove Village . . . the outer ring suburbs. They come off the highway . . . teach and then get back on the highway. Do they really care about the school community?

Placing greater responsibility and accountability on the administration's visions and efforts to foster a culture of authentic inclusion and solidarity, Gina agreed that while this was true initially, putting on an administrative lens had compelled her to view the situation differently. She highlighted that the change in the school and district administrative structure, a newly developed middle school model, and the expectation that teachers participate in extracurricular activities and engage with students meaningfully had made Maywood schools highly sought-after institutions where teachers from different areas wanted to teach now.

Gina: A lot of time it is based on the administrator and what vision they had for the school. The vision has to drive the hunger to be in that school. There were white teachers who taught in the Melrose Park schools but wanted to get transferred to the Maywood schools because of the vision of the new administration. When I was an assistant principal, same thing. The principal's vision has to be about community and supporting teachers. If the principal wants the teachers to be at Parent Night . . . it depends on that principal and what their vision is for the school. So yeah, we had white teachers who drove farther to be at our Maywood schools to work with the new school administration. They come to the games now after school and the white teachers run the soccer programs. They do home visits, and the turnover rate is not what it used to be. But the majority are gone when the children are gone. So, I feel like the times have changed a bit and the district is evolving. But again, I credit the superintendent who had a vision for our district and is still here enacting change. He has been here for five years and his ideas are coming to fruition.

Author: What are some changes that brought about the greatest reform?

Gina: We have one to one services for students. We have a new culturally and linguistically responsive curriculum and Dr. Sharroky Hollie has been working with us for the last couple of years. It's allowing teachers to look outside of their own culture and understand what is happening in the student's home culture. We have a dual language academy that really focuses on the Hispanic population and the African American students who want them to learn Spanish on top of English. We have so many options here in the community based on what the school has to offer. I think that is where the buy in comes from. I remember having conversations with some white teachers that were saying they wish they lived in Maywood because they wanted their kids to go to the dual language school. They asked me if I was going to put my son in the dual language academy and I said that he is going to apply like everybody else. The district is just so different now [2020]. I feel like we are more competitive now with our teaching pool.

The dual language academy referenced here is now in its sixth year of implementation and has overcome many of the initial obstacles, hurdles, and dissent from the school community. In 2010, the former bilingual education director for the school district developed a proposal for a dual language school that was eventually approved by the school board after a year of contentious school board meetings in which the Black and Latinx parents discussed the benefits and challenges with such a program: (a) whether Black children are the best English-language role models for the Latinx children; (b) whether the Latinx children will need to get bussed from their homes north of the railroad tracks to the south of the tracks where the dual language academy was located; (c) whether the Latinx parents felt safe sending their children to the Black neighborhood in Maywood where the school was located; and (d) whether Black children can master Spanish as a second language in which there are not many speakers of it in their homes and in their segregated neighborhoods. The students were overwhelmingly in support of the idea of a dual language program while the support varied greatly among the adults. In one public board meeting, Melissa, a Latina bilingual teacher who lived in Melrose Park, stated that the district could not have a dual language program because there were not any white students in the school. Another teacher stated that the Black students would not be good role models for the English language. Many teachers felt it was a good idea but claimed that the school board would never allow it. When we formally surveyed the Black students on whether they would be interested in learning Spanish, there was an overwhelming response in favor of learning Spanish and the need for the schools to even offer a foreign language program in Spanish in elementary schools.

Recent critiques of dual language programs have cited the low representation of specific student populations such as Black and Asian American students, students with special needs, and students from lower SES backgrounds. In Madison, Wisconsin, there were concerns about its dual language programs because only 9% of the students in dual language programs were Black when in fact there were 34% Black student population in the entire district (DeFour, 2011). Furthermore, when one examines the database of dual language programs across the country devised by the Center for Applied Linguistics (2011), the majority of Black-Latinx dual language programs are in California; the dual language academy in Maywood is the first in the state of Illinois. If the argument is that dual language programs should integrate English proficient students with English learners, then why do we not find dual language programs in majority-minority school districts? Given the fact that racial integration is increasing for these two racial minority groups, the onus is upon the educational research community to examine the invisible racial inequity found in majority-minority school districts and what happens when it is never named.

At the research level, a dual language program is a form of bilingual education that brings together children who are from two different sociolinguistic and sociocultural backgrounds in the same classroom where they learn each other's languages, cultures, and identities (Hadi-Tabassum, 2006). The model in this school district brings together 50% Latinx children who are Spanish-dominant and 50% Black children who are English-dominant in the same classroom starting in kindergarten and all the way up to the middle grades in order for both populations to become bilingual in both English and Spanish. The curriculum is grounded in both languages, and both languages are used to teach the content areas such as literacy, math, science, social studies, and extracurricular activities like art and gym. Research shows that dual language programs are the strongest academically since English learners who spend their elementary school years in two-language programs have test scores, English proficiency levels, and reclassification rates that are, on average, as high as or higher than similar students who were in English-only classrooms and over a long-term trajectory (Umansky, Valentino, & Reardon, 2015). Here is a description of the Washington Dual Language Academy (2022) on this school district's website:

> Our Dual Language program, a highly sought-after program, where students learn Spanish and English at an early age. Our Dual Language program provides

students the opportunity to learn Spanish and English through content instruction. The cognitive benefits for students attending this program are backed by decades of research. Our program stands out as a microcosm of intercultural unity in an ever increasingly polarized society and demonstrates to the educational community that students can acquire a second language without compromising their other educational needs. It also showcases that people of very diverse backgrounds can work together harmoniously for the good of all children.

Our parents support our schools in so many ways. We have a fabulous PTO that volunteers countless hours to organize many events that bring our school community together. Everything the PTO does is based on ways to promote family engagement that builds a strong community. Parents make a difference by being engaged and involved in their child's education, by volunteering, participating in PTO sponsored events, supporting fundraisers, by attending school and classroom activities.

We hold fast to the belief that a student need not lose a language to learn another and that additive bilingualism benefits all students in the development of their cognitive, academic, linguistic and socio-cultural proficiencies.

Research also shows that dual language programs are stronger because they promote socialization between often isolated and segregated sociolinguistic and sociocultural groups, such as the Black and Latinx students in Maywood, help reduce discrimination, improve self-esteem, encourage mutual respect for diversity, and produce stronger cross-group relationships and inter-cultural connections (Cho, 2000; Wright & Tropp, 2005). At the same time, there have been ongoing criticisms of dual language programs because of unequal power dynamics between the two different racial and linguistic groups, often with white parents in Spanish-English dual language programs accessing power and leverage over Latinx parents who frequently lose agency and decision-making authority when dual language programs are implemented in their community (Valdés, 1997). This unequal power dynamic has been recently applied to Spanish-English dual language programs with Black and Latinx students, addressing the social justice concerns that have arisen surrounding anti-blackness in dual language programs, as well as the minimal success and dilemmas of Black students participating in dual language programs (Hadi-Tabassum; 2006; Negrette, 2021; Palmer, 2010).

In the dual language academy highlighted in this school district, there was a higher rate of Black children in the dual language program being suspended and removed from the early learning classrooms, leading to the integration of behavior specialists who were brought in to determine whether the behavior concerns were due to a lack of cultural and linguistic responsiveness from the school leaders and teachers. Black parents went to the school board meetings and demanded that their children not be punished for misunderstandings and miscommunication, as well as the academic difficulties on the part of their young children who were just beginning to learn Spanish as their second language. Therefore, it was imperative at the district level to define both the Latinx and Black students in Maywood as "emergent bilinguals" and erase the anti-blackness often found in bilingual programs (Flores, 2016).

In the end, the school district became intentional in considering the racial and cultural challenges within its latest dual language program and hired a new bilingual education director who was a former, respected school principal in the district. She created a team-teaching approach at the dual language academy in which a Spanish bilingual teacher, often Latinx, taught alongside an English-dominant teacher, often Black, within the same classroom so all children had race-matching advocates and role models. Her background in child development also led to discussions with us on how young children are very much aware of racial dynamics and act as social actors who can make meaning; therefore, the dual language curriculum must address the histories of both the Black and Latinx communities in Maywood as they expand grades. The school district engineered a program that met the needs of both populations through new leadership, consensus building, and an effective team-teaching model within the dual language academy. The school district also challenged the false binary of whether a dual language program should be "Latinx serving" or "Black serving" and thereby changed the school culture with a multiethnic, democratic approach in which no one race is the dominant majority.

Gary Orfield's (2017, p. 165S) seminal research on civil rights and equal opportunity in public schools has highlighted the rapid changes to school composition. One could argue that Maywood is like many places in our country that has an evolving multi-racial population and that it is very difficult for schools to keep up with "the multidimensional changes" in which they often receive no training, especially managing race relations to explore solutions to divisions and find ways to diminish polarization. We have substantial research on Black-white school integration, but we have minimal research on Black-Latinx integration. The Black Power Movement of the 1960s and leaders like Fred Hampton created powerful places like Maywood in which the Black community felt better off in controlling their own segregated schools as trained Black school administrators and teachers took over.

Both Mary and Gina's parents were a part of that movement and settled into Maywood to create a strong school district. Now a generation later, Maywood was becoming increasingly Latinx as families moved into Black neighborhoods and perplexed the older Black residents who now understandably felt like the minority in their own communities. The following sections of this chapter delve further into the classrooms and highlight the festering racial tensions and racial fears within the brick-and-mortar spaces, as well as moments of racial and cultural bridging, which is what happens when communities undergo massive changes that make their way into schools. We highlight deeply rooted issues of social division that never heal and lead to further separation and inequality. Nobody in our study was really trained on how to create positive Black-Latinx race relations in public schools, how to undermine stereotypes and biases, and how to develop interracial harmony across racial lines between two marginalized communities facing many of the same social and economic obstacles. There are also moments highlighted below when strong school leadership led to a continued commitment to integration, to cross-cultural collaboration and teamwork, and to fairness and equality among the different groups. Our hope is to build on the body of research to help us understand Black-Latinx relations in public schools so we can illuminate and resolve problems by using the lessons from our research study to extend to new contexts beyond Maywood.

BROWN/BLACK RELATIONS: LOS MORENOS AND THE MEXICANS

The Latinx adolescent students whom we followed in this study comprise a small Brown minority in a largely Black middle school; therefore, our initial hypothesis was that the Latinx students will mobilize themselves as a minority group and form a strong collective identity both defensively and offensively against the Other students or los morenos—a euphemism for Black students used by the Latinx students. The fear of being marginalized is what one would say can propel Latinx students to stick together, to form a monocultural defense, to form an identity antithetical against the Other or los morenos: we are us because we are not them. Schwartz (1997) goes as far as to claim that all forms of identity making are violent acts because they are acts of inclusion and exclusion, versus the selfless acts of plentitude and generosity. However, we did not find our initial hypothesis to be valid in Maywood where many of the Latinx students spoke about feeling fully accepted in a Black majority school through acts of inclusion but they also spoke about being most comfortable within the nexus of their own small group of Latinx friends who spoke Spanish, ate what they ate and listened to the same type of music and dance—a sign of homophily which states that we are attracted to those who are most like us in our social network (McPherson, Smith-Lovin, & Cook, 2001).

Homophily argues that similarity breeds connection and that we live in homogeneous spaces in which we receive the same information, form the same attitudes, and share the same experiences, therefore less taxing for our brains. We no longer feel the "fight/flight" tension and can find homeostasis when we are with our own tribe. Furthermore, social science research also points to how the structural diversity in integrated Black-Latinx classrooms and schools may not always lead to interactional diversity; rather, greater structural diversity may lead to fewer interracial friendships, especially among students of color who tend to stick with same-race peers (Bowman, 2012). White students on the other hand do benefit from structural diversity and are more likely to have interracial friendships, close friendships, and romantic relations across races when attending diverse schools.

In our study of Maywood, the number of in-group friendships was much larger than interracial friendships, perhaps because there was no academic tracking and both races were in the same classrooms. Pairs of students often socialized within their race/ethnicity and generally were more similar in attitudes and behaviors in school, at the same time, homophily was strongest among the Latinx students who made up the minority in numbers but were growing. Martin et al. (2007) state that many Black adolescents limit contact with other students and increase contact with same-race peers to help maintain positive self-esteem and minimize social stress. Our findings validate the body of research stating that same-race friendships with a sizable number provide social and emotional support in racially integrated schools (Quillian & Campbell, 2003).

One young Latina student we interviewed spoke about moving to the United States three years ago from Morales, Mexico, and coming directly to Maywood in the fourth grade. She began her elementary schooling in a Spanish fourth-grade bilingual classroom but then was transitioned to an English-only classroom by the time she reached sixth grade, not enough time to truly become literate in both languages. In middle school, she began hanging out with other Latina students in her social circle and stated that her elementary school was "más Latino" and now her middle school was mostly "moreno" and "me gustaría más Latinas." She spoke about how her elementary schooling was "más fácil" since all her teachers were bilingual and how she could respond to teachers in Spanish. Now she uses more English, but she does not enjoy it because she feels nervous: "Me siento nerviosa en en inglés y no puedo entender más." She also spoke about how the Black students were playful and why she did not want to play along with them: "Ellos siempre están jugando y no quiero jugar. No dije nada y no se como defenderme en inglés." It was apparent that she was used to a form of schooling in which students were expected to be quiet and docile, focused on procedural engagement rather than engage in student-centered instruction that was focused on interactive, call-response discourse.

Her family bought a house on the corner of 16th Avenue and Washington and only spoke Spanish at home. She spoke about how they loved their new Maywood home because "es más tranquilo aquí y más seguridad." She shared the home with eleven family members: her mother and father, six siblings, two sisters-in-law, and a three-old niece. They waved to their Black neighbors when they saw them, but there was no relation between them, as well as no relation with their Puerto Rican neighbor: "Los saludamos cuando los vemos pero es lo mismo con la familia puertorriqueña." In the end, she spoke about how they never faced any racism from their Black neighbors, and everyone just minded their own business but did not develop social ties and social networks: "No lo visto mucho racismo aquí."

Yet, in the everyday lives of classrooms and students, there were moments of racial microaggressions (commonplace verbal or behavioral indignities, whether intentional or unintentional, which communicate hostile, derogatory, or negative racial slights and insults) when a racially tinged comment would flare up and then become potentially harmful for the classroom environment—comments about a Latinx student's immigration status to comments about whom they would never date or comments about a Black student's hair or the election of our first Black president (Sue et al., 2007). We captured moments when adolescents were being mean to each other and calling each other "crack babies" and "fools" across racial lines as well as using terms of affection like "boo" and "nigga" across racial lines. There were also times when the Latinx students spoke to each other in Spanish with hushed tones when they wanted to share something private, important to only them, and/or jokes about their Black peers who sometimes asked, "Are you talking about me in Spanish?"

The following interview with Susanna, a science teacher of South Asian descent, captures the small rifts and ruptures, as she describes them, which can flare up at any point and occur mostly among the female students:

Susanna: When I first started, I think there was one Latina girl. Her brother was in the sixth grade. When he moved up to seventh, I had two Hispanic students. What I am personally seeing is that they are taking the Black identity upon themselves. Some of my students don't speak Spanish even though they are Hispanic. They can understand it but don't speak it fluently. I had two students in my classroom . . . two females this year who do speak it and one African American female student did say to her, "You need to speak English because you are in America." I have heard it. At the beginning of the school year, I used to have these huge rifts between my African American girls and my Latina girls.
Author: What was the rift about?
Susanna: Just the fact that they were different, and they didn't like it . . . they felt that the Latina girls had extra attention and had more resources . . . the prank that blew it up is when one of the African American girls drew a picture of a pit

bull and wrote, "Have you found Maria?" and then they slipped the paper into her desk. That blew it up and I had to address the situation. I told them that this was not something I personally wanted to deal with . . . you need to treat each other equally and fairly. So, then I started pairing them up. So, I kind of forced them to work with each other. Then they had no choice. Right now, everything is going well, but Maria recently just transferred out of the school.

In this scenario above, we saw the racial tensions when a few individual Latinx students started to enroll in predominantly Black schools. However, there were also racial tensions when Black students started to venture into these quickly shifting Latinx neighborhoods within Maywood. Such experiences are not surprising when considering the concept of a critical mass of same-ethnic peers that seem necessary for students, especially high school students, to positively navigate a school environment where their group is a racial/ethnic minority, and where until such mass is reached, increasing diversity may be positively related to perceptions of discrimination (Benner & Graham, 2009, 2011). Here is an interview with Mary, a Black teacher who grew up in Maywood and noted the demographic shifts and the raw memory of being called the N-word on a school bus:

Mary:- Obviously when I was young between ages 2 and 10, race wasn't a really big issue because you saw these same people all day and every day, and Maywood is only 21 blocks long so everybody kind of knew you by your last name. So, if you are a Wiley or Robinson or Terrell everybody kind of knew who you were. Everything started to shift once I got into like the middle school age when more Latinx students started to come, and we don't quite know who they were. I remember my first encounter with race. I was on a bus. And this is pretty harsh, but I'm just letting you know about my first encounter. I was on the bus and there was a student who was . . . you know how we're all going back 'cause it's for like the cool kid, right? You know everybody wants to go to the back of the bus. That's where you can hang out. There's not a lot of . . . it's less structured back there, right? It's just more fun, yeah. I remember a boy sat back there . . . a Latinx student and he said the N word. He said, "Nigger don't come back here." And I wasn't really a fighter in that sense, but I remember almost jumping out of my body and I grabbed him, and we were just on the bus, hustling and come . . . I got pulled off the bus by a white teacher because that's the other thing. It's not just the new influx of Latinx students . . . most of our teachers were white, you know, so I always feel like Black students . . . even me . . . I felt like they always took the side of Latinx students. Also, because their parents were so involved. My parents were involved, but I feel like all majority of Black students, their parents, were very hard workers, blue collars, and not that they weren't, but their [Latinx] parents really took time to . . . you know they were always at the school or always you know, on field trips with us. They always came. So, I feel like since the white teachers saw their [Latinx] parents, what they considered more or they contacted them more for positive things. When it came to things that they were doing, even if it was blatantly racist, the white teachers liked the Latinx kids more. They put me off the bus and I wasn't able to go on that field trip and that student laughed at me as they were riding off and I felt that really stuck with me. This was 1999 and not so long ago. And I never wanted to talk to white teachers after that. I did not want anything to do with them. I set an internal clock for myself. If something was to happen to me, I would never be protected.

Throughout American history, the federal government has classified and reclassified the racial identity of the Latinx population, leading to the official and unofficial segregation of Latinx students in white school districts (Donato & Hanson, 2017). In the example above, Mary points out that the white teachers clearly saw the Latinx students more favorably and perhaps saw the Latinx population as more racially like them. There was no uncertainty and ambiguity here; rather, the Latinx students were racially more white than the Black students in Maywood. The Latinx students seemed more integrated into the school system, according to Mary, than the invisible Black students, even though their schools were in Maywood, a historically Black community. Mary felt her white teachers had thereafter labeled her as "aggressive" and "disobedient" and she was wrongly punished, even though she was a good student whose father was a local pastor. There was indeed a "tri-racial stratification" here that displayed the variegated racism within the public schools and was indicative of a multi-racial America that needs to come to terms with its ideology of race and belonging (Anderson, 2017, p. 75S).

Additional Black and Latina teachers whom we interviewed for this study validated Mary's interpretation of her experience when they described how the majority of white teachers openly displayed a preference for the Latinx students and treated the Black students as second-class citizens. If there is the possibility of solidarity and symmetry among the Black and Latinx students themselves, a racialized social hierarchy subconsciously adopted by some of the white teachers at large was undermining the social dynamics of solidarity. Heightened differentiation between the Black and Latinx students crept up in school rituals but remained voiceless for the most part. Barajas and Ronnkvist (2007) would support the idea that the teachers in Maywood were raised in the color-blind ideology that asserts that teachers do not notice the race of the student and treat all students equally, regardless of if they are Black or Latinx. Some teachers did not treat the two student populations differently and used neutral practices, but the majority did due to differences in their own racial experiences, privilege, and biases, even if it was subtle such as complimenting the female students from one racial group or making assumptions about the students' backgrounds. In the schools, the organizational space of teachers was a white space and the teacher's lounge was a dominant white space.

There was also a lack of emphasis on Black heterogeneity within the student body, the effects of racial discrimination from the teachers and administrators on Black students, as well as a lack of focus on how "Blackness is reflected not only in the meanings students bring with them to school but also in the meanings that are imposed on them by school structures" (O'Connor, Lewis, & Mueller, 2007, p. 542). As stated earlier, some of the Black teachers we interviewed for this study also argued that teaching Black students in Maywood was a proxy for the white teachers' own ineffective pedagogy and how many came to teach in Maywood because they could not get a teaching job in predominantly white school districts.

Chandra, the Black teacher whom we interviewed, described the subtle ways in the actualization of culturally oriented racism. This was most evident when she represented the marginalized experiences of Latinx students with prejudice and stereotyping from white teachers but not with the same deep racism that Black students faced. Chandra attributed her opinion to implicit and explicit bias that some teachers projected onto their students, while placing a disproportionate emphasis on behavior that left both groups of students underserved. She recounted her colleagues erroneously equating the physically and verbally active participation of Black students in the school with disrespect and aggression but the quiet, docile mannerisms of the Latinx students as good behavior. According to Chandra, it was the white teachers' incessant need to compare Black and Latinx students, sometimes verbally and openly in the teacher's lounge, that emphasized superficial differences rather than encouraging the exploration of solidarity. Research shows that Black students are no less engaged in more disruptive behavior than other students of similar achievement levels and socioeconomic status; however, teachers perceive Black students as disruptive more than other racial groups and then rely on instructional methods that focus on creating an orderly classroom to minimize these "perceived" negative effects of disruption. In doing so, the resulting instructional approach is less engaging for Black students (Kelly, 2010).

Some of the Latinx students in our study bought into a few of their white teachers' labeling of Black students as "disruptive" and stated in their interviews about how their Black peers were disrespectful of their white teachers, creating a cycle of bias and misperception, perpetuating a false crisis of authority that inevitably led to a classroom environment that reduced interactive discourse and more seatwork. The Latinx students sometimes used their white teachers as the normative referent rather than their Black teachers and often adhered to the normative linguistic codes, learning styles, and social orientations of their white teachers (O'Connor, Lewis, & Mueller, 2007). The Latinx students we interviewed also were recent immigrants from countries like Mexico where there is greater "teacher-centered" instruction than the "student-centered" instruction more common in the United States where there is more give-and-take and more talk between teachers and students. Some of the Latinx students in our study expected their teachers to disseminate knowledge from lectures and in quiet classrooms where orderly rows of students write down notes and complete worksheets, follow procedures and directions, memorize information, and then regurgitate information on tests.

Furthermore, seminal research from Wade Boykin (1986), a psychology professor, pointed to the behavioral, thought, and interactional patterns of Black students and how they often clashed with white mainstream culture, leading to cultural discontinuity. Today we would argue that Black epistemology is founded on the cultural values of communalism in which learning is gained best in social groups; responsibility to the collective rather than the individual; an orientation to physical movement, music, and dance; and verve, which is a propensity for stimulation.

Research also shows that white teachers pathologize the transgressions of Black students even when they are the exact same behaviors of white students (Ferguson, 2001). Transgressions from Latinx students were seen as "innocent" and as behaviors that the teachers deemed not worthy of bringing forth to the school administration such as tardiness and cursing in class. Black students were disciplined more often every day in the integrated classrooms in Maywood, even though the achievement and socioeconomic levels were the same as the Latinx students, who in turn became the foil. We can also argue that in integrated Black-Latinx classrooms there is an issue of symbolic capital and how the phenotype of Latinx students influenced which bodies were privileged by the white teachers and a subsequent proximity to white privilege (O'Connor, Lewis, & Mueller, 2007). In addition to racial and cultural differences, the tensions between Black and Latinx students were also predicated on language and the unprecedented linguistic diversity that was changing the school landscape.

The Black Dialect: Getting Treated, Tweaking, and Going Spanish on Someone

One of the earliest entries in our journals regarding language and identity related to an incident in the seventh-grade science classroom. The South Asian science teacher, Susanna, was interrupted during a lesson when a parent walked into the classroom regarding disciplinary actions taken against her daughter by the science teacher. The teacher and parent went outside to discuss the matter and soon the discussion became heated. Darnell, a Black male student, class leader, and role model, turned to us, the assumed cultural outsider, and explained how the science teacher was being "treated" by the parent through a reflexive and self-deconstructing gaze:

"Tiara's mom is about to treat her," Darnell said to me, who then goes on to explain what "to treat" means as the science teacher steps out: "It means . . . it means they are talking about them to make them shut up. You feel so embarrassed that you shut up. It's a salty moment. You get mad. You huff and puff." Of course, the students claim the science teacher treated them sometimes: "Ms. A be treating some time."

In addition to being "treated," students also commonly used the verb "tweaking" [2008–2010] and went on to explain its meaning to us, the presumed cultural outsiders, even though we knew its definition: to be out of your mind when under the influence of drugs like methamphetamine and therefore act irrational and with excessive emotion (Brisman, 2006). The word "tweak" originated in the hip-hop/rap culture and its music which depicted the drug culture of that era. The Black students first circulated the word "tweak" in playful, ephemeral, and metaphorical ways but soon most or all of the Latinx students used the word "tweak" in their everyday speech. At the start of the research study, the verb "tweak" became a part of our idiolects as we heard the word several times during the day—from teachers to administrators to students—therefore creating a shared sociolinguistic space of cohesion and common gratification in its use. A male student dropped some garbage on the classroom floor and the teacher asked him to pick it up, but he initially refuses to pick up the garbage:

Student: Oh, you tweaking now Ms. Gerald.
Teacher: No, you tweaking. I asked you to pick that up.

The Black dialect or African American Vernacular English and its speakers are known to develop creative and unique neologisms like "Chiraq" and "trippin" that originate in the Black community, as well as innovate old words like "bad" and "sick" to resignify their inverse meanings of "good" (Gilyard, 2011). Eventually, some of the newly coined words from within the Black community circulate back into the white mainstream culture, and at that moment when white people use the word as a form of cultural appropriation, these neologisms are no longer used within the Black community (Calhoun, 2020; Rose, 1994; Tshidzumba, 2019). These neologisms are a direct resistance to white power and authority and a direct contrast to the syntax and semantics of white speech (Alim, 2004, 2009). The students in our study used colloquial words that came from an urban youth vernacular that contrasted starkly with the white suburban speech of their teachers who used words like "awesome" and "really," which were not a part of the lexicon for the students in Maywood. At the same time, the Latinx students did not deliberately take the coined words circulated by their Black peers and resignify them from an emic perspective as someone from the same social group and through subtle semantic moves. Instead, they assimilated and played along with the lexical inventiveness of their Black peers.

In terms of the use of Spanish in the classroom, we observed the Latinx students often code-switching between English and Spanish during informal class time and during group work, depending on the context, within their Latinx peer groups. Occasionally, some of the Black teachers used Spanish in an informal register, often when giving directives and commands to all students, even though they were not native speakers of Spanish. When the Black students had no idea what was literally being said in Spanish, they often used the phrase "going Spanish on someone" as a newfound action word in sync with "going rogue" on someone—thereby entering into a discursive relation with the Other:

Ms. Gerald: Dion, you need to sit down. ¡Cálmate!
Dion: What does that mean? Is that Spanish? Don't go Spanish on me!

Here is an interview response from a Black middle school teacher, Olivia, who taught social studies in a classroom with both Black and Latinx eighth-grade students and her interpretation of the new sociolinguistic landscape:

Olivia: In my opinion, Spanish can only be seen as an equal status today if individuals are willing to learn Spanish as another language. However, this can also become an issue because some Spanish can be different compared to how Mexicans and Puerto Ricans speak Spanish. [Her current husband was of Puerto Rican descent] Not only can the dialect be different, but there can appear to be some biases and misconceptions we have about Spanish speakers today. One time, an African American student had made a rude comment towards a Hispanic student and said, "Maybe you need to learn how to speak English or go back to your country." Hearing this from a person of color say this to an immigrant hurts me because we should not be like this towards different nationalities. Rather than being judgmental and saying rude comments, instead, we should find a better way as to how to communicate with individuals who may not know English. Another misconception individuals have towards Spanish speakers today is assuming their lack of understanding English. For example, we assume if someone does not speak the same language as us, then they do not comprehend the things we are saying. On the other hand . . . which is not the case because some individuals can understand English but struggle to respond in English.

While the Black students were navigating the sociolinguistic integration of Spanish in their classrooms, the Latinx students were also co-opting language and code-switching between Standard English, the Black dialect, and Spanish. Here is an interview with a Mexican American middle school language arts teacher, Claudia, who grew up in Maywood, and her positive attitude toward the use of the Black dialect in her Latinx community:

Claudia: Growing up in a minority community of predominantly African American and Mexican families, I was exposed to the Black dialect on a daily basis but did not realize that this was known as a dialect until I got to high school. I had never heard or been told of the negative beliefs and misconceptions that existed towards the Black dialect because the community I grew up in used the Black dialect when speaking to me and to others. I simply thought it was modifications to words that people used in order to sound cooler or communicate better. It is just a way that people used to communicate with one another just as I witnessed when I was growing up.

The role of Spanglish was also evident in the discourse within and among the Latinx children. Spanglish can be defined as a hybrid form of language use that demonstrates the integration of American English into the vernacular spoken by Mexican Americans here in the United States. Latinx children attending school in the United States transferred the lexical and morphological aspects of English onto words in everyday Spanish. An example of this linguistic hybridity is the Spanglish word "parquear" (Bazán-Figueras & Figueras, 2014). Many Spanish bilingual speakers who moved to the United States before cars became mainstream did not have a word for "to park" in the Spanish vernacular because there was never a cultural need for it (Bierly, 2019). Later, while living in the United States and when the concept of "to park a car" came about, Mexican Americans adopted the English word, "park" and used it with the morphological rules of Spanish—despite Spanish developing its own formal, dictionary word for "to park" at the same time (estacionar). In Spanish, adding the morpheme -ar to a noun creates a verb, and therefore, the term "parquear" was coined by a Latinx American.

Over time, Mexican American children and families traveled back and forth across the border, and now people in Mexico use the word "parquear" instead of the formal "estacionar." Even though scholars and language experts want to eradicate Spanglish and its informal use, this hybrid form of language plays a key role in the everyday lives of Latinx children in the United States. At the same time, it represents an amalgamation of diasporic Latinx culture found in the United States. Spanglish has become the de facto lingua franca for many people in the United States who describe themselves as Latinx; however, there are variations of Spanglish depending on the region

such as the Miamian Spanglish versus the Nuyorican Spanish first spoken by
Puerto Ricans in places like New York and Chicago.

In Maywood, the Latinx students who were recent immigrants were more
comfortable speaking fully in Spanish with their same-language Latinx peers;
however, there were also students who identified as "Chicano" and were first
or second-generation Mexican Americans who interspersed Spanish phrases
and words into their mostly English syntax, known as Spanglish. Maribel, a
Mexican American teacher from Maywood, interpreted the linguistic variation in Maywood first as a child and now as an adult:

Maribel: When I was younger all I spoke was Spanish. I did not know English
or that it existed because my world consisted of Spanish until I started school.
Once I started school, I began to speak Chicano English and slowly began to
transition into a more Standard English. Once I began to do this, I in a way
stopped identifying as Mexican and considered myself more American than
anything, even giving up speaking, writing, and reading Spanish. As I grew
older and began to connect more to my Mexican roots, I began to pick up Spanish again and my Spanish was not the best, being more Spanglish than anything, saying things like "pushes" "lonche," and "hangues." I thought this was
so funny because I did not think this was something others noticed. Slowly I got
away from these words and started saying "empujes, almuerzo, and cuelgues"
instead of the Spanglish versions and this all began when I started to consider
myself Mexican once again, spending time with my family, visiting Mexico
and going to family events.

Communicative flexibility between and among the Latinx and Black students was observed during daily life in the classrooms, increasingly negotiated by the cultural straddlers, border crossers, style shifters, code switchers,
and multilingual composers who went back and forth across the Latinx and
Black cultural and linguistic spaces (Hornberger, 2000). Many of these
cultural straddlers in our study did not hold onto the centuries-old negative
perceptions and stereotypes of the Black dialect or Spanish; rather, they were
attuned to the Black dialect and Spanish and did not display a communicative
disconnect. The cultural straddlers demonstrated communicative flexibility
by sounding like their familiar Others—from friends to teachers—and taking
on these "typified voices of their everyday lives" (Dyson et al., 2009, p. 978).
The typified voices of the Black dialect were literally absorbed by the Latinx
students as they interacted with Black dialect speakers daily.

They also exercised their agency as cultural straddlers by making a conscious or unconscious language choice in adopting aspects of the Black
dialect as a part of their idiolects. In the several student interviews, none of
the Latinx students identified the Black dialect of their peers with any negative connotation, unlike some white teachers who often denigrated the Black

students for their language use. There was no perception that their Black peers were speaking in an inferior manner and that somehow their language was ill formed. Yet even though the Latinx students adopted some aspects of the Black dialect while maintaining their Spanish and acquiring Standard English, it was not the linguistic push-pull dynamic that Black students may face when they themselves are moving back and forth between the Standard Dialect and the Black dialect. Cultural straddlers gain acceptance as "authentic" members of a social group, foster social solidarity, and gain self-worth and self-esteem through cross-cultural connections with peers across social boundaries and perhaps peers who share specific school practices such as band and basketball. Here is an interview with Manual, a Latinx cultural straddler in the eighth grade, talking about his linguistic appropriation:

Author: So how do you speak? Describe it to me.

Manual: I guess I speak with slang . . . you know . . . words . . .

Author: You use a lot of slang? Why do you think you use a lot of slang?

Manual: I guess I grew into it from over here. You know . . . you kind of find it easier to talk that way.

Author: Give me an example of something you use.

Manual: Like I says . . . something like . . . "man I ain't never" . . . like stuff like that . . . like instead of saying "never" I say "nevah" . . . like "I ain't" . . . like stuff like that.

Author: So how did you pick that up? Were you conscious that you were changing the way you were speaking? Do you find yourself switching at school and how you speak even at home?

Manual: Not so much . . . you know . . . at home I don't do it as much as I do it over here.

Author: Hmm. So how do your parents feel about that, when you say something like "ain't"?

Manual: No one pays too much mind to it.

Author: Ok. Do you feel like the other kids in your class speak that way?

Manual: Yeah . . . they have like . . . but to me like they have advanced slang.

Author: What do you mean advanced slang?

Manual: They speak like more slang than I do. Yeah . . . I only use like words . . . just to make it more easier to say.

Author: But they actually come up with the words?

Manual: Yeah.

Author: Give me an example of something funny that someone must have said that you think they came up with.

Manual: Okay. Once when we were listening to this rap on the computer, he said that . . . one of my friends . . . I don't know who it was, he said that the guy can "spit." And I asked him, "What's spit?" And he said, "That the guy can rap pretty good . . . he spitting it." (this is a reference from 2010-2011)

Author: Good . . . So it was a word unfamiliar to you and then you learned it. So do you want to know more words like this from your friends?

Manual: It helps you . . . you know . . . get conversations . . . you know at least I am not left out.

Author: So, did you feel left out when you first came to Maywood?

Manual: A little bit you know because . . . I didn't understand some of the words they were saying . . . so I didn't really understand much . . . so I couldn't really get into the conversation like they could.

Author: Do you think your friends want to learn more Spanish? Do they ask you to teach them?

Manual: Yeah, they always want to learn Spanish.

Author: So, what is an example?

Manual: They just say like, "Say something in Spanish. I don't care what it is just say something." So, I say little words like juice and milk in Spanish.

Although Manual's answers represented the experiences of many Latinx cultural straddlers in this middle school, it was also evident throughout our research study that the Latinx cultural straddlers were not fully a part of the Black fictive kinship system at the school in which friends become a part of one's extended family—a system traced back to slavery. They were never really "one of us" and never shared in the deep love among the Black students who looked out for each other and supported each other in their fictive brotherhood and sisterhood (Williams, 2018). Rather, the Latinx students did not seem to be a part of the larger collective Black identity in Maywood and the daily lives of their Black peers—they were solely looking into the circle from the margins. Cross-race friendships between Black and Latinx students have been documented as well as how one's friendship network is related to race and ethnicity. Peer groups demonstrate within-group similarities due to the tendency for peers to select friends who are similar or due to peers influencing those in the peer group (Seaton, Quintana, Verkuyten & Gee, 2017). For most students in Maywood, peer group homophily was evident in which Black students were close friends with other Black students and Latinx students were close friends with other Latinx students.

However, our observational data led us to a small group of intergroup students who befriended peers from a different racial group and had a cultural orientation that favored racial and linguistic diversity and were attracted to the differences across groups. We captured them in identity-defining social moments and interactions, such as when music was exchanged through headphones, words were adopted from each other's vernaculars, speech styles were accentuated, and clothing became defining—all ways to secure acceptance in this intergroup where both Black and Latinx peers were accepted, and outgroup peers were favored over in-group critics. The feedback they provided each other were moments of joy and pride creating a sense of belonging, a shared "us," but without shame and insecurity. These were the same students who were curious about us as South Asians and came up to us and asked if "we were Hindi" and how to say "I love you" in our native language. When we answered with the translation "Mai tum se pyar karta hoon," one of the Black cultural straddlers demonstrated metalinguistic awareness by asking "all that means I love you." As these students continued to ask for Hindi translations throughout the year, one proud student stated, "we're learning a new language."

We defined these students as border crossers and cultural straddlers whose enacted identities shifted according to fluctuating context and environment rather than a definitive sense of race. In a majority-minority school, cultural straddlers disrupt the existing social divisions, craft alternatives to racial hegemony, and demonstrate a bridging potential for positive interracial relations between them (Sharma, 2010). The majority-minority status of the school setting led some social actors to display behaviors and actions that were hybrid in nature, and therefore, a small social space was created within the middle schools in which students from both racial groups came together in unison (Bourdieu, 1992). Some of the Black students displayed cultural competency by stating openly their desire to learn Spanish and to even use the Spanish they knew in front of their Latinx peers, by creating a tight social network of friends in which there was a racial balance, by dating outside of their race, and playing with each other outside of school.

The Black cultural straddlers anchored themselves in the Latinx community but also developed strategies to subvert themselves from being excluded entirely from the greater Black majority. In many ways, they moved beyond the "double consciousness" and "double voicing" of Black students navigating a white-Black landscape and found themselves instead in a trivariate of sorts, navigating between the Standard English of white teachers, the Black dialect of their fictive kin, and the newfound Spanish of their peers (Kinloch, 2010). Here is an interview with Zenida, a middle school Mexican American female student who was a cultural straddler:

Author: I noticed that you use a lot of Spanish in class with Julia and Maria. Is that true?

Zenida: Yes.

Author: Why?

Zenida: Since we're used to it . . . like we talk a lot . . . like all of a sudden . . . if we're talking like in English and then . . . we can't say some words in English so we just say it in Spanish. Sometimes when we talk about things that we don't want people to know about [laughs].

Author: Sometimes you use it for private things?

Zenida: Yes.

Author: How does Ms. Gerald feel about you speaking in Spanish?

Zenida: She tells us to speak in English . . . the whole class does.

Author: Why do you think?

Zenida: I guess she doesn't want the other students to feel bad like if we're saying something about them . . . she doesn't want them to think we're saying something about them.

Author: How do the other students feel about you speaking in Spanish? What do they think when you, Julia and Maria are speaking in Spanish?

Zenida: They think we're talking about them but we're not always. We're mostly just talking about regular stuff. We're just talking in Spanish.

Author: So, do they want to learn Spanish also?

Zenida: Some students do. They would like to learn . . . um . . . from the other class Sharde . . . from my class . . . Portia would like to learn. Um . . . Ollie . . . Precious . . .

Author: So, do they pretend to speak in Spanish sometimes?

Zenida: Sometimes . . . yeah . . . they go rrrummrrumm [makes a fast motor-like /r/ sound].

Author: They kind of roll their tongue for the Spanish [r]?

Zenida: [laughs] Yeah.

The Latinx cultural straddlers displayed their cultural competency around hip-hop culture, the Black dialect and challenging normative notions of hair and skin color. Yet, they did not identify with the Black culture for the sake of identity politics, unlike other immigrant groups who may identify with the Black minority in America due to a political identity aligned with combating racism (Sharma, 2010). The Latinx students also did not identify with Black culture for the sake of increasing one's masculinity or for becoming fascinated by the exotic Other, unlike white males who consume Black culture as a form of social capital (Rose, 1994).

In one of our interviews, Maria, a Latina cultural straddler described her reasoning for the cultural appropriation of the Black culture, specifically language and hip-hop and R&B music as natural and intimate. The adoption of the Black cultural style and taste by the Latinx students can be attributed to the cultural capital found within the Black community. Instead of viewing communities of color as places void of culture, it is imperative that we recognize the cultural wealth found within minoritized populations in the United States (Yosso, 2005). The cultural knowledge possessed by their majority Black peers is what the minority Latinx students wanted—from knowing how to speak, to knowing how to dress, to knowing how to interact in certain social spaces. Even if there was at times a lack of social capital within this majority-minority setting, leading to weak social networks and connections between Black and Latinx students, there was always a reverence for Black cultural capital, which was hard to come by for Latinx students who lived along the margins in spaces dominated by the Black students. Many of the Latinx students were given new monikers by the Black students: Zitali was now called "Lollipop"; Juana was now "cookie"; Manuel was called "Shorty"; and so on.

This hybrid form of mixing a Black and Latinx identity has been coined as "Blaxican" and research points to the growing number of children in our schools who identify as "mixed race." In places like California, there is a growing number of children who have one parent who identifies as Black and one who identifies as Mexican (Rodriguez, 2003). Children and adolescents who identify as "Blaxican" often have more cultural affinity to the Black cultural world than to white America. Yet, Black and Brown students always push themselves into corners and challenge each other on identity markers and cancel those who do not fit their labels: Is that Latinx girl acting too white? Is that Black student Black enough? Does that Latina speak Spanish? Can you be Spanish speaking and be white? Does she sound too Black? Does that white singer have that Black sound? Do Latinx people rant about whites like Black people do? Do Black people see Latinx people as honorary whites? and so on.

We could argue that majority-minority schools are liminal spaces where Black and Latinx students transcend binary oppositions and identities, become aware of multiple relationalities and potentialities, and cross borders and switch languages and dialects. There are interruptions and disjuncture of identities in liminal spaces, across race, language, and culture, (Campbell, 2015). The cultural straddlers in our study chose cultural agency over invisibility; they were direct and broadened their social identities by choosing a logic in which one can improvise and self-fashion identity, thereby moving into the informed cultural center rather than remain on the periphery where identity is essentialized and separate.

At the same time, we witnessed the blending and mixing of languages and cultural identities but not the outright shedding of identity, or the downplaying of identity, or the remaking of a pre-existing identity through evasion, subversion, and/or concealment. There were no radical cultural transformations here, just familiar forms of hybridity in which Black and Latinx students mirrored each other. One can also argue that both groups of students were assimilating to each other and that assimilating requires you to adopt foreign behaviors and tastes, in more ways than one. But when the choice is between annihilation and assimilation, you assimilate. This was the case for our ancestors as it is for young, deracinated Latinx immigrants in Black America who must assimilate to their new landscapes. At the same time, humans are malleable, and we acquire new ways of living and have learned how to evolve over time. We incorporate new languages, behaviors, and ways of orienting ourselves in the world—with each new experience, "the tapestry is rewoven"—as was the case here with the cultural mixing and melding among the students (Fan, 2021, p. 49).

Interestingly, the one racial category that was used to create social isolates within this majority-minority school was the white racial category: "You so white" was a common insult thrown around by the adolescents. Black and Latinx students who did not fit into the broader school culture and identity were labeled with the "white" pejorative label and were often bullied by their peers for "acting white" and being gay, conflating racial identity with sexual identity. Cultural misfits, therefore, were rejected along with white identity and placed along the margins. In an interview, Julia, a Latina eighth-grade student, described how a peer, Anton, who was Black and was ostracized, was even punched by peers for proclaiming to dislike other Black individuals. She summed up Anton's bullying by stating, "I don't really want to talk to him cause you know he'll get on my nerves . . . I don't know how to explain him . . . he's just there." The Black and Latinx students who acted white were often ostracized and this racial profiling alludes to the hypersegregation of American schools in which there is now a strong divide and polarity between majority-minority Black/Latinx schools in Maywood and white/Asian schools in the wealthier nearby suburbs like River Forest and Oak Park. When watching educational videos with white people, the students often mimicked the white dialect and its feminine intonation:

S1: Aren't these batteries just so excellent? [laughing]
S2: Actually, they are exquisite! [laughing]

The only white individual we interviewed for this book, Alice, was a colleague of ours who grew up in Maywood, who dated Black male students, and is currently in a relationship with her high school sweetheart. Alice came from a family of hippies whose parents eventually divorced, leading Alice's mother to seek a job as a nurse in a major hospital in Maywood where apartment housing was affordable for a single mother in 1980. In high school, Alice attended AP classes, took French classes, and became a statistician for the East High School football team. There were very few non-Black families in her neighborhood, and this was different from the diverse intentional communities in which she spent her childhood on communes; however, she was also comfortable in Maywood:

Alice: I instantly became a part of multiple social circles because I was presenting a certain energy different from the other white kids there who might have felt that their families were doing them a disservice by sending them to a predominantly Black public school. I knew everybody and everybody knew of me.

It became a place that I blossomed after having been in a very small white community in southern Illinois. But the few other white students hated me because I was comfortable socializing with the other Black students.

Alice also did not venture into Melrose Park which was entirely Italian at that time since she was often the only white person in her social group. She was conscious of the fact that they would not be welcomed in Melrose Park then and still discourages it today for Black youth; rather, they hung around in local restaurants and social spots in Maywood like the Buddha Barbecue which was owned by her friend's family.

Therefore, there was no reason to leave Maywood. Alice ended up sleeping over in homes, staying for family dinners, and becoming a part of the fictive kinship system in the Black community. Alice also embodied a form of whiteness that was different from upper-middle-class white feminism in which white women are the experts and can speak over Black and Brown women in an effort to uphold privilege and perceived cultural superiority (Zakaria, 2021). Alice did not embody the tone and language of white women and she did not express any discomfort and alienation from challenging white supremacy. It was her lived experiences that documented an affirmation of humanity, solidarity, and the collective.

Everyone saw Alice as a member of the Black community, and she was one of two interracial couples at the high school. She was dating the Black quarterback and was a part of the athletic circle; meanwhile, Jim Rogers, a strong academic white student, was dating a strong Black academic female student at the school and both the students' fathers were businessmen in Maywood. Today, both Alice and Jim live in Maywood and are committed to their interracial families in Maywood. However, Alice talked about her brother, who was white and younger than her, who struggled with fitting in with the Black culture of Maywood. He was never a part of the commune and did not have that same exposure and he only hung out with other white students in Maywood. There were cultural and communication differences between Alice and her brother and how they interacted with their peers from the Black community, even though they came from the same family. It seemed that acceptance of white students into the Black community in their high school years was contingent less on gender but more on the deep and authentic connections that the students actively forged with Maywood.

In our study, there were times when there was a "communicative impasse" between the Latinx and Black students in terms of the Latinx students not understanding their Black peers and vice versa (Dyson, et. al, 2009). There was also a communicative impasse when the Black students from Maywood could not understand other Black students who had moved to Maywood from the South, places like Mississippi and Alabama, and sounded too "country" and had cultural patterns so different from their own sub/urban cultural worlds. One such student from Mississippi was ridiculed for his homely style of dress and his naivete around the local drug and gang culture in Maywood. The other students often joked that this student went to get his rifle to hunt raccoons, used an outhouse, and was "stupid and smart at the same time." At other times, there was a cultural bridge that stretched the meaning of words across race and language, therefore widening the Latinx students' sociolinguistic reper-toire, especially since the Black dialect was the lingua franca in this majority-minority school district. However, when it came to academic English, both the Latinx and Black students struggled with the pronunciation, meaning, and use of academic vocabulary, especially in the science class where we observed and recorded in our field notes that students often relied on the teacher's voice for the correct pronunciation and meaning of scientific words:

(January 15) Students are having difficulty pronouncing the word "allele" in the genetics chapter. Some pronounce it as "alley." Jumanah after a while does not even want to pronounce it and says "that A word" instead. At one point, a Latina female student pronounces "hereditary" as "hair-a-tee" so Ms. Abrams corrects her pronunciation. Another male student pronounces Gregor Mendel's last name as "men-dale." Maurice continues to pronounce "allele" as "alley." After a while, the teacher stops correcting their mispronunciation of the science words. They are also struggling to pin down a definition for each term based on their chapter reading in the textbook.

(March 8) Today both the Latinx and Black students had difficulty pronounc-ing and knowing the science words: thermosphere, mesosphere, stratosphere, and troposphere. Both groups struggled with the academic vocabulary in the science book.

(May 12) Today a Black male student, Marvin, in the 7th grade says "magnana" for the word "magnetic." The other students laughed aloud. After he was corrected by a female student, he said aloud, "I thought it was a bigger word than that!"

It was interesting to note, however, that both the Black and Latinx students were comfortable sharing their challenges with academic English and were not ashamed. The students did not try to pretend that they understood the words and their meanings or knew how to pronounce them accurately. They also did not develop coping behaviors to disguise their frustrations either, which are cultural practices more common in predominantly white schools (Phelan, Yu & Davidson, 1994). In turn, both the Black and Latinx students struggled with the academic language and Standard English often associated with white mainstream classrooms as found in our observations. Academic language can be defined as academic English, the formal language of schools and of those in power and it is different from the linguistic registers of what is spoken at home in terms of lexicon and grammar.

At the same time, many researchers state that a deficit perspective of academic literacy and language for Black and Latinx students is a form of racism that stemmed from the 1960s and 1970s framework of closing the academic gaps between various racial populations to ensure equality but without looking at the larger systemic inequities in place. The research of April Baker-Bell (2020) describes the anti-Black linguistic racism in schools and interrogates the notion of academic language:

> Anti-black linguistic racism refers to the linguistic violence, persecution, dehumanization, and marginalization that Black Language (BL) speakers endure when using their language in schools and in everyday life. It includes teachers' silencing, correcting, and policing students when they communicate in Black Language. It is the belief that there is something inherently wrong with Black Language; therefore, it should be eradicated (p. 9) . . . Linguistic justice in Black and Latinx classrooms would begin by acknowledging that academic language is a white norm of speech or White English and then acknowledging the truth that the use of academic language by white people is often weaponized against people of color to subjugate them and make them feel intellectually inferior when academic words are mispronounced or misused. By focusing on the mispronunciation of academic words by Black and Latinx students, the science teacher is in turn mismeasuring them against the dominant white culture and therefore committing a racist act. In our study, the students did not necessarily internalize the bias from the teachers, nor did they absorb the negative ideologies and in turn "display feelings of linguistic and cultural shame" (Baker-Bell, 2020, p. 11).

The frustration self-esteem model also holds that students who experience unsuccessful school outcomes over time, such as poor grades, may suffer an impaired perception of self (i.e., self-esteem, self-concept). Inherently, a devalued sense of self can lead to further frustration with school, and possibly adopting oppositional behavior such as truancy, absenteeism, and complete withdrawal from school (Griffin, 2002). Both Black and Latinx students have to confront the negative stereotypes that can threaten their academic performance, especially when the race is primed in the academic task and assessment (Steele, 1997). Sometimes Black and Latinx students must disidentify with their racial identity in order to protect their self-perception while in school where they may feel heightened isolation and powerlessness.

A culturally responsive pedagogy would instead point out the linguistic racism and white linguistic hegemony in the world of science and how lexicon from Latin and Greek in the sciences kept the discipline closed off from the masses and open to only an elite cadre of white wealthy men, even though

many of the scientific concepts had non-Western origins that made their way
to Europe during the Renaissance:

> But the foundations of modern science were laid long before this time and
> were particularly influenced by Islamic civilization. The Muslims were the
> leading scholars between the seventh and fifteenth centuries and were the heirs
> of the scientific traditions of Greece, India and Persia. After appropriation and
> assimilation, they built on these discoveries, and developed a truly Islamic
> science that led worldwide knowledge in all scientific fields, including medi-
> cine. These activities were cosmopolitan, in that the participants were Arabs,
> Persians, Central Asians, Christians and Jews, and later included Indians and
> Turks. The transfer of the knowledge of Islamic science to the West through
> various channels paved the way for the Renaissance, and for the scientific
> revolution in Europe. The public in the West is generally unaware of this
> important contribution to modern science and to the culture of the Middle
> Ages. (Iaccarino, 2003, p. 220)

To pronounce the science words correctly does not make a student superior; rather, the importance lies in understanding the meaning of words and
the scientific constructs the words are referencing. Today, a science teacher
may focus instead on the comprehension of the science words rather than
have students read a chapter aloud in class to assess pronunciation. The last
section of this chapter returns to the topic of race and culture; however, the
focus is on the differences within each racial group and how there is often
greater diversity within than across racial groups.

Differences from Within the Group

The incorporation of new immigrants has always been a topic of interest
to social scientists and its various theoretical models (Lee & Bean, 2004).
The straight-line model of assimilation would posit that the newcomers to
Maywood will both affect and be affected by the village life and in doing
so will become indistinguishable within a few generations. This model has
defined European immigration and the economic generational mobility. As
immigrants assimilate into their new American lives, they lose their cultural
distinctions and become indistinguishable from the host society, and eventually adopt an American identity. However, this model may not work for the
Latinx immigrants in Maywood. Then what model of assimilation accounts
for the experiences of new Latinx residents in a historically Black suburb?
Will the customs, practices, and ideals of the Latinx community mirror that
of the Black community and to what degree? What is the structural incorporation that needs to happen? Their assimilation is into the "minority underclass"
where there may be more of a selective assimilation in which they remain

immersed in their Latinx community and preserve the immigrant community's values and solidarity as a means of economic mobility and learn to accommodate to the Black community in Maywood but without complete assimilation.

Latinx identity is not rooted in the same historical legacy of slavery as the Black identity and with its systematic and persistent discrimination and inequality. Latinx people were not forcefully brought to this country as slaves but were enslaved by their Spaniard colonizers. Latinx people are nonetheless voluntary migrants, and their identities are more fluid than those of Black Americans who do not have racial options. Will there be a loosening of the boundaries in Maywood that allow for more flexibility and identity options? Will a reduction in the physical distance then also lead to a reduction in the social distance? Can we remain optimistic that there will be more border crossings in Maywood? Or will the color line remain tenacious? Will there be the blurring of lines? Do Latinx immigrants assimilate by using the same stereotypes against the Black population as used by the white population?

Zhou and Bankston (1998) presented their own model for immigration and the concept of "segmented assimilation" which states that there are differential outcomes for immigrants based on the communities into which they integrate. Assimilation looks different based on the local communities, for example, when immigrants moved into inner-city communities, there was often a negative implication for educational outcomes which led to the delinquency of Vietnamese immigrants in inner-city communities. We can also argue that the assimilation of Latinx students into Maywood looks different from immigration into the city of Chicago. However, in addition to navigating the racial binary found within the schools (Black students and white teachers), the Latinx students also had to navigate the diverse subcultures within their own racial group. Rather than viewing all Latinx students as a monolithic whole defined by macro boundary-making themes of immigration, language, and ethnic culture, our study calls into question who is the Self and who is the Other. There were moments in our study during which the Latinx students did not portray a collective sense of Self; instead, they saw each other also as a cultural Other due to differences in religion, dress, musical tastes, and region. For example, there was a clear division between the Latinx students who identified as Catholic and those who identified as evangelical.

According to the Pew Latino Center's publication titled "Changing Faiths: Latinos and the Transformation of the American Religion" (2007), there is a growing trend among Latinx Catholics to convert to evangelical churches, even though a third of all American Catholics are Latinx: "Half of Latino evangelicals (51%) are converts, and more than four-fifths of them (43% of Latino evangelicals overall) are former Catholics." The over-all decline in religious observance has shifted the Catholic landscape and religious spaces are becoming obsolete in our daily lives as well as undo-ing civic bonds. Within the United States, one-third of all Latinx Ameri-cans identify themselves with the Protestant evangelical movement that is emerging rapidly within Latin America and its neighboring nations due to a greater degree of choice and competition within the religious landscape (Sanchez-Walsh, 2003).

When describing a church service in a Latinx evangelical church, one can find "the mostly Latino audience shouting 'Amen' and waving as ministers preach about how God would protect them. For more than three hours, they pray and sing spirituals in Spanish" (Glanton, 2009). The Pew Latino study (2007) also cited "Protestant Hispanics" as being more conservative in their social views as well as their politics, especially in relation to abortion, school prayer, and same-sex marriage. Latinx evangelicals are twice as likely to vote for the Republican Party than Latinx Catholics, unlike the Black community that tends to vote overwhelmingly for the Democratic Party regardless of faith, religion, and social views—thereby challenging the often taken-for-granted Latinx Democratic vote (Kelly & Kelly, 2005).

The changing religious landscape within the Latinx community was evi-dent in our study as well; we found a distinct cultural difference between and among Latinx students who practiced Catholicism versus those who attended a local evangelical church. Both groups attended congregations with a largely Latinx constituency and clergy in Maywood; however, the amount of daily time spent at church services was a dividing factor among the students, as well as the ability to read scripture in the Spanish language. Two male Latinx students in particular spoke about spending entire weekends and two to three weekday evenings at their evangelical church and stated to us during their interviews—"Soy Cristiano"—I am Christian.

Both young men who identified themselves as Latinx evangelicals sat apart from the other Latinx students in the classroom and often displayed a Protes-tant conservative ideology in relation to how they dressed, how they spoke, and how they viewed the role of education in their lives. Shedding traditional notions of ethnicity and the trappings of group identity was accompanied by a renewed emphasis on being a good student for these two young male evangel-icals who tied themselves to ritual participation in their Protestant churches. Some claim there is a messianic orientation among the young Latinx evan-gelicals whose core identity is tied to the Protestant church, to Christ, and to "sola scriptura" or to scripture alone. While the other Latinx students in the middle school talked about spending their upcoming summer vacation rid-ing their bikes, swimming, or visiting relatives, these two evangelical male students talked about attending on-site church events and church camp and staying connected with other religious peers in their social networks.

There was an uncanny resemblance between the two male Latinx students whom we interviewed, even though they were in two separate grades and did not know each other outside of school: both were well groomed, well-coiffed, always wore black plastic crucifixes around their necks, and were quite intro-verted. They both spoke about only leaving the house as a family to go to church and never really venturing beyond their sub/urban neighborhood. Both came from large families with two parents intact, read the Bible in Spanish, and spoke to their families "siempre en español"—always in Spanish. In the classroom, both students embodied an academic cultural orientation toward school that reminded us of a young Fred Hampton, a native son of Maywood, who was bright, motivated, driven by tradition and purpose, and a dedicated youth leader. Yet, both were also social isolates among their peers and seemed socially distant even from the other academically driven Latinx students:

Author: ¿Cómo te sientes en la clase? No dice mucho.
[How do you feel in class? You do not say much.]
Juan: Me siento diferente. [I feel different.]
Author: ¿Y triste? [And sad?]
Juan: No . . . solo diferente de los otros estudiantes [No . . . just different from the other students.]

The two young male evangelicals are members of the small Latinx com-munity at the middle school; yet, they also feel apart from the others. Their emphasis on religious identity as a distinct form of difference within their peer culture caught us by surprise; it created a distancing effect as well as a sense of plurality within the school setting. Moreover, during interviews with the other Latinx students, when we asked who the social isolates within the school were, the majority consented that the evangelical students were too tied to their "Mexi-can culture" and too different from them, thereby conflating religious identity with nationhood as well as immigrant culture. By attaching themselves to an evangelical identity, we could argue that these young Latinx male students are bypassing the stages of cultural assimilation and forming a type of resilience needed for academic success in sub/urban schools with many risk factors. We could also argue that the Latinx Protestant students were characterized as assimilative and willing to subscribe to the cultural codes of academic success.

Furthermore, scholars have stated throughout the past decade that Latinx American churches and the clergy have become partners in the social and political struggles of the larger Latinx community within the United States such as providing sanctuary for undocumented families (Badillo, 2006; Suro,

2007). However, understanding this social and political transformation within the context of public schools is also needed. Researchers in education have attempted to analyze family and religion as protective factors for Latinx American students in relation to a constant struggle to preserve their cultural identity and physical well-being against larger societal risks such as gun violence, homicide, and drug use (Castro et al., 2007). In addition, bonding with prosocial sources like the church has the potential to influence youth resilience in the face of conflicting normative expectations for adolescents, low self-esteem, and harmful temptations such as drugs and alcohol. These transformations resonate with the findings of the Pew Research Center (2007) report about the relatively universal characteristics of the Latino ethnic church in which theology and culture have mixed to create a religious reality that is focused on family, children, and the immediate community. The same can be said of the Black culture within Maywood where there were distinct churches in every neighborhood. Therefore, interfaith coalitions can be a potential bridge between Latinx and Black Americans—two minoritized populations who are heavily involved in their local community churches—which we will discuss at length in chapter 4.

Kimberle Crenshaw (1989) is a renowned scholar in the field of law and civil rights and famously argued that we cannot examine human subjectivity through a "single-axis analysis" that fails to interrogate the intersection of race and gender. We should avoid generalizing claims that "all Black students in Maywood are . . ." and "all Latinx students in Maywood are . . ." because race and gender are not mutually exclusive categories of experience and analysis; rather, we need a multidimensional perspective that examines intersections like language and race and race and religion—just as we did here in this chapter. We distort the human condition and create disparities when we reduce complex phenomena such as racial discrimination into simple categories, binaries, and representations that are solely about "Blackness" and "Latinxness." Researchers should never have to choose between distinguishing one set of human experiences over the other and instead need to see where those experiences may be contradictory and conflicting. Although we did not interrogate the intersection of race and gender in our study to great depth, we are proposing that there needs to be continued research in Black and Brown communities that build on the compounded nature of their collective experiences and the hybridity of such multiethnic communities where there is no one group in power, but the privileging of whiteness and maleness may still exist.

CONCLUSION

Mapping the lived experiences in majority-minority schools and capturing their specific dynamics have not been covered at great length in the educational arena. Our research grounds itself in knowing what defines majority-minority schools, how students adapt to shifting demographics, and how such heteroglossia reflects our postmodern world where the complexities of hybridity make up the norm and everything is less stable and more fluid in imagined communities such as majority-minority schools (Anderson, 1983). Even though our study used a small sample of middle school classrooms, the observations are from natural settings and speak to the everyday lives of students.

Our study captured moments when students called each other out for "acting Spanish," "acting Mexican," "acting white," and "acting Black." With middle school students, we captured the intraracial and interracial peer dynamic and the in/out-group signifiers as determined by a cultural style focused on dress, music, hairstyle, and cultural tastes. We looked at group solidarity, the racial composition of friendships, and interracial dynamics as well as the intersection of race and gender dynamics. We saw students teasing each other for their cultural background but without vicious bullying. We saw evidence of race centrality and the degree to which students defined themselves by race as a principal part of who they are as well as the salience of this racial identity to their own self-concept (Carter, 2006). We examined events like school dances, classroom discourse, and athletic games and assessed to which degree the students defined themselves and others in relation to race, language, and culture. Of course, we also missed many of these moments and could not capture every aspect of the everyday when and where racial ideology manifested itself.

One of our key findings was how there was not much interracial conflict among the students; rather, we saw more evidence of interracial cooperation among the Black and Latinx students than racial conflicts, explosions, and spectacles. However, the greatest degree of interracial conflict and tension was among the adults leading and controlling the school district which will be highlighted in the next chapters: a revolving door of white teachers and administrators, volatile school board meetings, corrupt state elections chronicled in the local newspaper with closed door deals between politicians and the school boards and mayors, refusal to desegregate schools through the bussing of Latinx students in overcrowded schools to predominantly Black schools with more classroom space, and so on. The conclusions from our study support the conclusions that anthropologist Annegret Staiger also came to in her ethnographic study of a majority-minority high school in California titled *Learning Difference* (2006): deep racial fault lines among the adults occur often in a majority-minority school; students do not necessarily replicate the racializing practices found in the adult world; and students create their own racial order in which they reverse the racial hierarchy supported by the adults. Given the fact that racial integration is increasing for Black and Latinx communities, the onus is upon the educational research community to critically examine the in/visible race lines found in majority-minority school districts and what happens when they shift and change without keeping equity at the forefront.

Nevertheless, the hiring of a new Afro-Latino superintendent who has stayed for over a decade in the district has brought positive change, such as the hiring of Black and Latinx teachers, the extension of a high-performing dual language academy, the building of playgrounds and new structural changes to old brick buildings, and the consistent push for equity and equality. The strong leadership from this current superintendent, who came during the middle of our study and stayed in the school district, can be linked directly to the knowledge and skills needed to improve race relations within these schools. He brought in the "wraparound services" needed to give low-income communities equality of education by bringing more social workers and behavior interventionists into the schools, focusing on the non-educational aspects of the students' lives as well as examining what is happening directly in the classrooms—all with a calm language that prevents escalation and avoids power differentials. A skilled leader seeks to change frames of mind to redefine groups from being competing enemies to becoming allies defending the shared needs of children, families, and communities.

Furthermore, since we started this study almost a decade ago before the Black Lives Matter movement, there have been great changes to the discourse within the school district. Today teachers are talking about race, diversity, and inclusion and are assessing their own biases and misconceptions. Schools are analyzing MTSS (multi-tiered system of support) data to see where there are academic gaps and why there are such disparities and inequities in order to see how they can close those gaps through tiered interventions, individualized instruction, and learning opportunities. After the pandemic, parents are now asked to come into the school buildings and take part in their child's education. The district is also recruiting more diverse teachers who look like the students in the classrooms. The dual language academy is continuing to thrive and graduating eighth graders who are going to high school and continuing to maintain their bilingualism.

Mika Pollock in her book, *Schooltalk: Rethinking What We Say About and To Students Everyday* (2017), addresses the need for schools to have dialogue and conversations with youth on essential topics of interest to them to help shape their lives. We can no longer stand in front of our students and lecture, disseminate archaic knowledge, continue to test, and sort them into categories, and ultimately label them. Rather, we need to flip the script and start a dialogue with them about what it means to be smart and the different kinds of smartness, why there is inequality among them, how culture matters, how data can be used against them as well as to support them, why opportunity matters, and having talks about life and what matters most. Of course, schools are also where we need to have the "race talk" and open up about the core tensions in school around race. If we had done so as researchers working within the schools we observed for our study, we would have questioned why the term "ghetto" was being used by teachers to talk about the students, why a divide and conquer hidden agenda was being used to compare the Latinx students to the Black students, and how the teachers themselves needed greater cultural competency regarding their own students, who they are, where they come from and the untold stories of their lives and communities.

Many teachers and administrators often forget that neighborhood schools play a wider role in the community and are anchors for intergenerational families, sometimes leading to fundamental dissonance between these constituents due to a lack of interest convergence as to whose needs are being met by the school (Bell, 1980). Through research, Gewertz (2006) found that Black parents worried about equity more than white or Latinx parents and made sure their superintendents and teachers were doing a good job, had high standards, and that their children had an equal shot at success. Pollock (2005b) found that when Black and Brown families come to the state and federal offices, they are convinced that principals, middle-level administrators, and district superintendents have ignored their requests to help their children. Feeling rebuffed and trivialized in the face of the district's internal politics, these families then try to resolve complaints that require reopening lines of communication between parents and school district officials.

One needs to question who gets to define a school, who reflects the vision for the school, whether school reform is always top-down or can it also be bottom-up, why there is the rhetoric around failing schools in our community, and the role of political theater. Sociologist Eve Ewing's book, *Ghosts in the Schoolyard* (2018), examines the 2013 closing of predominantly Black elementary schools that were losing enrollment (6,000 plus Black students) in the Chicago Public Schools, due to variables such as the tearing down of nearby housing projects and historical segregation, and which were eventually shut down by then Superintendent Barbara Byrd-Bennett and Mayor Rahm Emanuel. Ewing chronicles the complexity of variables at play in this historical moment that greatly affected the intergenerational Black families on the West and South Sides of Chicago who embodied meaning and memory into the schools that had been a part of the collective identity, community knowing, and legacy. Frustrations can be heightened when we realize that political games are being played with the lives of vulnerable Black and Brown children. Sometimes we engage in the blame game and point fingers at the "bad" teachers, "bad" parents, "bad" students, "bad" principals, and so on, while also using a "veil" to hide behind our false intentions—an endless game that can seem aimless and stultifying (Ewing, 2018, p. 108). In the end, Black and Brown children lose out on a quality education without the adults acknowledging "the past harm caused to them, no honest reckoning of the present injustice, and an acceptance of their reality" (p. 124).

Lastly, this chapter examines the larger issues of race, language, and culture in public schools, given the distinctive histories, languages, realities, and cultural legacies that exist within the Maywood community. This chapter asks us to question what linguistic and cultural futures are possible when we gather together. Which traditions do the Black and Latinx students follow, and which traditions did they create together with shared consensus? How did they find their way to each other and build from there? What sociolinguistic and sociocultural world did they imagine for themselves? What linguistic spaces did they conjure together and form the particulars of their intersections? What language(s) can we break open to make room for others? Are we open to possibilities of developing new forms and concepts in such intersections?

In *Language, Mind and Power* (2020), Boisvert and Thiede argue that language is a cohesive device to bond us into tribes and into hyper-collective cultures as well as a divisive tool that can cause us to become violently triggered by people who speak different languages and dialects. We know today that race is an artificial system of taxonomy that we humans have created for ourselves to divide and conquer; however, Boisvert and Thiede argue that we need to have a reckoning with language and how it hard wires us to bond with our tribe, while also warring with the linguistic other. A shared language can provide a sense of safety for an in-group, but it also can be contaminated and weaponized. Subsequently, we are othered because of who we are but mostly because of how we speak. Can we make alliances when we do not know the language of the others? Learning the language of the other can also lead us to gain equality in that culture. Languages, therefore, can be exploited just like land but they can also heal, empower, liberate, and brainwash us. Language is indeed a contradiction—it can make us come together as well as split us apart. In the next chapter, we are at that crossroad in which we see the Black and Latinx communities in Maywood come together as well as split apart.

Chapter 3

Divide and Conquer

Division and Unrest over Power and Representation

Racism is a pervasive fact of life for the Black and Latinx students in Maywood. In this chapter, we will look at how racism robbed the students of their childhood and threatened the communities through gun violence, political corruption, and gang warfare. The critical discourse around the demographic shift in Maywood is just beginning, and we were able to capture the early discussions surrounding the potential impacts to a place where Black residents had been historically oppressed and a place where now Black residents were urged to build bridges of solidarity with the incoming Latinx residents. The participants in our study are hoping we get the story right and put forth a complex narrative, with some participants urging us to surrender the image of a diverse, harmonious community in order to deal with the self-inflicted problems that drove divisions into their village. The stories we share below are not all edifying; the stories are instead trying to make us realize the damage that racism had wrought in Maywood and the type of meanness and degradation that can result inside the belly of a beast (Ortiz, 2018).

FOLLOWING THE SUBURBAN DREAM: BLACK/BROWN PICKET FENCES

There are varied reasons why families migrate to different parts of the country. Fishman (2005), the American architect and writer, created a taxonomy to describe migration in the United States after European conquest: (a) the "first migration" was when European pioneers colonized and created settlements across the continent and eradicated the indigenous Native American population through acts of genocide and enslaved African populations to create a chattel economy; (b) the "second migration" was when the descendants of the European population migrated from farms to factories in the 1800s; (c) the "third migration" was the development of large metropolitan centers like New York and Chicago in the 1900s and the start of the Great Migration of African Americans from the South to the North; (d) the "fourth migration" was when white people depopulated the major cities and moved out to segregated suburbs; and (e) the "fifth migration" is the current reurbanism of cities, a new digital economy, and the gentrification of city neighborhoods from affluent newcomers, often the children who grew up in the suburbs in the earlier migration, who now are living in high-rise condos (Fishman, 2005).

This reurbanism is also pushing out Black and Latinx residents who could never leave the inner-city neighborhoods before due to job security and family ties but are now being pushed out by white gentrifiers as well as other economic and social conditions such as the elimination of public housing complexes like Cabrini Green and increased gun violence. Migrations occur in waves and the current reurbanism of Chicago led to the movement of Black and Latinx residents from the city of Chicago into the inner-ring suburbs like Maywood in the 2000s. Some scholars are stating that this reurbanism is leading to a reverse migration in which Black residents who have lived in Chicago over several generations are moving their families out to the inner-ring suburbs like Maywood, and even as far south as Atlanta, leaving the Black population of the city of Chicago to reach such low numbers as 10% and the subsequent closing of public schools in Black communities (Lee, 2021). The mass exodus of the Black population in Chicago is also leading to the loss of Black political power in a city that once had a 40% Black population and a thriving Black culture, community, and with towering figures of American history: Louis Armstrong, Duke Ellington, Bessie Smith, Ida B. Wells, Jesse Jackson, and Barack and Michelle Obama (Kapos, Perez Jr., Rayasam, & Li, 2021).

South and Crowder (1997) found that Black suburbanites tend to be concentrated in predominantly Black suburban communities like Maywood, usually adjacent to central cities and characterized by residential instability, weak property taxes, low average incomes, declining population, and high crime. At the same time, Black suburbs also provide significant social capital in the form of kinship, friendship, social networks, social services, minority-owned businesses, and faith-based institutions. Black suburbs also do not have the racial hostility, bias, and discrimination faced by Black residents in white suburbs. We could also argue that Maywood is an inner-ring suburb outside of Chicago but within a metropolitan area. Suburban residence represents a major step in the process of Black spatial assimilation and Black mobility and often leads to Black residents staying put in the suburbs in the Black city-Black suburb migration pattern noted in our study. Maywood also reduced spatial mismatch when Black workers had to drive very far for their jobs; instead, the Black residents of Maywood live and work close to the same community and reduced spatial distance from home to work.

In our study, there was an overwhelming response from the Latinx students for home ownership in Maywood: their families moved to this historically Black suburb to attain the American dream of purchasing their own house with a front and back yard, with open space, and with tree-lined streets. Their families, however, did not migrate out from the city of Chicago in an urban exodus, rather, they often migrated southward from the neighboring suburb of Melrose Park, a historically Italian American, working-class suburb that was also shifting in demographics and becoming more Latinx. Yet, Melrose Park still has an Italian officialdom in place with a power-wielding Italian mayor who is known to be a racist in the public arena and who controls an aging Italian constituency: "In a recording of the exchange, the suburban mayor can be heard using a slew of obscenities and a racial epithet for Black people" (Schuba, 2021). Many of the Black residents of Maywood did not venture into Melrose Park because of police harassment and how the police would chase them down to the south end and tell them to stay below Lake Street, the dividing border between Melrose Park and Maywood. Jeremy, a long-time Maywood resident, talks about how he avoided going into Melrose Park as a young Black man:

Jeremy: Melrose Park is the most racist village in the western suburbs. I worked at a grocery store there but then I had to be transferred to another store because I could not deal with that type of daily racial tension, man.

Author: What kind of racism did you face?

Jeremy: You know it was just a lot of Italian men always looking at me full of anger. They thought I was odd. I didn't fit their stereotype. I was a nerdy Black male. I did not understand what was happening because I treat people with respect. It got so bad that I had to leave. I could not deal with it anymore.

Author: Since Maywood is a food desert, many people have to go to Melrose Park to shop but they also do not feel safe there.

Jeremy: It's been like that for a long, long time. There is a racial border between 19th Avenue and Melrose Park. It divides Blacks who live in Maywood. It also divides the Latinos between the railroad and Lake Street. And then you have a lot of Italians living there right along Lake Street. I have been pulled over by the Melrose Park police once, all Italian men, and I stayed calm and showed him my driver's license. He said I went over the speed limit, but I know I did not. He made me so angry and then let me go after ten minutes. This was on Lake Street between 10th and 25th Avenue.

The Latinx families were leaving Melrose Park for some of the same political reasons as Jeremy, but the housing market in neighboring Maywood had lower home prices with options for larger Victorian homes instead of cramped apartments. Figure 3.1 shows a picture of a famous historic home in Maywood, the Jacob Bohlander House on North 4th Avenue, built in 1896. Bohlander was a wealthy white merchant, a former president of Maywood, and the first automobile owner (Romain, 2018).

So, the Latinx families moved from Melrose Park to Maywood in large numbers at the start of the economic recession in 2008 for better housing at lower costs—thereby leap-frogging over the tightly controlled, aging Italian American suburb and its small middle-class brick homes with a uniform streetscape of front lawns, concrete steps, and iron-wrought railings. Olivio and Avila (2005) also found that in the early 2000s, the Latinx population migrated out of the city and into suburbs like Melrose Park for many reasons: city neighborhoods were becoming gentrified by white residents; a surge of jobs occurred in suburban manufacturing plants; an abundance of restaurant and construction work; and they wanted to purchase a first-time home. It

Figure 3.1   Historical Homes in Maywood. *Source*: Bartholomew St. John.

also led to a political and cultural transformation as inner-ring suburbs like Melrose Park became populated with Latinx-owned businesses that helped revitalize decaying strip malls. Assembly-line Latinx workers were now purchasing three-bedroom homes for $150,000 in old-line suburbs, often sharing the costs with extended family members and moving into mixed-race communities like Maywood.

As first-time homeowners, this social and spatial migration was seen as a sign of pragmatism for the Latinx students since they now had more space for their multigenerational households, even though their parents often worked outside of Maywood. The Latinx families migrated in an atomized fashion with a slow racial transition into the northeast section of this historically Black suburb; this was a side-by-side integration of two minoritized populations. Over time, after the recession, a rapid block by block, wave-like turnover of Black neighborhoods on the northeastern edge of Maywood turned into predominantly Latinx neighborhoods. Maria, a Latinx middle school student, when interviewed about other Latinx families in her neighborhood, shows how her extended family lives on the same block when she states, "Well some of them are from my family because my brother lives like couple of houses down and then my other brother lives like two blocks away."

Enchautegui (1997) states that the exodus of human capital in Black neighborhoods produces deterioration and poverty concentration; however, in Latinx neighborhoods, poverty does not lead to deterioration, even though 40% or more of the residents are poor. Rather, Latinx neighborhoods become the vigor for new immigrants, and over time Latinx immigrant communities increase in human capital due to higher self-employment through labor-based job networks. The lack of higher education, female labor force, and English proficiency, along with spatial isolation from the mainstream and larger families, do not get in the way of immigrant entrepreneurs and earnings outcomes (Tienda, 1991). Immigrants are often praised for their self-reliance amid adversity, and employers praise immigrants for their work discipline. Eventually, there is an outmigration of earlier immigrants toward non-Latino neighborhoods, and eventually these long-term immigrants reduce poverty in their new neighborhood like Maywood.

Thus far, we found similar patterns of economic growth as Latinx families moved into Maywood where there are only signs of racial integration as opposed to racial turnover. The Black population is not fleeing because more and more Latinx families are moving into their all-Black neighborhoods, although not all-Black residents are happy about the demographic change. One can argue that Latinx immigrants washed up on the shores of desolate American sub/urban neighborhoods, reviving them before demographic collapse in urban fallow fields. In Maywood, however, it was not a wasteland that Latinx people were moving into. It was a historical village that was for the most part unfamiliar to the new Latinx arrivals.

Hwang and Mordock (1998) argue that the principle of homophily is central to several social science theories and can be applied to the study of population change in geographic areas. These theories predict racial homogeneity in residential settlement patterns and how the concentration of one group in an area is expected to attract same-group members while deterring others. Ingroup attraction and out-group avoidance have led to segregation and spatial assimilation in Maywood between the Black and Latinx communities. The place-stratification theory states that people avoid minoritized places because they are highly stratified by amenities, services, and other valuable resources. Such minoritized places are typified by substandard housing, poor health and sanitary conditions, higher rates of crimes and violence, poor education and services, and lack of economic opportunities, and are generally viewed as not nice places to raise children. However, the Latinx population did not avoid Maywood as the crime rose and when three schools were on academic watch. They did not buy into the negative externalities associated with Maywood. Instead, the increase in Latinx families correlated more with the desire to be close to fellow ethnic members, often extended family and to leverage the suburban housing market. In fact, the concentration of first-generation Mexican American families in Maywood functioned more as an incubator preparing vulnerable families to adapt to the host society.

The interview below with Mary, a Black teacher whom we interviewed in chapter 2 and a current behavior specialist in the middle school, examines the differences in aesthetics between the Black and Latinx homes in Maywood. Pierre Bourdieu's sociological theory of aesthetics has offered a powerful explication of "taste," in all its meanings, from choices in art through choices in dress, furniture, language, and the like, to taste in homes, both as a unified subject matter and as a method for producing and reproducing power differences among social classes (Loesberg, 1993). The aesthetics of what is a home and what a house should look like in Maywood can be seen as an act of power and social differentiation between the established Black residents and the new Latinx arrivals. Here we can hear Mary's voice and how aesthetics can also be a form of political resistance.

Mary: I remember being disappointed when our T-ball games were being canceled and replaced by soccer programs. Then there was the housing issue. Our houses were seen as a little raggedier than theirs. Me going back now and thinking about it . . . it wasn't. They were just outside all the time fixing their houses. They were outside gardening and that was just something that my family never did. They weren't outside putting flowers in the front right. Their houses always seemed so immaculate and colorful and well kept. Our houses seemed so rinky dinky. And most of my Black friends lived in apartments. So, my friends are living in these small one-bedroom apartments while these new Latinx families are coming and have these homes like . . . they took over. They came across the tracks and changed the demographics in Maywood. Now they are on both sides of the tracks.

Author: Why do you think the Latinx families moved into Maywood?

Mary: Maywood is an up-and-coming area. It is close to the city and cheap enough. You can find a nice home here, but it is not as expensive as Logan Square where now white families are coming to gentrify Latinx communities that already had businesses and restaurants there. Now they are coming into Maywood and bringing in big businesses and restaurants. "Hmmm . . . Maywood is not as expensive, but we can fix it up to our liking." There is free reign in Maywood. We can come and make it what we want it to be. Maywood offers space but we are also a food desert and there is no grocery store. We have blood banks, churches, and gas stations . . . Maywood was never quite finished. Now they have an opportunity to finish it in their own way. We'll make it pretty for our families. They stay together. They live together. They have pots of money that they put together. Then they built new businesses and get new homes. Then they pass it on to their children.

Author: Do they come because there is more space for more than one family?

Mary: Yes, and the homes here in Maywood are spacious inside and beautiful. My god sister lives on 20th . . . the whole side of that street used to be all Black and now is all Latino. She's like, "It's just crazy." She says she does not remember a time when people felt comfortable enough to go outside and ride bikes, walk dogs, and play outside. Maywood has not always been safe. It's almost like the Latinx families are gentrifying Maywood. But it's hard to say gentrification because it is other Brown people.

Author: Do you think this Latinx gentrification is a good thing?

Mary: Hmm . . . actually I don't. To be honest . . . it is not because . . . I have Latinx friends. I am faith based and I love my community and the people that are in it. I think it is difficult to watch it change. Especially for my god sister because that house is her father's and he passed away recently. He was the police chief in Maywood and now the police chief is Latinx. For them to have that potential and then all the homes they are building. Her dad worked so hard to get that house and then they just came in and took over. All bright and shiny. We never grew up with any of that stuff. For most elders who own the homes it is hard.

Authors: Do the elders talk to the new Latinx families? Is there a language and cultural divide?

Mary: I think my god sister started to wave at her neighbors and left it there. Even when I am with her, and we are on the porch . . . she is not smiling much. Then she says, "Now they're building something else on the back of the house!" It's always something like that. It's no harm no foul but the change has been difficult

because of the language barrier. But then there is also some kind of jealousy
. . . from our end. It is hard to see change when we don't even interact with the
Latino families. If we interact with them, it is almost as if we are allowing it to
happen. Most of us just don't want to interact with them. They're there. We are
not going to exist in this big change. So now she says "hi" and waves. But they
are not realizing that their homes were filled with Black people first. They're
just living in that house, and they do not know about us and who was the first
Black family on their block. Yes, they have a house in Maywood, but do you
know about Maywood. We're communicating and they're not collaborating.

Mary went on to talk about the rich history of Maywood and how each
block has a set of pioneers who settled into that pocket of Maywood, which
the Latinx families are unaware of and may not want to know either. For
Mary, there is great importance on personal history and telling stories in the
Black culture, but the Latinx arrivals are not learning about these pioneer
stories. In similar neighborhoods within the city of Chicago, Brown/Black
neighborhoods reach a tipping point, and one racial group starts to exit as
opposed to staying loyal to the changing community—questioning whether
the Black community will stay intact in Maywood twenty years from now
(Wilson, 2006).

The intersectionality of gender and place is another common theme in
Maywood's early settlement story when acknowledging the pivotal role that
women played in establishing homes in the community. The following interview with Melissa, a bilingual teacher who grew up in Maywood, continues
this narrative as she marks her grandmother as one of the early Latinx pioneers who came to settle:

Author: When did your family move into Maywood?
Melissa: My mother is the oldest in the family . . . she is fifty now. They moved
to Maywood when she was fourteen. She was a freshman in high school. She
was the oldest.
Author: Where did she go to high school?
Melissa: Actually . . . freshman year she had started at a Catholic school in Chicago. She finished . . . they moved in the middle of the school year. She ended
up living with my aunt and coming home on the weekends through her freshman year. Then her sophomore year she went to the [Maywood high school]
. . . she had two younger sisters and a younger brother, and they went to an
[elementary school] in Maywood.
Author: Where did they live in the city of Chicago?
Melissa: Around Drake and Taylor Street? In Little Italy.
Author: Why did they move to the city to Maywood?
Melissa: My grandmother had just remarried and . . . when they lived in Chicago,
she lived with . . . my grandmother who lived with her brother and his family.

So, there was a lot of them in the house. You know . . . she met my grandfather and they moved and bought a house in Maywood.

Author: Why Maywood? Do you remember them telling you why?

Melissa: I don't recall . . . I know that in talking to my mom . . . she said there was one other Hispanic family. And it is such a small world because the other Hispanic family that lived across the street . . . umm . . . my grandmother is really good friends with this woman and her grandson is my sister's husband now. But they both brought their families to Maywood and their grandchildren ended up together!

Author: Were they the first Latinx family to move into Maywood?

Melissa: They were the first Mexican family. She did say that there were some Cubans at the time. But the majority was Caucasian in that part of Maywood. She said that through Roosevelt they were all Caucasian. My dad was from Melrose Park but he went to the local high school in Maywood also, so he knew Maywood fairly well and . . . he said that there were African Americans from between St. Charles up to Madison and Washington. From 19th to 9th and that was it. Everything else was Italian and Caucasian.

Author: Do you remember what your grandmother said about demographics changing?

Melissa: There's far more Hispanics now on the north side of Maywood. And even now . . . I can see Hispanics on the south side of Maywood.

Author: Why do you think there is a migration of Latinx families to Maywood now even though your grandmother was a pioneer in 1972? Why now?

Melissa: I think . . . moving away from the city . . . like Chicago . . . and moving into the suburb. I think that . . . what I see is a lot of Hispanics coming in and redoing the houses that are there. So, a lot of them are rundown and you know . . . they buy the house, and they fix it up and that's where they start their life.

Author: Do you think it is about the idea of having a house? The space? The yard?

Melissa: I believe so because . . . in the city . . . and I still have family that lives in the city . . . in the bungalows and the apartments . . . there isn't much of a yard. Then there is only one apartment for a lot of people. I definitely think space plays a role.

Author: Do you see the Latinx families migrating in chains with their brothers and sisters? Uncles and aunts?

Melissa: I do believe that because . . . my grandma is one of the youngest. One of her sisters lived . . . on 5th and she may have moved there because my aunt and her husband lived down there. But my grandma moved to 6th . . . I do believe that because my grandma moved there. Growing up I lived in Melrose Park . . . and then we moved across the street in Maywood to be close to my grandma. And then . . . and my father was okay with it even though he was from Melrose Park. Then my grandma's sister who lived on 5th then moved across the street from us on 6th. Then my mom's sister moved on to that street across from us so there are now four houses on the block with our family. I think that staying close to the family plays a major role.

Author: Now that you teach in Maywood, does it help to live in the same neighborhood as your students?

Melissa: Definitely. I got a house and a mortgage in Maywood . . . I love being around my family . . . and you know . . . staying in touch with the community I teach in . . . knowing who is who and what the mayor is doing and what politics are going on . . . and having a say in that.

Unlike the Black pioneers before them who migrated to Maywood to seek the American dream, even during white resistance, the Latinx subjects in our study never spoke of Black resistance toward their hejira to the suburbs. The middle school students also talked about how this historically Black suburb was secluded from white racism as well as white surveillance and provided more freedom; the master-slave narrative that applied to white-Black integration in the post-WWII suburbs no longer applies to the context of Black/Brown integration here.

The social and spatial inroads for the Latinx migration into Maywood were similar to the previous century's Black suburban migration; however, the recent Latinx suburbanites did not have to overcome racial barriers to purchase their home in this historically Black suburb. Our research setting, like many mature Black suburbs, is a symbol of cultural affirmation and racial pride; yet these historical precedents of Black pioneers building a safe cultural and racial space in the suburbs were never addressed by the Latinx subjects in our study. At times, they spoke of feeling isolated in a Black suburb as a Latinx minority; however, they never spoke of feeling uncomfortable either, even though racial isolation is often cited in interracial suburbs. The kinship networks created by the town's early Black pioneers were nonetheless missing in this new Latinx migration in which some Latinx families lived in isolation from other Latinx families in Maywood and kept to themselves. Many of the Latinx families in Maywood transcended place by maintaining ties to other Latinx enclaves and within places like Chicago, Cicero, and Berwyn, all outside of this Black suburb, logging in miles on the weekends in their cars by attending church elsewhere and visiting relatives whenever they could.

Even though the Latinx student population is the largest in the elementary and middle school district, there is only one Latina member on the school board who currently is the board president. The Latinx families in this suburban community are slowly building social capital among themselves and accruing leverage for social services such as Spanish language translation at public meetings, and eventually greater political power. However, the political machinery in Maywood is like the political machinery in the city of Chicago in which politicians play dirty and the name of the game is winning loyal votes for your political party. There is corruption at all levels from local to state elected officials, money is laundered, bribery and kickback schemes are inevitable, and superintendents who ask about missing funding clash with school boards until they are asked to leave within one contract cycle. An April 3, 2007, newspaper article in *The Chicago Tribune* chronicled the reelection of the power-wielding Italian mayor in Melrose Park, Mayor Serpico, and allegations of corruption of school board funds and cronyism cited by his Freedom Party contenders (Brosinski, 2007):

> Freedom Party candidate Roberto Rios, a 37-year-old computer-aided design operator, said the growing Hispanic population is under-represented in village government. Rios also said spending needs greater oversight. According to the 2005 audit, the village ran a $1.1 million deficit in the general fund. But village Comptroller John Gregor said 2006 audit numbers, which have not been released, should show a surplus. Freedom Party candidate Pat Allegrini, 42, said he's wary of the village's $100 million debt in 2005. "We need to be more responsible with finances," he said. But Mayor Serpico said indebtedness includes bonds sold for capital projects and six tax-increment finance districts, which hold surpluses.

The following interview with a Spanish bilingual teacher who grew up in Maywood, Stephanie, chronicles the volleying of power between the Black and Italian school board members all the while amid cultivating the increasing Latinx vote for school board positions, which can be won with just 20 to 30 votes sometimes in the local elections:

Author: Do you think the Latinx community will gain political power in Melrose Park now that they are the majority?

Stephanie: I feel that there is now a Hispanic majority in the school district but not enough numbers in Maywood, but we are the majority in Melrose Park. There are still many . . . Italians where . . . they're not ready to let up power in Melrose Park . . . I guess that is what you would say . . . control over the school district . . . even though they don't have children in the schools. There is still Italian power and control over the school district.

Author: Is there a lot of corrupt politics there?

Stephanie: I believe so . . . I feel like that when I was younger, I did not know it as much but now that I am older . . . it is a part of life. The Italian power is preventing the Blacks and the Hispanics . . . because they're still in the school district . . . whether it is family or not . . . they're still present . . . and I think that . . . even looking at . . . the politics of it . . . I have been to fundraisers for people who are running politically and . . . feel that the African American and Hispanic populations have come together . . . um . . . but there still is a divide between . . . you know . . . I think there are some that have gone along with the Italians but . . . I don't think . . . they have bought into it.

Author: So, is there discussion among your family members in terms of Latinx families siding politically with the African American school board members or the Italian school board members?

Stephanie: Yes . . . because one of my aunts is very close with the Italian mayor
and . . . some of my family members don't agree with the Italian mayor . . . yes,
he is doing things . . . for Hispanics in the community [Melrose Park] but . . . it
is kind of like . . . we'll just give them a little bit so they can be quiet. What did
one of my cousins say . . . that's just their way of staying in power and keeping
us happy . . . keep voting for him . . . even though we're the growing majority
now and we should have the power.

Author: So, if there was a Latinx contender for the mayoral race in Melrose Park
then would the current Italian mayor be challenged?

Stephanie: Oh yes. There was a contender named Martinez and it got pretty heated . . . my sister's boyfriend went to help to be one of the volunteers at the poll
and anyone who looked Hispanic . . . they asked for their IDs but the old Italian
people that were coming to vote were not asked. We went to grade school here
and we went to a private school with a lot of Italians, and we know a lot of
them, and we know that they don't live in Melrose Park anymore, but they were
coming in and voting . . . they brought everybody. They were bussing people. It
was pretty horrible. We were in disbelief that it was allowed . . . they kept telling the Hispanic people that this was not your voting area, and you have to go
somewhere else . . . but all the older Italian people were coming in their senior
citizen buses that the city paid for . . . like a shuttle.

Author: How close was the race?

Stephanie: I think it was 60 to 30 . . . . but it was . . . there was such a large group
of Hispanics that still voted for [Italian American mayor] because he had built
those relations. Hispanics voted for him because he is really good friends with
a Hispanic family that owns businesses here. They own that Mexican restaurant
on Main Street and the billiard place next to it. I went to grade school with
them. [Italian American mayor] goes to Mexico with the father. On Lake Street
and 18th and 19th . . . they have a Michoacán Museum there . . . they have a
very close relationship.

Author: Do you think the Black and Latinx communities will come together in
solidarity to vote out the Italian power base?

Stephanie: I would not be surprised. I think there is a push for the Black and
Hispanic communities to come together . . . my friend encourages us to get to
know our politics. I have seen them at the board meetings, and I also get the
newsletters at home also. I do believe that can happen . . . in both Melrose Park
and Maywood. Once you're in there . . . then you take care of your own friends
and family.

The racial politics brewing over who should become the mayor of these
majority-minority communities are indicative of the story occurring across
America in which Latinx voters are slowly gaining political power and presence as their numbers grow. The Machiavellian actors who controlled the
Black-Brown community in Maywood were named and identified by our

participants as well as their mobilizing efforts to retain power within the larger political network (Nespor, 1994). For example, the Facebook page "I Love Maywood" has 3,000 plus members, including us, but there was a recent decision by the Black administrators to not allow for Spanish writing on the site. This decision angered many of the Latinx members of the group and set off a tirade of angry posts and eventually many of the Latinx members splintered off and created their own page called "Maywood Unido." One post alluded to the divisiveness of this splinter: "I would think crime, property taxes, education, infrastructure & community development would take precedence over someone's primary language. Divide & conquer. Some residents bickering over minute issues while the surrounding suburbs sit around like the Romans in the Coliseum watching and laughing at the carnage. We've got to do better and not waste energy and resources" (Temple, 2011).

Young Latina voters like Stephanie and Melissa use social media, have stronger social ties and social capital, and are politically informed as to which candidate can best serve their interests and needs. The political calculus is changing and the century-old, Italian-Black machinery that migrated from the West Side of Chicago [after Little Italy was torn down for the University of Illinois college campus] to Maywood will soon become anachronistic in an increasing Latinx suburb (Fernandez, 2012). Michael Romain, the influential news reporter whom we interviewed for this book, talked about the hegemony of the Italian mayors in the inner-ring suburbs like Maywood:

Michael: The mayor of Melrose Park is nakedly paternalistic. He had a racist tirade on TV and called a white guy a "shine." He is used to using that language quite often. He apologized with a non-apology. He is running now for reelection uncontested. He knows it and he doesn't care. I have been in board meetings when his opponents wanted to make Melrose Park a sanctuary city like Oak Park. This was when Trump was in office. There were people there from PASO and other organizations lobbying Melrose Park to become a sanctuary city. I remember Serpico saying "I do enough for you all already. You have to trust me. We don't need to pass an ordinance. We do a lot of the stuff for you people that you are already telling me." He talked to them like that. "I do a lot for you people." My Hispanics. That's how they are . . . the Italian mayors. There's the Italian mayor of Hillside where 30% of the people are Black and 30% are Latinx. He is up for reelection, and he is running against a Black woman and keeps telling us what he is doing for the Black people. "Half my police force is Black." That's the way they talk.

In 2021, Mayor Nathaniel George Booker was voted in as the new, young Black mayor of Maywood who courted the Latinx vote and who brought in a diverse board of trustees as well as a progressive political agenda that attracted the Millennial and Gen X voters. Mayor George Booker included the Latinx residents of Maywood in his political agenda and sent a unifying message on his Facebook page: "Unity in the Community is not just a # It is a movement that surrounds every part of Moving Maywood Forward Together here in the Village of Maywood." During Hispanic Heritage Month in September 2021, Mayor Booker flew the Mexican flag over the village hall and unanimously passed a proclamation recognizing National Hispanic Heritage Month, stating that this act is "an important reminder of how much strength we draw as a nation from our immigrant roots and our values as a nation of immigrants" (Romain, 2021).

THE SUB/URBAN SPACE: VIOLENCE IN OUR EVERYDAY LIVES

The notion of suburbia for both the Black denizens and the recent Latinx arrivals in Maywood was acutely different from the bourgeois culture of family life, leisure, feminine domesticity, and nature that is often historically associated with white suburbs (Wiese, 2005). Drugs, gangs, and violence are now a part of this "at-risk" suburban landscape due to the effects of the 2008 economic recession as well as the recent pandemic, not to mention the political and economic inequities facing sub/urban communities like Maywood: "Eighty two percent of Blacks and Latinos who live in the suburbs are in at-risk suburbs compared to 52% for Whites" (Orfield, 2003). Many of the participants in our study stated that the outflow of poorer residents from the West Side of Chicago near this suburb, such as the Austin community, is what started its economic decline and subsequent increase in violence—creating a migration myth for themselves to explain the spike in crime and without looking at more complex factors. Yet, this spillover process of poorer residents from the West Side of Chicago to Maywood has been cited by sociologists to occur when poverty-stricken residents from the inner-city spill over into the aging inner-ring suburbs just outside the city limits, thereby creating contiguous "suburban ghettos" as they migrate just ten miles west from the city to the suburb (Murphy, 2007; Rury & Rife, 2018). The middle school students we observed in Maywood often talked about living in a "ghetto suburb"—now a part of the vernacular used even among the white teachers.

If Maywood was now coined a suburban ghetto, then it still does not negate the fact that the suburbanization process and its philosophy of self-help and progress was also a part of the town's history and allowed countless working-class families to purchase homes, raise families and build communities—just as it did for the new Latinx families. The private space of their suburban homes became places of refuge from the violence and crime outside their homes. Basketball hoops in the backyard prevented getting into tussles in the neighborhood park; the shelter of the backyard protected against the world of the deceptively quiet, tree-lined suburban streets. In 2012, the crime rate had spiked in Maywood; however, the rates have since been dropping significantly for most areas of crime minus violent crime:

> In 2016, the village of just under 24,000 residents was home to only 165 violent crimes—murder, non-negligent manslaughter, rape, robbery and aggravated assault, showing a 35% decrease, according to FBI data. However, in 2012, that number was 238 violent crimes. A total of 235 violent crimes were reported in 2015. Similarly, property crimes, which includes burglary; larceny; motor vehicle theft and arson, have decreased by about 10 percent overall. Reported property crimes in Maywood have been steadily decreasing for some time. Since 2012, property crime reports have decreased 53 percent, going from a total of 988 reports to 572 in 2016. Violent crime reporting has had a bumpier road. Reporting for violent offenses increased in 2014 and 2015. (Roach, 2017).

In the following interview with Manuel, a Latinx eighth-grade male student, we can see how adolescents in Maywood are coping with the ebb and flow of community violence:

Author: What do your parents think of the violence and crime in the area?
Manual: I guess they are used to it. I think it's worse in Humboldt Park in the city than here . . . to me it's worse than here because . . . my grandmother still lives out there. You know when we go visit her in the city . . . we're not even allowed to go out of the house.
Author: Why do you think?
Manual: Because it's dangerous.
Author: You think Maywood is becoming more dangerous?
Manual: Well . . . recent shootings probably.
Author: What are some of the recent shootings?
Manual: A girl was killed the other day, shot in the head . . . I am not sure why . . . Some kind of trouble from like . . . I think they said from the West Side of Chicago, and she came over here and she got shot in the head.
Author: So, it started in the West Side and then she came here, and they found her . . .
Manual: And they shot her. That's what I heard. I am not sure if it's true or not.
Author: How about you? Do you talk about it?
Manual: Not really cause I don't really hang around Maywood.
Author: Where do you go?
Manual: If I go outside, I usually go to . . . because Andrew lives down the street from me. So, I usually go over to his house to hang out. Or if I go out somewhere then I go out with a friend. We usually go to McDonalds. Not too far like you know from the area . . . probably like four or five blocks away.

In the post-WWII era, new suburbanites wanted not only green space for their children but also good schools, along with safe and quiet environments—essentially a sense of a civic community. Yet, the families in this study did not refer to these quintessential conditions. They were focused mostly on the actual physical house and its physical space. Suburbanization was not necessarily a means to an end—better schools and better social services—for the new Latinx families. To have access to these advantages, a few of the students we observed throughout the span of our research moved to the affluent, liberal, racially diverse suburb nearby in order to attain a better high school education. One of the Black male students in this research study picked up on the idea that location was the root of inequality and that schools in the affluent, liberal, racially diverse suburb directly east of them had an infrastructure that led to student success and made the following comment openly in class during a social studies lesson: "They should make school more interesting here. This is fucking bullshit. I'm never gonna send my kids here. I will put them in the suburbs. Fuck this shit. Schools with all white people. Here it's a majority of Black students with some Mexicans. At least in Oak Park, they teach you something and make it more interesting." Ironically, this student did not think Maywood was a "suburb," even though it is indeed by definition a suburb.

The violence in Maywood was also glorified in the local hip-hop and rap culture and the suburb was given the metonym of "Murder Woods." Local rappers coined the term and here is a description of its origin from the Urban Dictionary website (2012):

> Used by Suburbians of Chicago to refer to the near west suburb of [Maywood] and/or Bellwood, Illinois. Also used in an ironic attempt to try and put on for themselves to gain street credit and give the suburb(s) a harder-core image. Murder Woods is known for their increasing crime rate which includes, but is not limited to terrorism, gang activity, drug trafficking, rape, arson, treason, burglary, kidnapping, robbery, and of course Murder (hence the name Murder Woods). Not to be mistaken for or used interchangeably with Chiraq [the metonym for Chicago where the violence was higher than Iraq].

Girl: Ay boy, where you stay at?
Boy: I'm from da Woods, Murder Woods! All day!
Girl: Nigga! You weak as hell! Chiraq all day & night baby!

On the YouTube portal, there is a 40-minute documentary titled "Only The Strong Survive" posted in November 2013 by Atwill Williams, a Maywood resident, which depicts how violence affects the everyday life of the Maywood community. The video received over 50,000 viewers from all over the world who had diverse opinions about the documentary. Williams states on the website that "we're not doing it to glorify the 'hood,' we're doing it so it could spark conversations in people that will maybe turn into action." Yet the documentary also exposes the gendered nature of crime in the city, with the individuals embroiled in violence almost always portrayed as male. The comments posted below the YouTube video ranged from supportive to challenging the idea of how a clean and nice suburb can be depicted as violent, even though it was cited as a documentary:

- Oh how I miss the old Maywood. I will forever be a Maywoodian & continue to pray all the way from Arizona.
- This was so strong. I've lived in Maywood for 21 years out of the 23 years I've been on this earth. I loved living in Maywood. Now that I'm in college, living back in Maywood would NEVER happen, unless there is change.
- This documentary is interesting. I attended East High School and graduated in 2003, top 40 of my classmates. I look at this from two perspectives. Ever since I traveled to Maywood, I see years of disinvestment from vacant lots, abandoned buildings, and not enough people coming back to start their own businesses, being politically active, and being a teacher to mentor our youth. I also see that some parents having children at a young age, and are not being "parents" of teaching their children values and morals. This is why people need to vote and let the mayor of Maywood be accountable of their actions on how to not let this town be a "murder town."
- I knew some former classmates that were victims of gun violence, due to being in a gang, or just hanging with the wrong crowd.
- 4th and Warren, proud to be from Maywood and have survived. R.I.P. IQ.
- Maywood changed when they tore down the projects. Instead of coming to Maywood for a better life they just brought that low life mentality with them. Sad!
- This is NOT the Maywood I grew up in. Thank God I was a 70's kid and an 80's teen and was able to enjoy a safe and productive childhood. Great film . . . glad to be 20 years removed from it.
- how the hell can 21 blocks be this bad?
- Maywood is mostly Four Corner Hustlers 4CH's and Gangster Disciples GD's today, still have Vice Lords VL's sets, as well as Black Disciples BD's, also Black P. Stones BPS, and Mickey Cobras in the area, and Latin Kings to the north.
- Maywooooood up to no good.
- What a bunch of fake ass tough guys beating up on women walking around with their underwear showing what a joke they don't scare me at all I'll from Humboldt Park we laugh at these clowns!!!
- I live in Maywood it's not even that bad . . .

- Salute . . . Maywood born and raised 6th and Madison/school st. Maywood has DEFINITELY changed. There's NO activities for these children. Nowhere for them to go. I hate coming even driving thru Maywood. The feeling is so COLD and so sad. These children killing each other over what . . . for what!!!!! Modern day lynching . . .
- Mexicans are buying up the large Victorian homes and fixing them up. Family structure is vital for a community. Just need to figure out where the bust outs will go once property values start rising.
- I GREW UP IN MAYWOOD 640 S 17TH MOVED TO BOLINGBROOK IN 98 THIS DOCUMENTARY MADE ME MISS THE CRIB N GROWING UP THERE.. WHEN I RIDE THROUGH N VISIT MY GRANNY OR JUS BEND N BURN I DNT KNOW ANYONE ANYMORE! THE VIOLENCE GOTTA STOP PEACE TO EVERYBODY STILL THERE MAKING IT. #MAYWOOD

There was also a considerable backlash from the Maywood civic community toward this YouTube documentary that had left a tainted image of Maywood and gave it "a black eye" because it explored Maywood's criminal underbelly (Romain, 2016). The documentary did interview gang leaders and drug dealers, along with the mayor, police officers, local anti-violence activists, and former NBA players and coaches who came from the local high school. We did get to interview Mr. Williams for this book, who created the documentary as a class assignment while an undergraduate student at Columbia College. Atwill did confirm that he faced a lot of criticism for showing the dark side of Maywood, while others commended him for bringing an honest conversation to the community. He received the greatest backlash from the "street cats" (drug dealers and gang leaders) because the Maywood police also saw the documentary and started harassing them. Mr. Williams reminded them of the signed contract but took the YouTube video down for a few days, fearful of retaliation, and then decided to put it back up and it is still there.

West Side Migration and Gang Lines

Many of the Black participants in this study talked about their migration story to Maywood and when, where, and how they settled into this suburb. There were some participants who grew up in Maywood because that was where their grandparents moved to in the post-WWII era to work at the American Can Company, which produced the majority of metal cans in the United States. Maywood lost close to 8,000 jobs when the factory closed in the late 1970s and after a large fire destroyed the property (Romain, 2019). Others talked about migrating to Maywood in the 1980s when drugs and crime were rising in the nearby West Side of Chicago in the Austin neighborhood, and they came to

Maywood to escape violence. In terms of the younger students, there were some Black families who had recently moved to Maywood during the recession era in 2008–2010. There was also a small number who could trace their roots to Mississippi and ancestors who migrated to Maywood during the early waves of the Great Migration from the South to the North in the 1920s. We interviewed Michael Romain, a journalist for the Village Free Press, whom we cite extensively in our book and a native son of Maywood and current resident:

Michael: I was born and raised in Maywood. We moved there in 1985. My dad was from Chicago. I was like a lot of students back then and still now who come from the West Side to Maywood. But my mom's family goes way back in Maywood at least four generations. I actually wrote an article on my great, great grandfather Charles Linyard and my great, great grandmother Novella. The Linyards are a family of a few hundred. But I don't know where they actually came from. Charles was a chauffeur for a white family in Oak Park. They had nine children and one of them was my great, grandmother. Maywood is no more than five miles, but back then Black people were confined to a certain area of Maywood. It was no more than six or seven square blocks. They could only go to one elementary school which was Washington, which is ironic since that is now the dual language academy. The older Black folks from Maywood come from that area near Washington. They all went to the Second Baptist Church which is one of the oldest Black churches. I learned all this in the museum on 5th Avenue. It was a tight knit Black community full of laborers and blue-collar workers for the most part. Back then we lived alongside Jews. Jews and Blacks lived in the same area. We could not live beyond those borders. There were restrictive covenants, and you could not sell your house to a Black person because the mortgage company said they can sue you. Of course, there were clauses for servant quarters. We could only live in the white part of Maywood if we were servants. That was the history of my mom's family.

Figure 3.2 is of a synagogue in Maywood in 1905 when there was a Jewish population.

Michael then talked about his schooling in Maywood, his father moving back to the Austin community in Chicago, and his mother remarrying and staying in Maywood with his stepfather who was an artist and had a gallery in Oak Park. His mother was reticent about transferring Michael to nearby Oak Park where being Black was harder. Michael talked about how his father sold drugs in high school and was "pushing a lot of volume in Chicago" and had an extensive operation on college campuses like Bradley University, where he ended up graduating from but then went to prison for seven years after being arrested for selling drugs. The story of incarceration was familiar to young people in Maywood, especially since the Maywood County courthouse was at the center of town, but there were stories of redemption as well and

Figure 3.2   A 1905 Image of a Synagogue in Maywood with Children Playing. *Source*: Photo from the Chicago History Museum archives and taken by the Chicago Daily News.

how Michael's father went into rehab and now runs a community center in Peoria. After graduating from the University of Illinois-Urbana Champaign as a journalism major, Michael continued to live with his mother in Maywood in his grandmother's house and helped start a community newspaper, which chronicled stories of crime and corruption as well as stories of hope, community collaboration, and coalition building.

Michael: There is a perverse pride in living in Maywood. Your pride grows as you get further away from the town [laughs]. It is great to be from Maywood, but you don't want to live here. If you live here, the pride turns into something dark. But then I started the blog which turned into a highly circulated newspaper and my pride in Maywood started. It is a really interesting thing.

As the Latinx population was moving into Maywood, the majority from nearby Melrose Park, neighborhoods became territorial, and gang lines were drawn to see who would control the cocaine drug market in Maywood (Gibson, 1986). The Latin Kings made their way into Maywood in the 1970s from the city of Chicago to protect Latinx-owned businesses opening up on the main Lake Street business corridor as well as protecting the Latinx community from racism. The history of the Latin Kings in Maywood parallels the history of the Latin Kings in other parts of the country such as Los Angeles where Latinx gangs were created to protect against white racism, discrimination, and targeted violence. During the 1970s recession, more gangs from Chicago settled into the affordable suburb of Maywood where there were still industrial-based jobs nearby:

> Two federal criminal indictments were brought against a total of 34 Latin King gang members, one group on Chicago's far South Side and far south suburbs, the other in the western suburbs of Maywood and Melrose Park. One indictment identified two specific Latin King operational areas. One is called 'M-town,' mostly in Maywood in an area bounded by east of 25th Avenue on the west, 1st Avenue on the east, Lake Street on the south and North Avenue to the north in Melrose Park. The other area, '18th and Bloomingdale,' is in an industrial area north of North Avenue. (Dwyer, 2016)

Gangs from the West Side of Chicago migrated to Maywood such as the Black Gangster Disciples and the Four Corner Hustlers who were warring gangs that also fought with the Latin Kings. In the 1980s, the Imperial Gangsters from Melrose Park began warring with the Maywood Latin Kings; moreover, the Latinx gangs in Maywood never fought the Black gangs in Maywood and only fought among other Latinx gangs outside of Maywood. In 2002–2003, there were 20 murders and 150 arrests of gang members and drug dealers in a village with just 27,000 people, three times the murders per capita of Chicago and more homicides than any other suburban Cook County town (Rozas, 2004).

The gang fights made their way into the local high school and today the gangs use social media apps like SnapChat to taunt rival gangs when they cross over into their territories (Romain, 2018). When we discussed this territorial difference between Black students who came from the West Side of Chicago versus the Black students who were Maywood residents, some of the Black participants dismissed the difference while others marked it. One participant, Alice, talked about how students from the West Side of Chicago attended high school in Maywood by giving their grandmother's address in Maywood even though they technically lived with their mothers in Austin: "They took the Madison Avenue bus in the morning and stayed to themselves. They had a different positionality within the school. The kids from the city did not feel a sense of ownership. The Maywood girls liked the boys from the city because there was an allure."

The culture of violence in "Murder Woods" inevitably spilled over into the classroom. Students during one science lab were making gun signs with their fingers and brushing each other's heads with their gun fingers. Before conducting that lab, the science teacher stated a few times "no stabbing, no punching, no beating during the lab." The psychological trauma from sense-less violence in unsafe neighborhoods due to arson, drugs, gangs, and random murders has made its way into the suburbs. Understanding the effects of such trauma on young students is gaining greater attention as we struggle as a nation with a spike in violent crimes and gun violence. During our research, we knew of one student who was murdered at gunpoint outside one of our schools in the afternoon hours (Trottie, 2017). On another day, there was gunfire outside a school playground during lunch and we all scrambled back into the school and were in lockdown for the rest of the day. The field notes below capture the culture of violence in their daily lives:

> What was interesting to note is that the students referred to the spike in crime within Maywood as a key demographic change within their community—it was so noticeable to them. When Ms. Alexander was talking about conducting autopsies in science class, the students opened up about personal experiences with family members murdered and watching their physical autopsies in person. It was quite emotional.

Hypervigilance, anxiety, depression, blackouts, and flashbacks are some common effects of the trauma that students face today in violent communi-ties, but their stories are much more complex than bad people moving into the suburbs, and now they are behaving badly and causing the violence (Smith, Voisin, Yang, & Tung, 2019). One story told by a Latinx bilingual teacher reflected the traumatic stress and emotional numbing from the cycle of vio-lence that had slowly crept into the once-safe suburb. The bilingual teacher grew up in Maywood, then commuted to a local university, received her education degree and now was back teaching in the same neighborhood and in the same elementary school that she had attended as a child:

Author: So, tell me about this violent incident that occurred on your block. I remember you telling me about it . . .

Georgina: That was in 2008 . . . It was 1 AM and the whole block was blocked off and I was wondering what was going on. There were a lot of ambulances there. I didn't know what happened until the next day and someone told us . . . I can't remember who but some neighbor told us that the guys next door . . . they were troublemakers but they didn't mess with us. They were very polite to us. But um . . . I guess somebody got into an argument in the house . . . somebody shot somebody else, and they left the body on the porch. Just dragged him out and left him there. So, everybody else that lived there . . . just fled . . . to not return until a couple of weeks . . . and I want to say a month or two later. They came back into the house and tried to burn it down. I share . . . we kind of share a yard together . . . so I see smoke coming out. We called the cops. We called 911. I guess they came back to burn the house down so there is no evidence . . .

we really don't know what the scuffle was about. What the rumor was that it was over a girl. I think a family acquaintance and they got into a scuffle over a girl, and they shot him, and they just left him there. He died. And so, the house was abandoned for a really long time. About three years.

Author: Then the Colombian couple moved in there?

Georgina: Yes, but the house was in pretty bad condition, and they had to do a lot of work on it.

Author: What happened to the young man?

Georgina: Not sure. They fled. They never came back. He actually graduated from my school. He looked really young. He didn't look 16. He didn't look my age at that time, and I was the same age. He looked young. I don't remember him at our high school.

Maywood faced elevated rates of violent crime throughout the 30-plus years between 1985 and 2015. Violence is often disproportionately represented in socioeconomically disadvantaged communities like Maywood; neighborhood boundaries vacillate between rigidly defensive and porous, which impacts residents' ability to enact collective efficacy and positive change. People like Georgina feel like strangers in their own neighborhoods which then results in rigidly defended boundaries and a lack of trust (Brown & Weil, 2020). As crime and violence decrease in the community, the sense of collective efficacy increases, resources flow back into the neighborhoods, and the boundaries become more porous. Research suggests that in Black and Latinx communities like Maywood, there is a greater likelihood of crime when the in-group bonding is stronger and there is less social bridging and cohesion with people from the out-group—the more segregated Black and Latinx residents are in Maywood then the rate of crime and violence goes up (Weil et al., 2019).

Social capital in high-crime neighborhoods matters, and the more connected we are as neighbors, the less likely that violence and violence retribution will increase. Simultaneously, the subcultural values of the young Black and Latinx men who joined gangs for social identity, respect, and control also matters—the more racially segregated the gangs are in Maywood then the rate of violence and violence retribution also increases. In Maywood, there were either all-Latinx gangs or all-Black gangs. To counteract the subculture of gangs, neighbors in Maywood have to build trust and prosocial values with each other across racial lines to ensure their own safety. Strong internal social networks, large extended families, residential stability, and a strong cultural identity are all factors that can create high out-group bridging, porous boundaries between neighborhoods, and more resources flowing, thus avoiding the "us v. them" power dynamic that can tear apart interracial communities.

Boundary Making and Drawing Lines in the Sand

When discussing identity theory in a Black/Brown setting, it is inevitable that we discuss acts of boundary making and drawing lines between cultural insiders and outsiders and between different racial groups. We use facial recognition that is wired in our brain to study the faces of others and recognize those faces from our in-group immediately. We have the power to choose who we bring into the group and use recognition bias to create boundaries, whether good or bad. The type of inter-group dynamic, however, between distinct racial groups can be reflected in the school climate and culture, regardless of how many homogenous student in-groups there are present. Those in the minority group often remain invisible until their numbers start to go up, just as they did for the Latinx residents in Maywood. As the landscape becomes more heterogeneous, differences are no longer ignored, and our salient identities come to the forefront. How can we rehumanize ourselves so that we make more human contact and learn from different racial groups? How can we stop demonizing the out-group so that we can reach common goals? We are living in a divisive moment in history where it is easier to attack and punish each other for being different than to sit down and find commonality among ourselves as a human race.

Chandra is a Black music teacher in Maywood who was raised in the same community in which she now teaches, similar to many of the teachers in this study. The issues related to racial and cultural boundaries between Black and Latinx students were present even when Chandra went to school there in the 1980–1990s, along with tensions from the remaining white residents:

Author: As someone who has lived in Maywood for a long time . . . what was your reaction to the Latinx population moving into Maywood?
Chandra: As a child I don't remember people thinking negatively about it . . . or having a problem with it. I remember the spark in me . . . I always wanted to speak Spanish because of attending school with my Spanish friends or going to one of their houses for dinner and things like that. From what I remember in grammar school is that we got along . . . we were all friends . . . now sometimes some of us did not hang with each other as much outside of school. But in school there was not a beef . . . not an "all Spanish here" and an "all Black here." Or anything like that. I think everyone got along fairly well and there didn't seem to be a problem . . . now I am not quite sure how the white counterparts felt. I can remember my neighbors when we first moved there . . . there was an older white couple that had been there a long time. And one of their first questions to my parents was, "Are you renting or buying?" My mom was like that is none of your business. You know. We could tell that they were not thrilled . . . when we first moved into that community as a matter of fact there were white neighbors on both sides of us. We lived a couple of blocks north

of Chicago Avenue. And there were a lot of whites in the area when we first moved out there. And there were Mexicans around too. And Black also. So, it was kind of mixed. But it was still . . . people socialized with their own. Now people probably spoke, and chit chatted here and there but . . . spending time in each other's homes and going and doing things together . . . was you know . . .

Author: How about interracial dating?

Chandra: In grammar school . . . you know the Black boys would date the Hispanic girls . . . even then they would . . . and they dated us too . . . for them it was whoever was the cute girl . . . they didn't care . . . whoever was the hot girl. You know. They will find them, and you know they dated whomever. I can remember vividly even at that time that Black girls tended not to date outside of their race as much . . . boys were a lot more experimental. Even then. They would date girls fairly easy . . . no matter the race. But Black females tended not to.

Author: So, were there close friendships between Hispanics and Blacks?

Chandra: Some. There were some. Like I said . . . I had some. I can remember Elizabeth very well. I remember eating at her home. I had been to her house before. More than once . . . I remember hanging out with her even outside of school. There were some friendships.

Author: Now did she come to your house?

Chandra: She never came to my house. I know another good girlfriend, Laurie, who was Black and was good friends with a Mexican girl, Lenore. They hung out at each other's homes and did things together. And went places together and things like that. So, they were very close. And that lasted even up to high school.

Author: Why do you think some kids crossed that racial line and others didn't?

Chandra: Sometimes I think it may be . . . like commonality. Things that both of you have in common. Like both of us really love music. You know . . . that brings us together. So, I think sometimes that's it. Maybe sometimes there's prejudice already built up from how they're brought up in their household and they're told that they can't hang with this person. Or they can't go over there. But I think a lot of it has to do with personality and what you have in common.

Chandra had an optimistic outlook and wanted to personally build bridges rather than boundaries and borders with people from the out-groups. It was interesting to note how race and gender intersected in her memories of romantic relations when she recounted male adolescents having more fluid interracial boundaries with respect to dating compared to female youth. However, she was waxing nostalgic about when she was a student in Maywood and had cross-racial friendships with other Latinx students. But was she also revisioning what Maywood in the past was like in her present recollection of childhood?

Scholars have examined acts of historical revisionism and its destructive yearning to restore transparent unity and meaning as an effect of the community's loss of hope and progress as its ultimate source of self-legit-imation (Ivy, 1995). Against the anomie and instability of living again in Maywood, Chandra represents racial tensions as acts of boundary making that are at once organized and organizing, legitimate and legitimating—a nostalgic memory where the cultural residues of an interracial community are reimag-ined (Haratounian, 2010). Chandra sheds critical light on this rhetoric by iden-tifying its resonance with the discourse of young Black and Latinx adolescents spending time in each other's homes after school. The prospect of catching up and Maywood becoming a truly harmonious interracial community also implies the status of a temporal latecomer for Maywood and a distance that still had to be covered between a lived past and the present, which can be called a "time-lag" for Maywood. The perception of Maywood lagging behind other multiethnic communities when it comes to peace and prosperity created an optical doubling—seeing Maywood as two communities, one Black and one Latinx, yet assuming at the same time that they are the same. Rather, should we perceive Maywood as two distinct and different communities?

This optical doubling, according to historian Harry Haratounian's theo-ries of nostalgia and memory (2010), was further reinforced by the multiple temporalities of Maywood (Maywood in the past; Maywood in the present; Maywood in the future) and grounded in different experiences and places, as well as active agents of the past as anachronisms in the present time (the revival of Fred Hampton and creating a center for him in Maywood). In fact, we noted the repeated narrative of loss, nostalgia, and recovery mediated by the ghastly images of violence and death scattered in many of the interviews for this book.

The landscape in the present for Maywood has changed dramatically within the last two decades when gangs and guns became part of the milieu for many of the young adolescents today and far removed from the era of Chandra's schooling. The interview below is with Norma Hernandez, a young Latinx leader in the progressive political movement taking over May-wood. She was elected to the board of trustees of the large local community college, Triton College, and helped create a Fred Hampton Center at East High School, which we will discuss in the conclusion of our book. Norma sits on the elected board with many of the Italian and Black leaders in the western suburbs who also have a political stake in the community college. Here Norma shared her story with us as to how she struggled with the racial and cultural boundaries she faced as a high school student in Maywood but which she was able to transgress later in life as a young adult and now as a newly elected public official representing Maywood students:

Norma: I grew up in Mexico and then moved to Melrose Park when I was little. I went to school at Stevenson when the school was mostly Italian. I remember the kids writing "go back to Mexico" on my desk. I was learning English so I could not defend myself. When I told the teachers, they just told me to wash it off. Fast forward to high school . . . now I noticed the racial divide between African Americans and Hispanics. That's when I noticed the racial tension. I had never been to a school that was mostly African American. My freshman year was actually very rough. My cousin was killed the first week of freshman year. That Monday was when the shooting occurred, and it was in the 8th period. It was my cousin Herman who was killed by the Latin Kings from Maywood. My cousin was an IG [Imperial Gangster] from the opposite gang in Melrose Park. That was my welcome to high school. Then there were all these fights happening around homecoming week. You had the Black gangs fight with each other first and then the Hispanic gangs would fight with each other. In my sophomore year in 2005, there was a really huge bomb threat, and the school was evacuated. But that bomb threat turned into a race war. It was Blacks against Mexicans. One day during the second period . . . I was going into class and then suddenly, we had to evacuate the building in the middle of November. We were huddled outside and did not know what was going on. Tensions were building between the Black and Brown men. We all stayed together with our click of friends. There were twenty of us . . . my cousins and my friends. Then a circle of men came toward us and surrounded us. The guys started hitting my friends and it turns into a huge brawl. The girls stood back and held the jackets. But then my cousin was being jumped by three guys and I jumped in to defend him. I accidentally hit one of their girlfriends and then the next day this girl put a "hit" on my name and was going to kill me. She's describing me to people, who I am and how she is going to jump me.

In the end, Norma banded with the other Mexican American high school students for safety as she walked to and from school each day and was often followed by a mob of students throughout the school, eventually leading to many more brawls. Norma said the school expelled most of the Mexican American students and not the Black students, according to her memory. However, one of the Black school officers was a witness to these brawls and stated that Norma was using self-defense and should not be expelled, especially as an honor student. Norma's recollections once again highlighted the gendered nature of conflict in Maywood, where it may be easy to deduce that much of the violence is often male-dominated, yet females are increasingly pulled into the downward spiral as unfortunate victims and sometimes as inadvertent participants, which mirrors the national trend. In the National Youth Gang Survey conducted annually by the National Gang Center founded by the Office of Juvenile Justice and Delinquency Prevention, the Office of Justice Programs, and the US Department of Justice (DOJ), responding agencies report gang membership as being overwhelmingly male (~93%), but with a small presence of females primarily in gangs outside of large urban cities (National Gang Center, 2022).

In Norma's situation, the Latinx parents were never notified that their children were being jumped, and when Norma's working mom found out, the Latinx parents banded together and complained about the lack of safety for their children. Norma's mother even brought in Representative Chris Welch, the local Black politician who went on to lead the Democratic Party in Illinois through his political climb in Maywood, to come speak to the school board and protect the Latinx students from gang violence and violence retribution. By senior year, the gang violence decreased due to Mr. Hardy, a new high school principal who brought in structure, rules, and order in 2015 and helped reclaim the school. In 2021, Mr. Hardy was not planning to leave the high school principal position but the new superintendent, whom we will meet in the next chapter, set the stage for a major administrative overhaul, reclassifying, or failing to renew the contracts of dozens of individuals (Maxham, 2021). However, the racial tensions between the Black and Latinx community are still there at the local high school, and we will examine the volatile politics tearing the school board apart in the next chapter.

CONCLUSION

In 2016, there was a fledgling but a growing political movement led by young Black activists addressing the systemic inequities affecting Black Americans from a broken criminal justice system to police brutality and violence. The Black Lives Matter (BLM) movement was born during the presidency of our first Black President, Barack Obama, and it was a movement quite different from the Civil Rights Movement of the 1960s. Following the Occupy Movement from the 2011 to 2012 recession era that challenged economic inequities through protests and physical squatter camps built on public sites, BLM uses similar tactics and strategies that defy hierarchy and the centralized leadership found in the earlier Democratic movements. The BLM movement gained recognition during the concatenation of violent events that addressed Black rights on the national stage such as the George Zimmerman trial in Florida for the murder of Trayvon Martin; Michael Brown's murder in Ferguson, Missouri, at the hands of a white police officer; and the massacre of Black lives at the Emanuel A.M.E. Church, in Charleston, South Carolina, by a white male gunman (Jobb, 2016). The discourse around race that BLM pushed forward has realigned every institution in America to the point where everyone and every organization now addresses diversity, equity, and inclusion with the hope of being anti-racist.

Our book was written in the shadows of the BLM movement as we participated in and watched the marches in our hometown of Chicago, where we protested the murder of Laquan McDonald, a young Black teenager who was shot by a white police officer and whose death was being covered up by then-Mayor Rahm Emmanuel, who once served as President Obama's chief of staff. Within these marches, one could find protest signs that addressed intersectionality such as "Latinos Unidos con Black Lives Matter" and "Black Trans Lives Matter." The national sentiment we read on social media claimed that we are stronger and united as people of color so that police brutality can end with this generation. Many of the faces leading BLM do not belong to a political organization or pulpit; rather, they are young folk who are connected to each other through social media platforms and online activism. Yet, the core idea of BLM is that Black Americans should be treated as equals with dignity and rights but that we as a nation also need to undo the systemic inequities and injustices against Black America. There was also a need for the movement to be determined by Black Americans as opposed to white progressives and the movement became a counterpoint to President Obama's rhetoric for calm and order amid organized protests erupting in major US cities and mirroring the rhetoric coming out of the national Democratic Party.

As BLM grew in presence and size, the national discourse turned to systemic and structural racism found throughout American society—from young Black boys being expelled in preschools to the use of bail to keep Black and Brown people in jails. The discourse also turned to the Civil Rights Movement of the 1960s and why we had not seen the changes we needed in these systems and structures. In fact, leaders from the Civil Rights Era like Jesse Jackson were booed by the young protestors in Ferguson, Missouri, where there was a push for horizontal leadership at the grassroots level that was inclusive and went beyond the talented tenth in the Black community (Cobb, 2016). The inclusive and progressive politics of the grassroots youth movements of today like "Sunrise Movement" and "Justice Democrats" were brought forth by the BLM movement and this opened the political space for more inclusive voices to be heard (Wickenden, 2021). The local 2021 elections in Maywood brought in young Black and Latinx activists and leaders, such as Mayor Nathaniel Georg Booker and Trustee Norma Hernandez, who argued for an inclusive platform leading to cross-racial solidarity and alliance.

The Latinx community has always been in solidarity with the BLM movement; however, the Latinx community was careful not to take over the spotlight from another minoritized population. Many argue that BLM led to greater cross-race solidarity between Black and Latinx communities while also acknowledging that prejudice, oppression, and inequalities like racial profiling and police brutality also affect the Latinx community. Carlos Ingram-Lopez and Erik Salgado were young Latinx men who were murdered by police officers and represent the national statistic in which the Latinx community is close to 17.1% of the national population but disproportionately accounted for 18.3% of police shootings between 2016 and 2018 (Koran, 2020; Foster-Frau, 2021). In the State of California, where the largest number of police killings occur followed by Georgia and Texas, 46% of those killed by police are Latinx while 15.2% killed by police are Black and 32.4% killed by police are white (Rosenhall, 2021). According to the *PBS News Hour*, there has been a national spotlight on high-profile cases of Black Americans killed in police custody due to activists taking to social media to protest; however, there tends to be an absence of media coverage about Latinx Americans killed in police brutality, even when there are the same patterns of violent interactions (Downs, 2016). Black Americans are the largest group to be killed by police, and Latinx Americans are the second highest group, but many people believe that the media is silencing Latinx voices when it comes to police brutality.

Leaders in the Latinx community also pointed out how the same unchecked police power was being used simultaneously to separate undocumented children from their families at the US-Mexico border and place them in cages within crowded, dysfunctional holding centers. Racial profiling and police killings are common in large Latinx communities like Los Angeles. Yet, members of the Latinx community who identify as Afro-Latinx, almost 25% of the Latinx community, have also spoken out about colorism and the internal anti-Black racism within the Latinx community (Rodriguez, 2021). Members of the Afro-Latinx community find both the slogans "Latinos for Black Lives Matter," "Las vidas negras importan," and "Brown Lives Matter" to be contradictory and illogical, even though they hope to benefit from the current pro-Black ethos in our country (Hatzipanagos, 2020).

While the BLM movement took center stage during the writing of this book, the immigrant rights movement within the Latinx community was also running in parallel form. Issues such as deportation, DACA, and border politics took center stage as multiple American presidents tried to address immigration and how to support the millions of undocumented families in our country. DACA, for example, protected the rights of 700,000 immigrant children who were brought here by their parents and allowed them to stay here to complete their education and receive work permits to work legally and receive benefits (Nieto del Rio, 2021).

DACA legislation was enacted under President Obama, and the first recipients are known as Dreamers; however, President Trump tried to stop the legislation during his years in power, which left many Latinx residents in Maywood fearful of deportation and of family separation. Furthermore, critics of DACA have cited its inability to provide a path to citizenship for neither the child nor their family, which has left many feeling panicked and anxious about their livelihoods. Newly elected President Biden has stated that he wants to maintain DACA as well as fortify it while we all wait to see whether immigration reform will bring the promise of permanent legal status and residency. However, there are lawsuits against DACA from Republican lawmakers and the Mexican American Legal Defense Fund is legally supporting the now 800,000 DACA recipients and the original verdict (Nieto del Rio, 2021).

In the book *An African American and Latinx History of the United States* (2018), Paul Ortiz chronicles the voices and experiences of people from the African and Latinx diasporas and examines periods in American history when these two racial groups intersected, organized themselves, and engaged in collective struggles for self-determination: "Here we retrace the odysseys of African American and Latinx thinkers as they theorized outside the nation's borders and beyond its mythologies of innocence and exceptionalism to challenge the crises facing them inside of the belly of the beast" (p. 5). Ortiz grounds his book in the concept of "emancipatory internationalism," a concept born out of slavery and colonialism, depicting historical moments in time and place when people of color realized that they shared the same oppression: (a) when freedom and sanctuary was granted for Black slaves in Mexico; (b) when the slave revolts in the Caribbean in Haiti and Cuba inspired those still enslaved in the Americas; (c) when Black journalists and the Black press wrote against the war with Mexico; (d) when Dr. Martin Luther King, Jr. reached out to Caesar Chavez and supported the rights of Mexican and Filipino farm workers in California; and (e) when we go beyond the white-Black racial binary and acknowledge our mixed ancestry of Afro-Latinx, Indo-African, Blaxican, Afro-Mexican, moreno, mestizo, la raza cosmica, biracial, multiracial, and many more mixed racial identities.

The markers of self-identity have nonetheless changed over time as Mexican became Chicano and now Latinx, as Negro became African American and now Black, yet the struggle for equality and fairness has remained the same for both groups—"you might become we; we might become us" (Rodriguez, 2003). Emancipatory internationalism asks us to "raise up the voices of the people who build democracy across borders and helped us overcome the paralyzing nationalistic myths that have divided people in this hemisphere for too long" (Ortiz, 2018, p. 10).

Chapter 4

People of the Dream

Tearing Ourselves Apart while Building Spiritual Connections to Belong

As the racial composition of the nation changes, intergroup interactions are increasingly common in our daily lives as different racial groups work alongside each other as well as volley for power, attention, and resources. At the same time, the field of neuroscience is delving into research about how our brain adapts to the rapid shifts in demographics and whether our brain is rewiring itself as it perceives people from a greater number of different racial backgrounds. There has been an increased focus on how our brain processes the new human diversity that is coming toward us in terms of differences in phenotype—what we look like on the outside—and that for thousands of years we mostly existed in homogenous tribes.

The emerging research on race and the brain has informed our writing here and how we perceive, recognize, and respond to people who are different from us and how this difference in phenotype is new in relation to one's epigenetic background a few generations back. For example, the elder Black community members in Maywood began to interact with Latinx neighbors for the first time in their lives, both very quickly and on a larger scale, who were different from them. These interracial interactions were very new for the elders since they had never lived alongside immigrants who were racially, culturally, and linguistically different from their known Black-white world.

We know through this research in neuroscience that "a network of interacting brain regions is important in the unintentional, implicit expression of racial attitudes and its control," otherwise known as our implicit biases (Kubota, Banaji, & Phelps, 2012, p. 940). Our beliefs and attitudes about people from other races start off in our brain and how we perceive this human variation within our immediate environment. The types of social behaviors that result from how we categorize race has yielded insights into the consequences of racial perception such as bias, misconceptions, prejudice, and hatred. The amygdala, a structure located in the anterior-temporal lobe, is the brain area that has been reported with the greatest frequency in studies of race attitudes, beliefs, and social decision making. The amygdala is where we learn emotions like fear and learn to read and code stimuli in the environment through our perceptions and the subsequent internalization of our emotions in relation to that specific stimulus. Our daily experiences are coded for these flight v. fight v. freeze moments that can result in fear and anxiety.

Race relations in the United States have always been grounded in salient emotions such as fear, mistrust, and hostility, and research today is trying to locate where and how these emotions get processed in the brain. Greater activity has been recorded in the amygdala through MRI scans when we perceive faces and skin tones outside of our own racial category; however, there have also been inconsistencies with that general result reported in a few studies (Ronquillo, Denson, Lickel, Lu, Nandy, & Maddox, 2007). The Implicit Association Test from Harvard University is one of the more famous psychological tests that measure racial biases, both good and bad, toward the faces of Black individuals versus white individuals and has collected aggregated data on these findings. Associations such as "Black and bad" and "white and good" are measured with results showing that the white popula-tion tends to have positive stereotypes of white faces rather than Black faces (Kubota, Banaji, & Phelps, 2012). The white participants even demonstrated a physiological response to Black faces with a "startled eye-blink" (p. 942). However, with Black participants, 40% show a preference for white faces, 40% for Black faces, and 20% as neutral to race preference.

The variability of race attitudes within the Black community can also be found in our study and a wide variation as to how the Black community in Maywood responded to the changing demographics and the increasing Latinx population. In some of the interviews conducted with Black residents, we heard explicit preference for the Black community while in other interviews the topic was avoided to remain neutral, and/or perhaps there was an implicit racial preference for the inner group. The variation within the interviews of Black community members in Maywood reflects cultural and social learning of race attitudes and stereotypes from different contexts. At the same time, equality norms in Black society dictate that behaving in a racially biased manner is unacceptable, given their own history of Civil Rights and why many Black Americans share that aspiration of equality for all. Although Black society may consciously stress equality and fairness, there still may be negative associations with Latinx community members based on whom we spoke with in the study. Our data highlight the conflict between upholding the egalitarian goals of equality in Black history while also admitting to negative attitudes and stereotypes of the Latinx community. The detection of conflict between these two extremes is the first step in regulating and controlling one's unwanted and implicit racial attitudes and biases.

Research in neuroscience has also mapped where in our brain inhibition is activated when we are in interracial interactions that might be uncomfortable and/or unfamiliar to us and we need to inhibit our emotions, language, and behaviors. The dorsolateral prefrontal cortex (DLPFC) is a region in the brain that has been shown across a range of cognitive tasks to be involved in top-down executive control such as the cognitive regulation of emotions, attention control, performance monitoring, and working memory (Stanley, Phelps, & Banaji, 2008). The DLPFC is a regulatory mechanism that controls unwanted, implicit racial associations and keeps us emotionally regulated. We all have the capability and effort to control negative racial attitudes in the interracial context, especially when there is an interference with our implicit racial preference. Experience also matters and research has shown that we process faces faster when they are from our own familiar racial group, pointing to the concept that we process faces from outside our racial group differently and see the Other-group faces as categorically different from the individuated faces from our ingroup (Young & Hugenberg, 2012).

The failure to encode individual variation to people outside of our race group leads to "perceptual homogeneity which may then contribute to poor memory for racial outgroup members and negative implicit evaluations" (Kubota, Banaji, & Phelps, 2012, p. 943). In other words, some of us fail in perception and categorize people who are different from us as a homogeneous group, lumping everyone from a different racial group all together into one scheme and do not see them as individuals with variations such as differences in personality traits, levels of education, regional dialects, generational divides, and so on. We can therefore conclude that the amygdala monitors for racial bias while the DLPFC helps regulate racial bias and that not all of us process these interactions in the same way due to neurological differences.

Alongside these neurological processes, personal and societal motivations also exert control over our implicit racial biases, as well as our years of lived experiences. We know that internal conflicts occur when people are unintentional in their indications of racial bias, even when they are personally motivated not to be prejudiced as dictated by societal norms (Costandi, 2012). Internal conflicts also occur when we are socially excluded from people within our own racial group. We also know that the stereotypes we carry of different people act in a top-down way to sort people into categories and affect our visual perception at the bottom-up level when we encounter individuals from different categories. Understanding how people process and evaluate social groups is invaluable to our study of Maywood. Racially biased decision making in specific social scenarios is highlighted in this chapter. We know that teachers use racially biased decision making when comparing Latinx students to Black students. We know that school board members use racially biased decision making when it comes to hiring practices in schools, use of budgetary funds, and curricular decisions. We are all wired to be biased against those outside of our tribal group.

Our study captures those implicit biases and reflects on the socially relevant consequences of those biases. In our interviews, Black and Latinx participants were able to reappraise or re-interpret an emotionally salient event regarding racial bias explicitly in an effort to alter its emotional effect, whether that was a name-calling incident or a warning not to walk in certain neighborhoods. Many interviews led to perspective-shifting in the participants as we posed questions that asked the participants to re-interpret and reappraise negative attitudes of the out-group. Yet, one can also argue that a participant, such as a school board member or teacher, can and should increase cognitive control of their racial biases as a public official; however, "the original negative associations with the racial group [often] remain intact" (Kubota, Banaji, & Phelps, 2012, p. 946). How do we change the original negative association with an individual from an out-group, thereby eliminating the need for cognitive control?

One proposition is to reconsolidate those original memories of the negative racial encounter and/or event. Memories are fragile and can be reprogrammed and disrupted to provide an altered response instead—a response that is not full of prejudice and hatred. It is also about undoing those negative associations one has with out-group individuals and our underlying unwanted implicit race attitudes and stereotypes. But there is also tribalism and a sense of fear and anxiety that occurs when we are seen as a minority in a different tribe's territory. Your intuition tells you that the person who looks different from you, who dresses differently, speaks differently, and eats different foods, does not belong in your tribe. But you must fight this intuition for the greater good.

We can reflect on and override these intuitions with conscious reason. It is harder to resist segregating ourselves from the Other to protect ourselves, but we also have the capacity to reconfigure our world and reconfigure the threat of the Other. Those who are in power also have the privilege of Othering and pushing aside those who do not belong to the tribe into the desert, doomed to fight for survival. The following sections of the chapter focus on two influential areas of Maywood in which there were significant interracial interactions between the Latinx and Black populations; however, there were many more intersections that we were unable to capture and chronicle and can only provide a partial narrative here. We will start with the role of religious institutions in Maywood and their ability to build bridges between the two racial groups and then end the chapter with the politically divided high school board in which racial tensions were heightened to the point of spectacle.

UNDERSTANDING THE ROLE OF RELIGION

Ethnographic studies in the postmodern era have pointed to the concept of culture being fluid and flexible, especially as the human experience has been transformed by "migration, race relations and the opportunity structure in the United States" (Louie, 2004, p. xxx). Culture and structure, furthermore, work in tandem with each other and inform each other in a feedback loop (Park, 2012). The prevalence of certain structures such as schools and churches in a community greatly influences its culture and the ever-changing dynamic of culture in turn informs the structures of that very same community (Williams, 1966). Over time, the demographics of Maywood shifted and informed its social structures which in turn changed its culture as a community. This cycle of culture and structure is tracked in this book, and how the children and families living inside this community are shaped by the structural conditions at multiple levels, in places like schools and churches, and how these intersections and forces of culture/structure can either deter and/or create social networks and pathways of opportunities.

Communities vary widely in how and why they build social capital and social networks, provide social services to residents such as new immigrants, develop the civic skills of its members, and shape residents' identities. Local leadership and group characteristics much more than ethnic origin or religious tradition shape the level and kind of civic engagement that communities like Maywood foster. Particularly, where leaders are civically engaged, they provide personal and organizational links to the wider American society and promote civic engagement by its members. Furthermore, "a strong sense of religious and ethnic identity, far from alienating immigrants from American society, promotes higher levels of civic engagement in immigrant communities" (Foley & Hoge, 2007). Scholar Angela Banks (2020) argues that we need to broaden dialogue in the field of civic education beyond "what types of citizens do we need" through the exploration of both de jure and de facto citizenship, arguing for a lens that focuses on societal citizenship rather than individual citizenship and individual rights. In a Black and Latinx community like Maywood, this theoretical framework presents a more inclusive civic education that acknowledges and embraces all peoples in society, regardless of their legal citizenship status. We can only achieve a democratic ideal in a multiracial society when we create a civic identity that has space at the table for the undocumented, the incarcerated, and those outside the membership of what we define as the "good citizen" in society.

Furthermore, contemporary multiracial religious congregations in the United States are poised to better understand the future of race relations in our country and often are more racially diverse than their neighborhoods, even though they make up just 7% of all congregations (Emerson & Woo,

2006). Understanding the multiracial gatherings of religious people allowed us to observe how such religious organizations can play a mediating role between the small private worlds of individuals and families and the large public world of Maywood. Even though there are variations nonetheless in immigration histories, group-level socioeconomic characteristics, patterns of incorporation and community organization, and host society reception, we focused our attention on how congregations in Maywood that have been historically Black, and are now becoming more Latinx, are contributing to improved race relations and equality (Zhou, 2009, p. 165).

In Maywood, there is a growing network of ethnically based businesses and civic organizations that are helping to facilitate the flow of information and resources within and across the Black and Latinx neighborhoods (Park, 2012). Religious centers and churches are still vital to the community and provide social capital, human capital, and economic capital for all races (Yosso, 2005). Religious institutions in Maywood also help connect students to their educational needs with structural support such as after-school programming and tutoring. Students from nearby affluent communities have access to very expensive after-school programming and tutoring services that can cost thousands of dollars.

Here in Maywood religious organizations are also providing supplementary, after-school education at no cost to families. Religious involvement here becomes a form of capital and can potentially affect academic achievement for low SES families. In Asia, after-school academic programs are seen as a form of "shadow education" in countries like China and India that provide supplemental tutoring and testing support but at a great financial cost for the impoverished families (Zhou, 2009). One of the authors of this book (Persis Driver) was a part of this shadow education system in India, both as a student and an educator. Immigrant families may recognize this form of shadow education when they come to the United States and look for ways to support their children's education through religious institutions.

When faced with marginalization, racism, and downward mobility, religious organizations can target education as a form of social mobility for their children (Louie, 2004). Religious organizations and institutions are "where culture and structure interact, where values and community forces allow for upward social mobility beyond survival" (Zhou & Kim, 2006, p. 6). Churches and civic centers in Maywood have historically provided ethnic and racial social structures to create pathways for cultural adaptation, develop social ties among parishioners, and facilitate the flow of information and resources such as providing food drives, vaccine sites, immigration support, and community violence prevention—public services that are found readily in more affluent areas.

However, churches do not exist in a vacuum; they are a part of a community's infrastructure and help propel the ideals, values, and aspirations of a community to fruition. The after-school programming for youth in the local churches gave immigrant families in particular a sense of safety because of long working hours and language barriers. Mary, a current Black middle school teacher in Maywood whose father is a beloved local pastor, spoke about how Latinx parents "invest" in their children and seek out resources for their families from the community, regardless of differences in social class. In particular, the mothers who attended church services in Maywood become the cultural brokers for their children and send their children to Bible study so the children can gain cultural capital, knowing they themselves lack the levels of education needed to do well economically in the United States. The hope is that the churches and civic centers in Maywood will give their children the know-how to go beyond just survival in this country.

Churches connect Black and Latinx families to a network of peers and adults who exchange knowledge about the community and what and when resources are available, how to navigate systems such as schools, and ways to succeed regardless of a lack of economic capital. Through religious participation, children gain access to multiple parents in the church who look after them in the community, who reinforce the same values and beliefs, and who share the same identity and narrative. Without participation in religious and civic organizations, children may not hear the same message about academic success reinforced outside of school and are often disconnected from other youth who promote prosocial behaviors such as coping and perseverance through faith (Park, 2012). Religious service attendance has been noted as a factor for academic support in low-income communities. In this study, the Latinx adolescents who identified as Evangelical and attended after-school programming such as Wednesday Bible Study at their churches like the First Baptist Church talked about their enhanced resiliency, social ties, and higher educational outcomes in comparison to their Catholic Latinx peers who did not attend service regularly and had low religiosity. The majority of Latinx students identify as Catholic but their religious affiliation does not necessarily lead to the supplementary educational opportunities found in Protestant churches such as the historical Baptist and Lutheran churches in Maywood (Andrews, 2011).

In our ethnographic work, we saw the Evangelical Latinx students exchanging information about school and homework, information about navigating the after-school program for gifted students, thus reinforcing normative expectations about school success. They also held informal study sessions in pods with their desks turned toward each other before exams and quizzes. Research shows that friendship-based study groups can be helpful in maintaining academic achievement. Here we can argue that the habitus of the Evangelical Latinx students matches the habitus of white, upper-middle-class families where these behaviors are expected and assumed. Protestant churches have been cited to have greater participation from youth which then allows them to connect with a youth network that keeps them in high school and on track (Zhai & Strokes, 2009). The egalitarian messages of the Evangelical church led to the Great Awakening in the mid-1700s when Blacks and whites gathered together in religious context (Emerson & Woo, 2006). However, Black Americans have always challenged the genuineness of white churches due to slavery, white supremacy, and the traumatic violence of lynching. By the 1900s, Black Catholics and Protestants attended racially segregated churches. Since the 1960s, racially integrated congregations with white and Black parishioners may not happen anytime soon but Black- and Latinx-integrated congregations may become a reality in under-resourced communities and in drastically changing communities like Maywood.

For many of the students in the school district, these academic behaviors may seem foreign to them since the adults in their lives often were uncertain of what was expected from them outside of school hours and what was needed for college later down the road such as the need to form study groups and learn content that cannot always be covered in class. However, our ethnographic study does not measure actual gains in the Protestant and Evangelical Latinx students in the college-going process. We can only speak to how their religious affiliation fosters out-of-school resources and opportunities for academic achievement and provides an infrastructure that promotes literacy and learning, especially in the Spanish language. The religious congregations in Maywood are building an infrastructure to help support families gain educational advantages; however, we did not measure the student outcomes from these resources in Maywood.

The churches in Maywood are nonetheless mostly racially divided, as reflected in most of America where parishioners attend services with people who are from the same racial and socioeconomic background and who are bound by a single language, ethnic homogeneity, and tighter social networks (Emerson &Woo, 2006). Within Maywood, ethnic communities are geographically bound with Black churches in the Black areas of town; however, the Latinx population is more dispersed and relies on churches they drive to for community functions outside of Maywood. Established in the late 1800s by Italian immigrants, Our Lady of Mount Carmel in Melrose Park offers Catholic services in Italian, English, and Spanish throughout the day and in that order for its parish but does not offer the after-school programming needed for youth.

Citizenship and religion also played a role in the lives of undocumented Latinx families who were seeking a church in Maywood that could also provide a sanctuary for them when and if family members were split due to arrests by ICE (Immigration and Customs Enforcement) since raids had occurred in neighboring suburbs like Melrose Park. The inequality of citizenship prevents access to certain social networks, resources, and social capital due to the fear of being deported at any moment. In 2017, Maywood was considering becoming a sanctuary city due to the increasing Latinx population:

> Citing the large Hispanic population in the village, Trustee Isiah Brandon has proposed that the village go on record as being welcoming of all immigrants. "We're a community of diversity," Brandon said, "We need to send a message that 'This is your village, that you are welcome in the village of Maywood.'" He said he wants Hispanics and others in the community to feel "Maywood is my home." (West Suburban Journal, 2017)

Trustee Brandon wanted to create a safe space for the growing number of immigrants in Maywood, as well as follow the lead of neighboring communities like Oak Park, a diverse and affluent suburb nearby, that made the evening news for being one of the first suburban communities to become a sanctuary suburb that "forbids local government or the police department from giving ICE agents access to any village databases or to use local facilities such as schools" (Lotus, 2017). However, other members of the village board challenged Isiah Brandon due to the fear of losing federal dollars under President Trump's administration that threatened cities that stopped deportation. At the same time, Village Manager Willie Norfleet Jr. stated clearly that the amount of federal money the village receives is very limited, but he also wanted to attend the National League of Cities Conference before making a final decision as a village. At the national conference, Isiah Brandon along with others heard that every city's workforce growth is due to the influx of immigrants and immigrant-owned businesses that account for many cities' annual revenue such as $770 million in annual main street business earnings (Lotus, 2017). Maywood never became a sanctuary city and neither did Melrose Park; however, in 2021, the Illinois General Assembly passed a sweeping immigration bill that would close all immigrant detention centers in the state and severely restrict how local law enforcement can collaborate with federal immigration agents (Ballesteros, 2021).

Meanwhile, Maywood was moving toward integrating its religious institutions as the size of the Black congregation continued to decrease in capacity and power, and the Latinx congregation was burgeoning and required church services in Spanish and English. Churches were now mixing races and people from different class backgrounds as well as different generations. Maywood leaders were encouraging people of different races to engage in life together, at least side by side, in the classrooms, pews, and consumer lines and knew these social ties may be more casual and secondary but can help lessen social isolation. This new mixed-identity in Maywood churches was distinct from the historical single-identity congregations. Research also shows that when religious congregations are more diverse in terms of race and class there may be enhanced opportunities and outcomes such as community mobilization and activism (Zhou & Bankston, 1998). Rather than seeing communities of color from a deficit lens, religious and civic organizations can tap into the cultural wealth and structural support these communities offer (Yosso, 2005).

Multiracial congregations are atypical and are filled with people who are cultural straddlers and like to float across religious lines and borders. But they could also be places of risk such as when power gets abused and one racial group is suppressed in relation to the other and certain cultural practices are cut off. We were never able to access the inner workings of the multiracial congregations and question whether there were conflicts as well underneath the surface of public meetings. However, as multiracial congregations collapse together and start anew in order to survive, they need to define their goals and mission, maintain boundaries to define who they represent and what they do, set up meetings to decide on services to make available to the congregation, and determine worship and youth events.

In the end, multiracial religious congregations build social ties, trusting interpersonal relationships, and "bonding and bridging social capital" that comes from micro-bonds made between individuals in well-established, inward-looking groups in which people may not share common histories and identities (Emerson & Woo, 2017, p. 93). Of course, the bonding social capital creates ingroup bonds that can override prejudice and discrimination and help develop bridges across obstacles that separate cultures and races. Places of worship then create expanding rings of social ties in which the bonds created at church extend into the neighborhoods, friendship circles, and schools. The Holy Corinthian Baptist Church shown in figure 4.1 is described as a "beacon of light in the neighborhood" on its website but began its journey in the 1970s from the West Side of Chicago to the present location in the heart of Maywood.

Building Coalitions and a Sense of Belonging

One nonprofit organization that is supporting the mixed-race, *mestizaje* community in parallel with religious institutions is the Coalition for Spiritual and Public Leadership (CSPL) in Maywood. It is a grassroots organization that campaigns to change racial, economic, social, and environmental structures by developing leaders rooted in and inspired by the Catholic traditions. On their website (2022), they state their beliefs and values:

Vision: CSPL envisions a conscienticized and spiritually rooted movement of
    people organizing from the grassroots to transform and build liberative and

Figure 4.1   Local Baptist Corner Church in the Black Community of Maywood. *Source*: Samina Hadi-Tabassum.

democratic systems in the ongoing journey toward achieving a greater approximation of God's Kin-dom.

Mission: CSPL is a multi-racial, multi-ethnic, multi-generational spiritually rooted organization that labors to transform racial, economic, social and environmental systemic structures through grassroots coalition building, community organizing, and liberative formation.

We accomplish our mission through these core strategic priorities (Methodology):

1. Building a powerful and dynamic coalition of member congregations, worker-owned cooperatives, universities, community organizations and institutions that can act boldly together in our communities and across society. (Coalition Building)
2. Organizing to transform and build systems and structures that advance racial, economic, social and environmental justice through community organizing and direct action. (Community Organizing)
3. Co-forming grassroots leaders and communities to be critically conscious, strategic and spirit-rooted through leadership and theological formation that is deeply grounded in the liberative Catholic and Christian traditions and popular education. (Liberative Formation)

Term Glossary:

Conscienticized—Comes from the English term conscientization. The term originally derives from the French term "conscienciser" used in Frantz Fanon's 1952 book, "Black Skins, White Masks." In 1970, Brazilian educator, activist, and theorist, Paulo Freire, popularized this term, "conscientização," which means "critical consciousness" and "consciousness raising" through his book, "Pedagogy of the Oppressed." Freire focused on how conscientization allows for marginalized and oppressed peoples to achieve a critical and in-depth understanding of systemic structures and oppression. Through critical consciousness, people are then able to take action to create a new world free from those oppressive structures.

Kin-dom—Coined by Sister Georgene Wilson, O.S.F and later introduced into public discourse by mujerista feminist, Ada Maria Isasi-Diaz, the "Kin-dom" of God is a radical vision and statement of the world we are working to build. Jesus used the "Kingdom of God" to describe an alternative kingdom opposite of the oppressive regime of the Roman Empire. Jesus was describing a world rooted in kin-ship, equal distribution of resources and justice for the most marginalized.

Liberative—Any theory, action, or effort contributing and related to bringing justice, liberation and full humanization in the world.

Grassroots—Rather than taking a top-down approach, grassroots organizations and movements are rooted in a bottom-up approach in which residents, organic leaders and people at the local level who are most impacted by systemic injustices are the central protagonists who inform, guide, sustain and drive the organization's mission and work. Grassroots organizations center democratic values and practices such as participatory decision-making, shared leadership, engaged listening, and by taking collective responsibility for their communities.

Spiritually-rooted—Engaged in an active way of life and set of spiritual practices that fosters a deep connection to God, to oneself, to others and to Mother Nature and that brings deeper awareness of our interconnectedness and co-responsibility for one another.

Faith-based organizations like CSPL have built a bi-racial religious community in Maywood with services in Spanish and English, trying to fight the growing racial tensions and to find common issues brought to the forefront so the two populations can work with each other. Even though they might not have enough power at the political level, they are trying to build important coalitions across the Black and Latinx populations. The CSPL is very concerned with the Latinx Catholic population in Maywood, but they also have Black Catholic members as well, especially those connected to the local clergy. The flier below is a call to action and a way to recruit new members into their organization for a fee of five dollars a month.

One of their more successful coalition-building projects was the Smart Routes program which started almost five years ago in 2017. CSPL created safe crossings for children walking to and from Maywood schools as crime and violence spiked. They were able to gain $40,000 in funding from the elementary school district, the village, and the township to fund this initiative that is still ongoing and dependent on community interest. They employed adults in the community to stand on corners in designated spots so they could stop fights and other violent acts as children were coming to and from school. The Smart Routes to school program gave CSPL presence and engagement with the school community in Maywood and its base of children and families. However, the Italian leadership in Melrose Park was against this initiative because, according to Mayor Serpico, these problems of community violence and safety do not exist in Melrose Park—that's a Maywood problem (Romain, 2019). In this statement, Mayor Serpico lumped all BIPOC constituents when it was convenient for him while also

Figure 4.2   An Instagram Flyer of the CSPL's Work in the Field. *Source*: Image found on the CSPL Instagram page: https://www.instagram.com/csplaction/. Citation: Arturo Gonzalez, VP of Communications at the CSPL.

keeping the Black and Latinx people out of the reach of power in Melrose Park. Grassroots coalitions in Maywood pushed for the safe passage program and the township leadership agreed with them because it would help stabilize the schools. The Smart Routes campaign benefits the community overall and it also led to conversations between the Black moms and Latinx moms in the PTOs when there was minimal contact there before.

The CSPL organized the community and brought in Black and Latinx parents and held several public meetings. The Smart Routes project brought hope and organized energy to the Maywood community and was borrowed from the Chicago Public Schools. There was also institutional support coming in from beyond Maywood such as the local university partner, our employer, sending student teachers into the classrooms as well as theology students working with the CSPL. This interfaith organization is also unique in the sense that it can be bilingual when it comes to public meetings and presentations, which other Maywood organizations may not have the capacity to do so. The public meetings held at the village hall and in school board meetings still lack Spanish language translations, which disempowers the growing Latinx community from civic engagement. At the same time, CSPL is asking the Latinx residents of Maywood to hold that space on their own and not have someone else hold it for them on their behalf. Subsequently, the CSPL is starting to see more Latinx representation in Maywood and is working to build new leaders in the community who can also hopefully run for political office. John Dewey, the philosopher, argues that we must address equality in education when we engage with those who bear the burden of inequality (Roger & Oakes, 2005). Change needs to be grassroots rather than a top-down structural change. The Safe Routes program showed citizens engaged in public inquiry how to create new and useful systems of knowledge as the basis of action. Such organizing promises a Deweyan social inquiry in which the status quo of schooling is challenged, and the masses are mobilized to generate sufficient pressure to change structures and practices. Social movement organizing has a history of engaging the poor and working-class communities, pushing the limits, and agitating mainstream society. The Coalition for Spiritual Leadership was constantly developing new strategies and skills, engaging in political action, creating common understandings within the Black and Latinx communities, and requiring broad participation, educating its constituents, developing relationships, and creating networks to develop social ties and solidarity—all to advance the community's interests in Maywood.

Moreover, the young progressive Black leaders of Maywood like Mayor Nathaniel George Booker, along with a new cadre of trustees, wanted to support a shared platform and did not have the xenophobia and anti-immigrant sentiments of their elders who attached a certain degree of whiteness to their

Copy of Irving Safe Routes

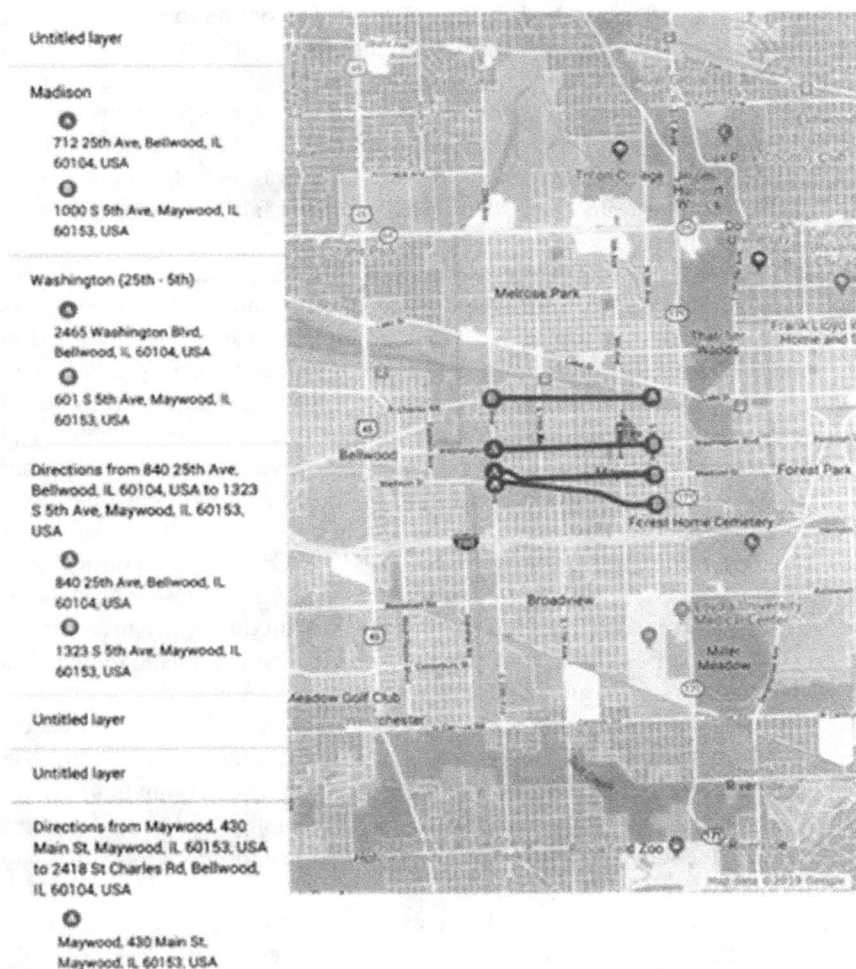

Untitled layer

Madison

○ 712 25th Ave, Bellwood, IL 60104, USA

○ 1000 S 5th Ave, Maywood, IL 60153, USA

Washington (25th - 5th)

○ 2465 Washington Blvd, Bellwood, IL 60104, USA

○ 601 S 5th Ave, Maywood, IL 60153, USA

Directions from 840 25th Ave, Bellwood, IL 60104, USA to 1323 S 5th Ave, Maywood, IL 60153, USA

○ 840 25th Ave, Bellwood, IL 60104, USA

○ 1323 S 5th Ave, Maywood, IL 60153, USA

Untitled layer

Untitled layer

Directions from Maywood, 430 Main St, Maywood, IL 60153, USA to 2418 St Charles Rd, Bellwood, IL 60104, USA

○ Maywood, 430 Main St, Maywood, IL 60153, USA

Figure 4.3   2019 Map of the Smart Routes Developed by the CSPL. Village Free Press, March 24, 2019. *Source*: Michael Romain; Arturo Gonzalez, VP of Communications at the CSPL, Coalition for Spiritual and Public Leadership (CSPL).

new Latinx neighbors. Yet, many elders in the Black community saw their new light-skinned, Mexican American neighbors as "honorary whites" who have some of the same privileges as the white Americans who fled Maywood in the 1980s when they moved into the neighborhood (Alba & Nee, 2003). Though progressive Black leaders in Maywood have formed real relationships with the Latinx community through organizations like CSPL and Neighbors of Maywood Community Organization, there is still a degree of disconnect and distrust. In fact, the CSPL held an online forum in 2021 for the political candidates in Maywood to discuss their platform before the local mayoral elections, addressing questions that directly affected the Latinx residents and race relations in Maywood. This political forum brought together Black and Latinx community leaders who wanted to hold all elected officials accountable and are not partisan-based. The forum was recorded on Facebook and was well orchestrated since there was a sense of fairness and impartiality to no one candidate.

We were also cautioned to not write a single story about the local election and how the Latinx vote does not depend on undocumented residents of Maywood; rather, many in the Latinx community came out and voted in the local elections. The census work that the CSPL conducted showed there was a lot of fear in the community and a lack of familiarity with the local political processes and entry points. The role of CSPL was to do the critical work and to identify the entry points and then give people the leadership skills to engage the Maywood community, which we would define as "civic self-agency." This agency is essential to becoming engaged citizens and having a public life regardless of immigration status. Creating the political will to disrupt unequal schooling requires powerful actions by those who stand to benefit the most: low-income students, parents, and community members of color in Maywood. Building power is necessary if CSPL wants to increase its resources and to create good schools and stronger communities. The CSPL sees openings of promise and hope and wants to work with the Black leadership in Maywood to build Black-Brown coalitions, which was not the case with the Italian leadership in Melrose Park. The Maywood community is now waiting to see if this new progressive Black leadership will create policies deliberately to address the racial divide and tear down those sociocultural and sociolinguistic walls.

The President of the Board of Directors for the CSPL is a colleague of ours from the Catholic university where we are employed. We formally interviewed Joshua and began to better understand the history and direction of CSPL. Joshua graduated from college, worked for the Interfaith Committee for Worker Justice in San Diego, and was trained by the Industrial Areas Foundation, a global interfaith worker justice group focusing on community organizing. According to their website, the Industrial Areas Foundation was founded in the 1940s and is the nation's largest and longest-standing network of local faith and community-based organizations. There he met with Kim Bobo, an early pioneer in faith-based organizing and worker rights issues and currently the Executive Director of Interfaith Worker Justice located in Chicago. Kim Bobo is the author of *Wage Theft in America: Why Millions of*

Working Americans Are Not Getting Paid—And What We Can Do About It (2008), a book that documents the practice of employers failing to pay workers the full wages to which they are legally entitled.

Joshua retained his training in community organizing while he became a trained clinical social worker and found these sets of skills valuable. Joshua later received a doctorate in Hispanic Theology and Ministry from Catholic Theological Union in Chicago. His community organizing and ministry work brought him to the local Catholic university where we work and where he combines the work of the church with the work of the university. His goal is to bring the university in line with the local community and not engage in the typical extractive work of universities where they draw students from the community but do not give back to the community. Rather, his role was to engage in asset-based community development at the university.

Joshua's work in Maywood began when he was at a civic organization conference and a Catholic sister and administrator from the university encouraged him to work with the Quinn Center which was based out of a Catholic church in Maywood, St. Eulalia, even though Maywood had a historical Baptist, Evangelical, and Lutheran religious base. Joshua was a parishioner at St. Eulalia for a year before being invited onto the Board of the Quinn Center. However, he had been engaged with students in the community for at least a year before becoming a parishioner at St. Eulalia. The university ministry wanted to develop strong ties with the Maywood community and had only completed limited activities in Maywood, even though they were in neighboring communities and shared the same street boundaries. The university ministry had previously helped support the soup kitchen on Tuesday nights at the Quinn Center. Joshua helped serve packaged meals from the university dining hall at a discounted rate at the Quinn Center since the undergraduates could not invest the time needed to prepare meals for a large number of families at the soup kitchen due to their own need to work.

One of the women who volunteered at the Quinn Center, Martha Minnich, encouraged Joshua to formally join the church with his family. St. Eulalia is a Black Catholic church and Joshua is an Italian American middle-aged man who does not live in Maywood but who still felt a spiritual connection to St. Eulalia. After service, everyone walked around during the circle of peace and talked to each other for a few minutes, while the music was playing in the background. For Joshua, it was a powerful connection, a revelatory moment, and the parishioners welcomed his family and hoped they would stay in the congregation, which they did. Joshua paralleled that revelatory moment with his subsequent experiences in Maywood where people welcomed him and his ministry work both personally and professionally.

Joshua joined the board at the Quinn Center where he met others who wanted to start faith-based organizing in the Catholic tradition within Maywood. Joshua was clear about his need to bring in college students from the university who could also be trained in community organizing that was grounded in Catholic social and spiritual traditions since there were no other local organizations doing that work. The university has many first-generation college Latinx students who have practical barriers preventing them from engaging in civic engagement such as financial burdens to support themselves and their immigrant families. So, Joshua and his university team had to be thoughtful about how to create those community-building experiences and to make sure they were situated near the campus and not too far away.

After many meetings, this partnership with the Catholic university and the Catholic church in Maywood led to the development of the 501C3, CSPL. The university partnership was important, but it was the conversations among like-minded organizers and people of faith that resulted in the creation of CSPL. The university became an early partner in that because of their interest in what CSPL was doing right from the beginning. Joshua is now the President of the Board, and since its founding in 2017, CSPL has grown leaps and bounds from an organization with a $50,000 budget to now an organization with a $500,000 budget and six employees. The executive director of CSPL is also a good colleague within the university ministry department, Matthew, a faith-based community organizer with nearly ten years of experience in criminal justice, immigration reform, worker rights, and economic justice. In the end, the CSPL worked on development in education, mental health, and food insecurity because those are the immediate issues that affect Maywood. Joshua also knows that there are issues the CSPL cannot control such as the economic infrastructure of Maywood and the need to increase business development and revenue and keep taxes down for the residents.

The mission statement of CSPL is focused on racial equity and justice as a means to a common purpose, as well as accountability to live up to this institutional commitment. A key goal for CSPL is to ensure that both Black and Latinx parishioners come to be and feel like insiders at CSPL, that they belong and have a voice, and where issues can be talked about (Emerson & Woo, 2017). The leadership of Joshua and Matthew is deeply committed to racial equity, and without their personal commitment and resolve, multicultural congregations can fall short and disintegrate, especially when there is a misuse of power. However, since Joshua and Matthew are not from Maywood and neither Black nor Latinx, they are only able to operate in these spaces as neutral figures and from the periphery. Joshua identifies as Italian American while Matthew is biracial and identifies as Mexican-Polish.

During our interview, Joshua talked about fighting the undercurrent of racialized politics in Maywood from the sidelines and watching from the balcony as to how the Latinx population was complicating that historical white-Black binary. He also noted that there is a spectrum of racial and cultural identification within the Latinx community that includes a whole series of contextualized experiences such as when recent immigrants work alongside second and third-generation Latinx families in these multiracial congregations. Maria Franco is one of the leading community organizers in the CSPL who grew up in Bensenville, an inner-ring suburb with an immigrant population and where the author was also raised (Samina Hadi-Tabassum), then moved to Maywood and married someone who is a recent immigrant and who sees how these two subgroups within the Latinx community are linked to each other through ministry.

Nonetheless, CSPL has stronger roots in the Latinx Catholic community in Maywood, but they know the frontier work has to be intercultural and they must have strong Black members in the organization. In *House by House, Block by Block (2004)*, Alexander von Hoffman tells the remarkable stories of how local activists and community groups helped turn around blighted areas in America. For sixty years, federal policy has attempted with little success to solve the problems of housing and poverty in America's inner cities. Yet increasingly, local organizations are picking up where Washington has left off. Von Hoffman also shows that grassroots work can't do it alone: successful revitalization needs the support of local government and access to business and foundation capital. Human agency is needed for economic revival. Here is an excerpt from our interview with Joshua addressing the multicultural commitment needed in Maywood to turn itself around through human agency:

Author: Do you think the Black churches need to open up to the incoming Latinx residents?

Joshua: I think that they do but they do not have enough resources to meet their needs either. The Black churches have an aging population and there is a lot of anxiety and pressure around being able to do things in both communities that are purely ministerial and pastoral. There are unique particularities to both communities, and it is hard to meet both their needs. The intersectional work is hard. It takes time and it takes a lot of confidence building. It will also take time for the Latinx constituents to be at the table and have decision-making power in the room. It needs time and there needs to be more trust building. Our organization might be a good place to start because there are not a whole lot of expectations. We have to show up and hold true to our word. And we continue to show up . . . then good things can happen. We have a role as the local university in a community wide conversation that is very complex. The university is situated in a predominantly white affluent suburb that is adjacent to a historically Black suburb that is transforming . . . that had a deep history of resisting racism. But also, a deep history of entrenched racism. When you talk to 80-year-old Black residents who have been there their whole life, they remember being cordoned off to four blocks. There are logical reasons as to why they need to stay firmly engaged in the political power structure. They don't want to go back to that experience of being oppressed. We are hoping to have conversations that ferret out that history, bring it to light, bring it to the surface, and say that all of these communities have work to do. The Latinx community has a lot of deep work to do to understand this historical context and the injustices that their Black neighbors have experienced. White communities have to own the ways that they have contributed to this oppression. Even structurally . . . do you know there are no sidewalks that go from River Forest to Maywood? That was on purpose. We need to have race dialogues that get at racial healing.

Author: We saw differences in the Latinx student population and talked about how some of the Latinx families are moving to Maywood because of the evangelical churches that provide services in Spanish and on many days of the week and even after school. Do you see that trend as well?

Joshua: Yes, we see that general trend here as well. There is an evangelization occurring among Roman Catholic Latinx groups. The Latinx community is also becoming secular at the same rate as everyone else in America. Both the Black church and the Catholic church are aging. Young Latinx families are going where services exist for them, where learning is also occurring.

Joshua agreed that we see the same families in Maywood who are engaged with their children's lives at school as well as their children's lives at church. There was also growing hope as well when the historical Sacred Heart Catholic Church in Melrose Park closed in 2021 due to low numbers of parishioners and ended up combining with St. Eulalia in Maywood—connecting worshippers from both sides of the railroad tracks—and offering religious education for children in after-school and weekend programs through the Quinn Center. Sacred Heart and St. Eulalia merged as part of Renew My Church, a program of renewed evangelization and resource consolidation run by the Archdiocese of Chicago. Technically, both churches became worship sites in the new parishes named, "Sacred Heart-St. Eulalia." At the end of the day, community organizing is about giving people the sense that they have the power to act and that they do not have to live under these challenging circumstances. "We are in control now . . . the people are in control collectively. We don't have to assimilate. We can hold onto both the Black and Latinx cultures in Maywood," said Joshua at the end of our interview. Joshua can be categorized as an "organizer" who develops relationships by linking community members to one another in networks, building power, and taking social action.

Organizers and community members engage one another in dialogue about their situations and generate more hopeful alternatives and reframe problems.

The dialogic pedagogy developed by Paulo Freire was evident in the CSPL and allowed the residents of Maywood to construct a story of who they are, what they do, and why they do it. That collective story then motivates the group to strategize ways to realize the hopeful possibilities. It would also be naive to overlook the considerable challenges in Maywood that the CSPL faced such as the political asymmetries in local governance, not enough financial resources and social capital, the inequities, and tragedies of daily life in Maywood, and weak cross-race coalitions.

Currently, the CSPL is conducting listening sessions with the community and continuing to meet their needs such as the mental health sessions for the youth in the high school. There were three suicides before and during the pandemic year at the local high school in Maywood: one was a Black female student, another a Latina student, and one male Latino student (Romain, 2019). The Maywood community came together after these three deaths to find solutions to the rising suicide rate, and with over a hundred people in the meeting, solutions included how churches should work together and open their doors more often to young people; schools should be open during Spring Break; parents should be more vigilant when monitoring their kids' social media accounts for signs that a child is considering suicide or going through a depressive episode; and more mentoring activities.

The high school district also asked for more coalition building during this community crisis and reached out to CSPL for mental health support for their students. The CSPL was very much aware of the social stigma around therapy and mental health support in Black and Brown communities, often denying that mental challenges exist for many adolescents. CSPL provided mental health training for parents in which they learned how to better listen to their children, put down their phones and pay attention, become tolerant of their children's differences, examine the role of social media and their child's degree of social isolation and connectedness, and look for the multiple signals of possible suicide.

In this next section of the chapter, we will move away from interfaith organizations as positive sites of coalition building and move into the high school setting in Maywood. Even though we only conducted ethnographic observations in the three K-8 school buildings in Maywood, mostly focusing on adolescents in the middle grades, the high school loomed large at the end of the study as a site where the discourse of power and authority became enacted to such heightened frenzy that every interaction seemed like a spectacle of race. In *The Society of the Spectacle* (1967), Guy Debord, a French scholar, writes about the divisions in modern democratic societies and how they lead to spectacles in the public eye that can lead to generalized separation among social groups. Debord argues that the spectacle is not a collection of images; rather, it is "a social relationship between people that is mediated by images" (p. 12). When attending the high school events, the images we consumed led us to believe that the spectacle is both the outcome and goal of these public meetings, thus a spectacle is "tautological" since the means and ends are identical. The very unreal spectacles we witnessed, and their invented appearances epitomized the racial tensions between the Black and Latinx communities in Maywood, and at the root of all spectacles, is the specialization of power.

Though we never conducted observations inside East High School in Maywood, we did attend the virtual school board meetings and began to interview constituents who made salient arguments during those broadcasted public sessions. The public discourse was polarizing, discriminatory, and full of racist rhetoric, along with exclusionary practices. The regime changes in leadership within the school board spoke to the political and economic privileges of dominant groups and powerful actors at the expense of subordinated ones, along with barriers to true political membership (Hanchard, 2018).

THE SCHOOL BOARD AS SPECTACLE AND THE CHALLENGE OF AVOIDING RACIAL LANDMINES

A recent opinion piece in the *New York Times* spoke about the chaos and seemingly irrational behaviors exhibited by American adults in school board meetings that often get videotaped and aired on television (Cottle, 2021). The pandemic caused by the COVID virus set off many emotions from parents about safety procedures, mask mandates, vaccination requirements, teacher protection, and bussing concerns, leading to contentious board meetings. Today one can find a cabal of parents protesting outside the district headquarters before the school board members arrive for their public meetings, sometimes arriving from back doors to avoid passing through the large mobs in front. There is viral video footage of physical brawls occurring in these school board meetings, hair pulling and shoving at the lines to speak at the microphone, use of foul language and expletives, fascist salutes, voiced conspiracy theories, accusations and retaliation plans, the use of scripture, and threatening language full of rage. School board meetings were often nonpartisan spaces where community members discussed the budget for various programs, curricular topics, and other administrative issues that seemed for the most part innocuous. In the past, key issues such as sex education and desegregation did get discussed in school board meetings, and as heated as the debates were, there was decorum nonetheless and lots of common sense.

Today, local school boards have become the stage for the national culture wars and their differences in values, conservative versus liberal, that are tearing our nation apart and have subsequently fueled greater division among the populace, as well as ugly behavior from fearful adults that seems shocking and strange and goes beyond the expected cheering and booing. The power of local politics has also increased along with the community pressuring of board members and board takeovers to change the slate. The weird behavior often caught on tape also mirrors the excessive parenting from this generation of helicopter parents who want to hover over their frightened children and control all aspects of their existence for the so-called good of the children— children who are often afraid of the adults and their actions in these school board meetings. This "politics of petulance" has led the National School Boards Association, a group that has represented school boards since 1940, to ask the federal government to use executive power and authority to prosecute violent offenders who are being compared to domestic terrorists (Talbot, 2021). Attorney General Merrick Garland asked the FBI to investigate the angry violent crowds at school board meetings, some of them who go on to "overthrow" the school board. Maywood was no exception, especially in its high school board meetings, which took on a spectral aura.

School boards today face the same pressure as schools to present a positive image of the community and are held accountable for the academic perfor-mance and public image of the students (Walser, 2009). Oftentimes when deficiencies and errors are publicized, it is the role of the school board to defuse any fallout from bad press and from angry parents. High-functioning boards can recognize when conditions are out of their hand and understand the limitations of the structures in place. In the end, what is most essential is that the board keeps the interests of the students at the front center and remains engaged with improving and reforming the school district. In the 1800s, the role of the school board was to hold the superintendent account-able, especially when it came to missing monies. Now the board functions more as a co-leader directing the school district along with the superintendent in terms of student performance and teacher accountability.

However, to be successful in administration, the school board must rely on the expert knowledge and technical expertise of the superintendent and not just on themselves. School boards should be concerned with the *what* of governance while the superintendent should be concerned with the *how* of governance (Walser, 2009). Boards are there to provide resources and support for the superintendent, school administration, teachers, and staff. School boards hire the superintendent, approve budgets developed by the school administrators, approve policies written by school leaders, and influ-ence the local community to support the passage of levies and bonds to help fund infrastructure improvements (Alsbury & Gore, 2015). But in the high school board in Maywood, there were many gray areas in governance and in how much power the board should exert with regard to decision making and its relationship to the superintendent. High-functioning boards are able to negotiate and reach a consensus to the satisfaction of multiple parties. For a board to function appropriately and constructively, it must see itself as a partner in the reform process and be willing to learn from others across and within the community.

In our study, the high school board was not working productively and seemed to be ruling from the dais with absolute power. The distal board members were shifting the power to them and using the platform for their own political machinations and, in doing so, brought large turnouts of discontented parents to the board meetings whose numbers grew during the pandemic. A core value of a school board is shared leadership which was not evident here; in fact, many of the board members displayed bad board behavior such as name-calling and grandstanding. We did see the high school board create and sustain initiatives and engage in continuous improvement; however, there were many other functions that were missing such as providing a supportive environment for school sites, staff, and parents. This board was aware of how goals and initiatives were being carried out in school sites but often spoke negatively about each other, sometimes the community members, and school staff in public meetings. The board rarely used data to make decisions and often made decisions behind closed doors.

In well-governed school districts, a successful school board has six distinct characteristics: (a) stable members over time on the board to avoid turnover in leadership; (b) short regular meetings that focus on goal setting and data analysis; (c) effective management that includes problem solving with all the constituents; (d) a communicative school board president who is a cultural broker between the superintendent, teachers, and parents; (e) a focus on student achievement and its evidence in the budget and policies; and (f) an ability to work well together in a collaborative manner and with great trust (Walser, 2009). Effective boards work together to establish a shared mission and vision, articulate results with the community, and create policies that allow for the effective use of resources and forms of capital. However, these traits were not evident in the high school board in Maywood and eventually even Representative Chris Welch, a lawyer and the Speaker of the Illinois House of Representatives, had to step in when the board president and superintendent refused to meet with the teachers union and students were at home for two weeks until a federal mediator stepped into the negotiations (Romain, 2022).

All of the members of the high school board campaigned for their seats and were then catapulted into making decisions without much training. There was commitment and partial support but there was no trust, even though the cameras were on, and microphones were cued. Collaboration requires consensus building and not everyone will agree all the time. However, to promote conflict and dissension was also not savvy on the part of Mr. Arlington, board president, a Black male parent who was formerly in the military and currently a senior parole agent according to the district website, and his ongoing feud with Ms. Morales, a Latinx female parent who directed a local Montessori preschool. This was not the healthy conflict that generates ideas and leads to better policies. Coming together on a decision as a whole board and not a fractured board is best practice and postponing voting until alternative solutions are used can bring the board together. Instead, there were side-stepping diversions that made the board meetings go off task, single issues took center stage with split votes, and a few board members were cast off as outliers. There were often TV crews in the boardroom and some issues, such as the teacher strike, made the ten o'clock news, sometimes capturing blows on camera (Chronis, 2022).

Many of the board meetings reflected the by-gone discourse of Chicago ward bosses and the "locals" in contentious public city council meetings as well as the private meetings that occur behind closed doors and without the constituents listening to their heated discussions. It is also important to note that less than 10% of the American population votes in their local school board elections, and many feel that this voting is undemocratic because boards are often not responsive to the citizen's demands (Wasler, 2009). Here are observational notes from a school board meeting that we attended regarding the racial politics that became a specter of how the school district codifies, compares, judges, and places different races into a social hierarchy (Hanchard, 2018). Our notes also capture a purely spectacular rebelliousness that was concerted and diffused throughout the evening and founded on real, repressed contradictions in race relations:

On June 15, 2021, a teachers union representative spoke in a live video recording commenting that Mr. Arlington came to their union meeting and stated he wanted to change the school counselors since East had mostly Hispanic guidance counselors, West had mostly Black guidance counselors and the math and science academy had mostly white guidance counselors. "This is a false statement," said the union representative and that the racial composition of the counselors was diverse across the district. She then stated that Mr. Arlington said they have to take it on themselves to relocate. If the counselors did not relocate themselves, Mr. Arlington would do what he had to do. The counselors declined to relocate themselves. On June 21st, an email was sent to Mr. Harrington, the superintendent, from the teachers union stating that this will cause harm to the students and that we need to think about this change more carefully. She stated that the union wanted to meet with the superintendent, but they never received a response, even after ccing the school board. They chided the superintendent for not being transparent and unwilling to sit down with the teachers. On July 2nd, six guidance counselors received a notice of transfer. The teachers union representative was pleading to stop this transfer since the students were already attached to their counselors and a return to campus after the pandemic was already a shaky transition. However, Mr. Arlington did not comment and moved onto the next item agenda.

Even though Mr. Arlington was correct in his racial classification of the counselors across the three high schools, based on our follow-up research, Mr. Arlington nonetheless saw himself as the CEO of the board and took on a corporate persona, held the primary responsibility of running the show while sitting right in the middle of the dais, the camera on him all the time. Even though it seemed as if Mr. Arlington was a cultural fit for the Maywood community and had the right mix of experiences, his "my way or the highway" mantra led to great conflict with the multiracial community in the larger Proviso township that wanted to build bridges across the Black, Latinx, and white residents. The superintendent, Mr. Harrington, also a Black male leader, was boxed in with Mr. Arlington when it came to governance and management and they both pushed against the teachers union as well as the parents and public. Mr. Arlington often took his time telling stories while offering personal quips and quotes, leading to board meetings that were sometimes six hours plus in length, reinforcing the idea that spectacles are quintessentially dogmatic.

The school board meeting spectacles were often a self-portrait of power as the superintendent and school board president tried to keep a tight grip on their leadership, and in doing so, they took on a fetishistic appearance, concealing their true character as human beings and leaving the audience confused. Occasionally, Mr. Arlington was apologetic of his behavior in these spectacles, his "spectatorial inclinations," and sometimes claimed "authorized amnesia" with respect to his past behaviors and sometimes found himself "between the fake despair of a nondialectical critique on the one hand and the fake optimism of a plain and simple boosting of the system on the other hand" (Debord, 1967, p. 139).

Meanwhile, the unhealthy climate and culture of the schools was raging in the media with issues of violence and mental health concerns among the high school students across the three high schools: East High School located in Maywood, West High School located in Hillside which was a suburb farther west of Maywood, and the math and science academy located in nearby Forest Park. Figure 4.4 shows the front facade of East High School today and its neo-Gothic architecture with a clock tower.

In one Facebook post, a security guard was assaulted by a group of female students at East High School in Maywood who were fighting with each other in the outside parking lot. The superintendent responded immediately with punitive measures for these fighting students but was still not open to working

Figure 4.4 Front Facade of East High School in Maywood. *Source*: Samina Hadi-Tabassum.

with the teachers and the parents on larger safety measures. Instead, parents banded together and created a Facebook group to address these concerns and provide a platform for future collaboration that focused on the students' safety. In one board meeting, we transcribed a plea from a parent on the escalating school violence, concern for her daughter, and a lack of teachers: "Almost every single day is a fight—fighting in the homeroom, fighting in the streets, and fighting inside the school. What are you doing about safety? I would like to hear an answer. At the beginning of the year, my student went almost one month without a teacher. What's going on [there] too. [There's] poor communication with the parents. How is it possible you make robocalls about the games, everything, [but] nothing about the problems that happen in the school." Here is a Facebook post from a parent who lives in the township and created a parent response group to the board politics:

The community seems to be coming together and organizing—digging into the issues, discussing, rolling up their sleeves to do the work to make our schools great and hold the board and administration accountable here and via a group called P200 Cooperative. Check it out. Chime in. The more people working together, the stronger the voice to advocate for our schools (CB).

Irrespective of the meeting last night, moving never was and never will be the answer to educating children in the nation. Stay and advocate for what you want to see for ALL kids at ALL schools without making this be about personalities or demeanor at board meetings. I want to see all adults hold themselves to this standard, both at the Board table and in the community as they (looks like with some cause here) rebuke the powers that be. Thanks to the people who took time to live stream the meetings because this is a very basic element of transparency for the community. I appreciate that other municipalities and boards of Ed have also done this. Hopefully our district realizes that they can't escape public curiosity and interest. (JB)

Mr. Arlington, the board president, did not immediately respond to the parents' call on Facebook to address their concerns and did not model cross-collaboration from the top, shifting his priorities away from any active give and take with the broader school community. Such lack of responsiveness fueled perceptions of egotism and personal agendas on the parents' Facebook pages, accusing the administration of lacking the intuitive piece of the process, even though Mr. Arlington lived in the community with them and his well-respected son attended the high school. There was no working together in the spirit of mutual respect here, no deference, and no identification of any common ground. The local newspapers and social media buffs may have enjoyed the fighting between the school board members, but this type of attention does not do any good for anyone, especially the students who are looking at the infighting and seeing where the adults are crossing the line.

There was also role confusion since no one really understood the role of the board and its board president and what they can and cannot do. At one point, when some parents questioned why Mr. Arlington was not using his district email to respond to their questions and concerns, he instead encouraged them to use his personal email and cellphone, stating that this decision may push some parents to file an FOIA (Freedom of Information Act) to get a hold of the district emails formally. The parents wanted to know what is prohibited by executive limitations and what are the board norms and values for its operations, such as whether the board had adopted a policy of a single official voice to represent all persons on the board (Wasler, 2009). On the collective parent Facebook site, the racially diverse parents across the township voiced a need for public education on how school boards should operate at the state level. The high school board in Maywood was not following many of the more common norms of interaction such as building trusting relationships, respecting all persons on the board, accepting responsibilities as the ambassadors of the schools, communicating positively about the school community, and representing common interests rather than group factions.

It did not help that the board was not composed of professional educators, nor did they work in the trenches of these three high schools—they were distal leaders enacting policy from the balcony. Even when Mr. Arlington knew he was making the parents, teachers, students, and community leaders in the board meetings uncomfortable since the meetings went on into late evening hours, he was comfortable with others being uncomfortable and spent the first hour sharing his personal agenda from the dais and then more hours of an informational meeting with a back-and-forth discourse between board members. The spectators in the audience were either supporters of the administration or detractors, reinforcing the concepts of "one divides into two" and "two fuse into one." Like our polarized country, the boardroom spectacles at once united and divided us as researchers in the room and we became enveloped in this spectacular consumption. Any sense of unity split throughout the evening and reinforced the inherent contradiction: "division is presented as a unity and unity as division" (Debord, 1967, p. 36).

Thoroughgoing attacks on language emerged in these spectacles and any revolution was stomped down and buried by the board and its old Chicago machine culture, structure, and rules. As audience members took notes of what was being said and done, even we were taken aback by the "excesses" of the board meetings, and these excesses seemed alien to us as researchers as they were foreign to our everyday world. We overheard psychological and moral judgments being made about the school board and tried to be both consciously and unconsciously neutral, which was not always possible and evident in our chapter here.

There were not many board members playing the diplomatic role either, especially during infractions between Mr. Arlington and Ms. Morales. The pitting of Mr. Arlington and Ms. Morales invoked the specter of race, gender, and the fight for power and rule. There was no united front; rather, the Latinx community was invisible during board meetings, even though they were physically present but did not speak up during the public speaking sessions. The board also did not have translators for Spanish-speaking families, even though it is a state requirement. Was there a false unity between the Black and Latinx communities in Maywood? Was the school board anti-Latinx and therefore amplifying the idea that the Latinx students are honorary whites? Potential alliances between the Black and Latinx parents would make them invincible to the aggressions of the board, ambition and tyranny, and the plotting of machinations between board members that were undermining consensus for the betterment of their children. There needed to be more initiatives from the school board and administration under one banner for all—the question of Black versus Latinx is not what we want to get caught up in as parents and creating enemies and eliciting counterattacks from within the community.

Eventually one board member, Ms. Granger, a white female parent in the district, held a listening session at a union lodge to hear the multiracial parent group share its discontent in a public meeting that was live-streamed online. Many parents voiced concerns at the listening session that there were so many false rumors, half-truths, he-said-she-said scuttles, and the perpetuation of false narratives that they could not tell the difference between what was real and what was a spectacle. It is also assumed that the role of the superintendent is to serve as a shield by protecting their school board members from public criticism and discontent—but Mr. Harrington was nowhere to be found in the board meetings nor in the listening sessions unless he was invited by Mr. Arlington, the board president (Donlan & Whitaker, 2017).

Ms. Morales soon after conducted her own listening session at the local union lodge which was broadcasted on Facebook and included a wide range of parents and teachers who brought in Power Point presentations and speeches: the lack of bilingual services for parents and lack of translators; lack of basic resources at the predominantly Black high school such as bathrooms being closed due to low supplies and cutting the number of security guards in half; committed teachers who are getting paid less than neighboring communities; how the district spends less on students' instruction and teachers' salaries and more on the highest-paid school administration; the missing public dollars and the presumed channeling of funds to local politicians since it is only recently that the State of Illinois withdrew its emergency financial control over the district (Forest Park Review, 2021); the turnover of teachers which creates great instability; the movement of Black counselors by the superintendent to East High School from West High School and disrupting intact social relations; the firing of the IT department leading to 800 unresolved IT tickets since the school year started; the number of student fights; and the accusations from Mr. Alexander and Mr. Harrington that Ms. Morales is racist and anti-Black. The meeting ended with action steps that were small in scale as well as larger issues that will take time and perhaps a new board leadership. The parent collective has remained active in beating the drum on these issues and has created a collective political group to bring in their own slate candidates for the upcoming elections.

Simultaneously, the board members may not feel loved when they walk into the boardroom. Nobody sought them out before the meetings and referred to them by their name, minus Ms. O'Neil, who was a veteran board member—a Black female elder who had been on the board for decades and had the new high school football stadium named after her. The board members were not seen as selfless individuals who are the real drivers of positive change in the Maywood school district. Students did not show up to the board meetings to hand out positive cards and messages for the members; rather, most students were there to air grievances such as the dismantling of band classes and the violence on campus. In the end, one has to question whether the board members felt like they belonged when they arrived at the meetings since they were not greeted warmly by the public. There were no smiling faces in the audience making small conversations and there was no celebration of other board members' accomplishments. Everyone seemed serious. The board members did not feel heard by their constituents and felt the trickle-down effects of animosity toward the board president, who eventually stopped live-streaming the board meetings on the district website and stepped down by the end of our study.

When the parents asked to reinstate the live-streaming of the board meetings, here is the email response from Mr. Arlington, which alludes to gaslighting Ms. Morales, his Latinx opponent, instead of finding a solution. It also shows his passive-aggressive nature toward the personal battle with Ms. Morales with some parents calling for his resignation and others asking that this rivalry between board members not take center stage at board meetings:

Please see the below message we received from Board President Mr. Arlington in an email last night in response to our letter and petition:

> Good morning parents and thanks for your concern and the petition. As you may know Dr. Harrington does not run the board meetings or make the ultimate decision on how the board conducts its business. I do have some concerns though if you'll allow me to address them.
>
> 1. This very board has done nothing to suggest or even infer the lack of transparency or lack of communication? Why now is livestreaming an issue?
> 2. The unwarranted attacks on board members and the Superintendent are not a part of the board's responsibility to sit back and take? How would you suggest we conduct the business of the district when folk come to disrupt it?
> 3. There is an ugly racial overtone to all of this because there is not one infraction this board has done to warrant this transparency argument? No one has spoken up about the one board member that's in violation of her oath of office? Why not???? And what's not transparent that we're doing?
> 4. I should be held to a different standard of accountability. Why? We all got elected and we all have the exact same oath of office??? Why no petition about her???
> 5. The public can attend, speak at the appointed time, get the agenda the same time we do, and video the entire meeting if you want? Which was done??? What am I missing here??? What's not transparent???
> 6. Board policy says 3 minutes and 30 minutes overall. That's 10 comments per meeting. We listened to 22??? And have never used our policy to curtail speech? To ask for respect and courtesy from teachers. Who checks the community elected board signs is wrong? Where's the petition about that behavior?

The school board president's decision to stop live-streaming and recording board meetings backfired into a growing grassroots movement in the form of a closed Facebook group, an online petition, and a call for volunteers to fill the information void that decision had created by posting live board meetings onto Facebook from their own phones (Romain, 2021). A parent cooperative was launched to increase parent involvement and a petition was created to persuade the board president, Mr. Arlington, to immediately resume live-streaming and recording the district's regular board meetings, committee meetings, and any public forums it hosts. In an interview conducted by news reporter Michael Romain of the Village Free Press (2021), Mr. Arlington said that he has the authority to suspend live-streaming district meetings and "pointed out that live-streaming meetings is not a legal requirement, adding that he made the decisions to stop the practice because board meetings were getting too disorderly, a reality he blamed on the teachers union." The district is currently negotiating the contract with the teachers union. The parents on the other hand want to find a middle ground, work with the school administration while supporting teachers but most importantly advocate for the safety and education of their children. We observed a subsequent board meeting in which Mr. Arlington responded to a frustrated parent, angry about the marching band class being canceled due to low enrollment, with a speech of his own:

Mr. Arlington: I mean what I say, and I say what I mean. So, if I tell you that it is not true, then you can take that to the bank. If it is a misunderstanding, then we need to get to the bottom of it. But signing a petition and making a false claim and getting people riled up is not the responsible way. It is not my purview to do that. The board members have their numbers on their cards. You could have just called me. It is almost personal to be attacked like that. We have never canceled a class in the four years that we have been here. I want to thank the board for the privilege and honor of serving. I want to commend the Maywood community. We work for you even when we disagree. So, none of us sit up here with a big head. This is work. This is a lot of work. We do not get paid. We're parents just like you. I have a son who is a freshman. We're taxpayers just like you. I am not running for anything else. No one on the board has political aspirations. We are all here to serve you based upon our record. Judge us on that. We earned that respect from the community. I thought I knew service through my fraternity and through my religion. But I learned it here. We make sure every child gets the best education they can.

[He then goes on to list the personal sacrifices and histories of the board members.] When it comes to Ms. Morales, he says that she works "tirelessly" to educate children out of her home . . . advocating for students . . . fighting the good fight . . . twenty-four seven. Working her tail off. "We hardly ever agree but she is dedicated to whatever cause she believes in. Medical issues. Family. All of these things and we are still serving this community." [This board meeting went on for six hours.]

Mr. Arlington: "We are sometimes that lone voice telling it on that side of the mountain. You'all don't hear me. This woman, Mrs. O'Neil has dedicated 22 years of her life to this board, and she does not get a pension. I am blessed to be a part of the board. I just wanted to share tidbits about the board so when there is a misunderstanding you can say 'that's not them.' If there is something that we get wrong, we are human. We will apologize and we are trying to do the right thing."

[Mr. Arlington commended the superintendent for a smooth drive-by graduation that was meaningful. A wonderful summer school. An administrative retreat. Two town hall meetings. Ongoing contractual work and construction. Saving us all kinds of money. Adding all kinds of curriculum.]

Mr. Arlington: We are working to add to our students as scholars. We love our town. We want better for our students. We know it can be done. We're doing it. That is evident in the board. We don't have any losses here.

Mr. Arlington's role as the high school board president and his speech above echoed W.E.B DuBois' call for building national institutions, businesses, organizations, and communities to meet their own needs and respond to efforts from the white community to control the Black population and dehumanize them. Mr. Arlington played an influential role in the Maywood community and shielded the Black residents from the unfairness of the segregation that he had experienced in his life. He wanted to create a school board that served the social, political, and spiritual needs of the Black community in Maywood—from the new football stadium and its christening to the creation of a new Black history curriculum and to his own personal stories of being in a Black fraternity. He held a position as a school board president that was denied to the earlier Black residents of Maywood. His skills in oratory, organization, and leadership helped serve the needs of the Black community who had voted for him to protect them from the hostility of the outside white world.

The racial tensions between Mr. Arlington and Ms. Morales led to stagnation among the board even as the superintendent was moving ahead with restructuring plans for the three high schools. However, the animosity worked both ways, and there was public resentment toward Ms. Morales for sending out pamphlets in English and Spanish to the Maywood community disparaging Mr. Arlington, which led to an anti-defamation lawsuit as well as backlash from the Black community. Instead of sending pamphlets to the community sharing the mission and vision of the school board, there were instead defamation pamphlets mailed out by Ms. Morales against Mr.

Arlington, and many of the Black residents of Maywood did not approve of the disparaging material nor its Spanish translation. One could also argue that this political move was an emasculation of Mr. Arlington by a female Latina board member, perhaps due to her desire to outrank him on the board.

Brockenbrough's (2012) research would support the idea that both Mr. Arlington and Mr. Harrington have been positioned in the popular imagination as surrogate patriarchs for the Black community in Maywood. In response to the chronic struggles of young Black male students in American public schools, the research shows the importance of strong Black male leaders like Mr. Arlington in the educational arena to help restore a normative gender order in a predominantly female profession. Mr. Arlington and Mr. Harrington were cast as ideal surrogate father figures for Black male youth, especially Mr. Arlington who was uniquely poised as a real-life father with a rising star son who attended a high school in the same district. There was an underlying sentiment to retain and support both Black male leaders in the district. The salience of Blackness and Black masculinity proved critical in producing a blind eye to the spectacles unfurling during the weekly board meetings. We do not need to question whether Mr. Arlington experiences emasculation in his workplace under white supremacy (most likely) and where he faces the "psychosocial stresses of Black masculinity unfulfilled" (Brockenbrough, 2012, p. 30). To resist this emasculation, Black male leaders may take strategic efforts to resist that white supremacy power structure through masculinist posturing in their own community.

The contentious battle between Mr. Arlington and Ms. Morales became the single issue that plagued the board, even though both of them framed it as a "small concern" issue and highlighted the gender dynamics within the board. Both Mr. Arlington and Ms. Morales were coming from an authoritative position and used strikingly similar language to vent their frustrations. Mr. Arlington's predictable behavior was expected on the surface but what was causing his tensions with Ms. Morales lies deeper and no one in the public truly knows what influences their antagonistic behavior in private. Did gender unequivocally mediate our research lens on leadership in this study because of excessive assertions of power by the board president? Was Mr. Arlington reluctant to listen to women with authority? One can argue that there is a broader portrait of the tensions between Mr. Arlington and Ms. Morales that goes beyond the intersection of race and gender.

However, in one school board meeting regarding the cancelation of the marching band class brought forth by a white mother, the rancor between these two board members was evident through their antagonistic communicative style, abrasive rapport with each other, and prickly demeanor full of indignities:

Ms. Morales: Don't the teachers know which classes to offer beforehand? I'm a musician. We can't cancel the marching band class, or the band program will fall apart.

White mother: I agree. Marching band saved my son in the pandemic. I don't understand why the district is canceling it.

Mr. Arlington: Excuse me ma'am. I am not addressing you ma'am. I am just addressing what has transpired here. We're not going back and forth like this. I am just explaining what you just saw. You came out with a concern and the principal just explained to you and the person responsible for the band classes to just explain what happened. And you still hear this word "canceling" when that did not happen. You can't teach what is not there. That was explained. If the students come, then I am sure we will offer the class. But right now there are just four kids in the marching band and we do not have enough students to offer a marching band class.

Ms. Morales: The kids . . .

Mr. Arlington: [hand against her side of the room] Ms. Morales I have the floor . . . I am not going back and forth with you. I gave you the floor. Please give me the same respect. Thank you. We're done with that subject and now we are going onto the President's report.

Mr. Arlington's vigorous rhetorical style reflected a neoliberal era of education that resulted in unfettered democracies and social engineering. At the same time, Mr. Arlington had spectacular power, which was absolute and with "an unchallengeable internal logic," ensconced in powerful words, corrupted by the contempt he felt for Ms. Morales, and confirmed this contempt with the spectators in the audience (Debord, 1967). Parents at the board meetings were put on the line, without much time to deflect, and it was hard to diffuse an issue—everyone mastered the facial expressions, tones, and gestures to convey discontent. Even though serving on boards is a voluntary act, if the board is not doing its job correctly, it can hamper the school system. Most school boards' members are elected but it does not make them any more effective than school boards determined by the village mayor (Alsbury & Gore, 2015).

Many feel that elected school boards are an anachronism and we need to find better councils of people who can advise school administrators and teachers on how to improve student achievement and school climate, rather than have a plank of parents seeking power. At the same time, everyone who has gone to school presents themselves as an expert on schooling and thinks they know how to run schools. However, research shows that school boards do matter and can affect student achievement (Alsbury & Gore, 2015). The beliefs and values of the school board can affect the school culture, either positively or negatively.

The district is at a critical juncture now with heightened frustrations that can lead to high teacher turnover and administrative transitions. It needs to develop a set of operating principles such as not accepting personal complaints of an individual at a board meeting, making decisions based on the information and not personalities, and debating the issues and not each other. Yet, dysfunctional boards are the exception and not the norm. Shared leadership is more common today in school boards compared to the classical top-down leadership of the neoliberal era of the 1990s. Rather, shared leadership encourages the transparent and open exchange of information, shared responsibility for problems and solutions, and opportunities for learning that allow other community members to also contribute (Wasler, 2009). Furthermore, shared leadership encourages balanced governance, defined as an approach that discourages micromanaging as well as a disengaged stamp of approval by the board. There must be a balance of power and oversight as well as a need for the school board to only offer informed oversight on their part.

The concept of "hero making" can also be applied to Mr. Arlington, who is leading individuals with different backgrounds and viewpoints on the high school board, down a pathway as the fictional hero of his own story and enabled by others around him such as the superintendent (Donlon & Whitaker, 2017). A real hero would not be influenced by their own personal agendas because their personal agendas may not be what is best for the students in the school district. There was no building of common ground such as around issues of safety that the students brought to almost every board meeting. A school board president needs to instill trust, deference, assurance, and humility for optimal governance, which was not always evident in this board leadership (Donlan & Whitaker, 2017). At the same time, there were also constituents in support of Mr. Arlington's agenda who fueled his hero-making desires with knee-jerk assurances. Each constituent has an expectation when they enter a board meeting and soon those who share the same views as others start to band together as well as set up constituent groups that vary in motive. But Mr. Arlington is a steward of the community dollar and there are only so many resources to go around in a cash-strapped era and in a sub/urban community.

One issue that created a racial division in the community was an idea proposed by both Mr. Arlington, the board president, and Mr. Harrington, the superintendent—the development of a Black history course as a requirement for all students in the three high schools. However, according to Mr. Arlington, the district needed to invest at least $300,000 in public funds to develop the course as well as an obligation to de-invest in other areas such as the elimination of the bilingual education program at the high school level and its subsequent combination with the special education program. What is urgent and what is important were voiced by the board president and superintendent even though the community sentiment was not in agreement. They both want to be the heroes for the Black community in Maywood and use their power of influence to develop the required Black history course, which also included the backing of several prominent Black community members.

Even though we saw criticism from the public about Mr. Arlington, the older Black constituents wanted to be heard by Mr. Arlington and wanted him to keep the promises he made to the Black community. Their own personal experiences in high school, having been denied a required course in Black history while living in Maywood, the home of Black Panther Party leader Fred Hampton, was fueling the cause. Beyond the veneer, all constituents have fragile egos and need to have their individual needs met as well as promises kept, as the case in Maywood. Upon reflection, it may seem an insurmountable task to lead this group of individuals down a common path in Maywood when they have such dramatically differing backgrounds and viewpoints (Donlan & Whitaker, 2017). All school board members want to make a difference for their group of constituents, but their insecurities also arise. They want to be a hero for their group and accomplish group goals in a positive and productive fashion. However, individuals on the board are never a powerful force and do not have absolute authority; rather, it is only when they form groups that board members can do anything.

To better understand the racial tension behind the development of the required Black history course, we interviewed Michael Romain, the Black male newspaper reporter whose coverage of Maywood and its neighboring western suburbs in several newspapers provides much of the local knowledge in this book:

Michael: We are really feeling the tension now between Blacks and Latinx people. It's really, really deep, especially in the high school. I don't know how much you are paying attention to what is happening in the high school, but it is a real mess, and it is incredibly contentious. It's rooted in Black and Brown tensions and just last week in the board meeting . . . Mr. Arlington read aloud a really nasty letter that he said was sent to him by Ms. Morales, who is the only Latinx board member. It was nasty and claimed that she called him a scumbag and all this other stuff. He read it aloud in the public board meeting with the camera on. Then he claims that she only sent this letter about him to the two white board members. They just hired an African American superintendent, Mr. Harrington, to replace the previous superintendent, Mr. Roberto, who had been the superintendent for five years. Even then when I started my blog and started to write about the school district, Ms. Carter [a Black community leader in Maywood] calls me up and says, "This guy has a real thick accent. I don't understand what he is saying. A lot of the parents are telling me 'I don't understand him'." I wrote about that and how the Black community in Maywood was xenophobic. I actually miss Dr. Roberto. This is all very complicated. The

Black board members claim that Ms. Morales has a bias in favor of Hispanics. This is what I heard from many people, including Chris Welch [powerful local Black politician who is the head of the Democratic Party in Illinois]. It may or may not be the case. She was accused of doing some you know, crazy stuff. And, uh, she would visit him at all hours of the day and all kinds of crazy stuff. I don't think Dr. Roberto welcomed that behavior. He was a real competent superintendent. But most superintendents stay between three and five years and some leave even sooner. And then trade chaos baked into the transition. I think schools are too heavily administered. But with that amount of disruption . . . schools become inherently disruptive. It's less chaotic in wealthier schools. In our communities, kids do not need that disruption baked into their poor public schools. The changes that this new superintendent, Mr. Harrington, is making . . . they are asinine, and I cannot stress that enough. I know administrative realignments, but Harrington eliminated entire departments. If anyone criticizes Harrington, then Mr. Arlington gets up and says 'You're punishing a Black man. You're beating up on the Black man.' You can't criticize him because the guy's Black. There is so much race baiting going on at the board meetings. It's ridiculous and dangerous. Both Morales and Arlington are doing it. It doesn't do anything to heal the divisions. And it's really, really frustrating. You can't govern effectively because you are always stepping on manufactured racial landmines.

Michael Romain went ahead to explain how Mr. Arlington originally went into Maywood and spoke with the local preachers, the Ministerial Alliance Network people, and leaders like Ms. Carter to lobby for a required Black history course for students at the three high schools. This movement was led mostly by the Black men in Maywood and a successive line of male superintendents, with a noticeable passing up of Black female school leaders. The cost of developing one mandatory class was anywhere between $300,000 and $500,000 which the previous superintendent, Mr. Roberto, did not want to fund because of the budget crisis, and he instead put the money into the building infrastructure and capital investments. Mr. Arlington, on the other hand, is implementing curricular changes without having conversations with anyone, especially the parents. The autocratic behavior of the board president was tolerated in Maywood but perhaps would not be tolerated in nearby wealthier school districts. According to some of our study participants, they saw nothing wrong with Mr. Arlington's behavior and stated that he was aggressive in making changes but that he was making the changes needed for the Black community.

Many of the district administrators and teachers across all racial groups were not in agreement with the pace and rate of change and the type of changes that Mr. Arlington was proposing. The term xenophobia was used quite a bit in our interview with Michael and with others who challenged the actions of Mr. Arlington and stated that the dissent was not there when Mr. Roberto was the superintendent. When pushed further as to why the Black community did not renew the contract for Mr. Roberto, relatives of Michael Romain in Maywood stated to him directly that "they have to wait their turn." Many Black people in Maywood did not rally for Mr. Roberto because he was "Hispanic" and did not want to discuss his qualifications. There was an ugly xenophobia among some of the older Black residents of Maywood that was often boldly stated such as statements claiming they do not want "a bunch of Mexican people taking over Maywood." It is a valid reaction, though, to Black residents who have been historically left out of wealth, opportunity, and the American dream and had created a thriving Black suburban community on their own. The xenophobia is coming from a place of validity for them and a history of voter suppression for many Black residents; however, there is also a resentment that Mexican Americans are being allowed to come into this country and step ahead of them in the line of the zero-sum game.

Yet, not everyone in the Black community agreed with Mr. Arlington's actions. During a June 2021 board meeting, a public comment from a Black female parent was aired on Zoom in which she praised the district for bringing in more resources for African American history but also wanted the district to flush out a curriculum for Latinx history and Asian American history. On the topic of race, this same parent asked the board to not scapegoat the majority of white teaching staff and instead look at how they govern and spend funding that should be going to both the Brown and Black students. This parent went on to admonish the board for increasing the salaries of the administrators and not the salaries of the teachers closest to the students and the unlivable wages of the cafeteria staff. Yet, as Michael Romain pointed out, there should not be blame placed on the new Latinx arrivals who were not the ones suppressing the Black vote and rights in Maywood.

Various players within schools, communities, and districts are often in disagreement with not just what occurred, but they may also disagree over defining what racially inequitable treatment actually looks like in Maywood. While some parents may see a lack of translators as blatant acts of racial discrimination that are designed to harm their children because of race, different groups of people measured racial inequality treatment and opportunity with different rulers. Indeed, Maywood had many heated debates over racial harm, racial fairness, and even the relevance of race. How do parents, teachers, and school leaders show the intent to discriminate because of race? The board became more defensive rather than ready to negotiate with the community. The parents needed to show how the students have been harmed because of the discrimination. What are the proofs of racial harm and not just insinuations about the board's racist intentions and is there proof in leaked documents? Clearly, the Latinx parents were raising the board's defenses. Where the board's acts racially motivated?

We also interviewed a director at East High School, Dr. Brice, whose department for bilingual and ESL services was being dismantled by Superintendent Harrington and the school board, collapsing the Bilingual/ESL Department and combining it with the Special Education Department. The Bilingual/ESL Department had been audited by the State of Illinois before Dr. Brice took over the role of director in 2017 and after the district had been cited for twenty-two violations. Dr. Roberto hired Dr. Brice to fix the violations, repair bilingual services, and develop a dream program for the mostly Spanish-speaking bilingual students at East High School, along with a few Arabic and French-speaking immigrant students.

Dr. Brice: When I arrived, they were only offering services up to sophomore year which is a major violation. There were a whole lot of things not occurring for the bilingual students based on the compliance report from the state. When the state came out again, they found errors with our Home Language Survey as well as other program components and we changed what we could the following year in our strategic initiative. We were co-teaching freshman, sophomore and junior year with the SPED teachers pushed into the bilingual classrooms. Then we looked at math and science data and tried to develop language support and provide case managers who could provide student support, especially when they are not doing well. Our bilingual teachers were always reaching out. I pushed for our general education teachers to get ESL certification [through the local university where the authors are employed] and provided in-service training for staff. We created PLCs [professional learning communities] for ELs [English learners] on the PD [professional development] days. We also translated progress reports in Spanish but there were delays in translation and we do have some French-speaking and Arabic-speaking students. There are so many kids here and we could not do progress monitoring with infidelity and someone on the board did not understand this challenge. Parents loved meeting with me because I did speak in Spanish with them. I tried to connect with the 600 kids even though there was only one of me. Our bilingual parents do not feel comfortable coming into the buildings because they want them to speak in English. There is nobody in the office at East who can speak in Spanish with the bilingual parents. The Latinx kids wrote to the principal about not being treated equally by the school cafeteria staff and security guards for being Latinx. Educating Latinx children was his Achilles heel and he kept saying "I am not bilingual." We need equity and access for all of our students. This is horrible rhetoric in an educational community because it jeopardizes the success of our community. We need everyone on board. We cannot tear each other apart. Now that we have power . . . how can we ensure that others do not get oppressed? You cannot repeat the ugly vicious cycle of oppression.

In terms of student enrollment, at East High School in Maywood, there were 259 emergent bilingual students when Mr. Brice started and more than 100 were not receiving services. Now close to 300 students in the high school district who are emergent bilinguals are receiving the proper language services. Black teachers in the district who went ahead and completed course-work for their ESL certification thanked Dr. Brice for being able to "see language" in their teaching and how they became better teachers by keeping the linguistic needs of the Latinx students in the forefront. The teachers also spoke about how they gained knowledge of the Latinx students' cultural backgrounds and their hardships as immigrant students such as the need to work after school to support their families as well as helping with siblings at home. Across the three high schools, there are now more Latinx students (54%) than Black students, but the district leadership did not come to the realization that they are no longer a predominantly Black high school district.

For Dr. Brice, the rhetoric of the board president was not unifying, and he could not justify the cost of developing the required Black history class. Instead, Dr. Brice was advocating for a course on the history of Maywood that would include the rich history of so many famous people from Maywood like Black Panther Party leader Fred Hampton, famous astronauts like Eugene Cernan, and singers like John Prine, as well as the race riots and political rallies. A required class on Maywood could unify the district, not be at odds and address the same concepts of hate, oppression, and acts of violence. Even though Dr. Brice left the Maywood school district in 2021 due to the restructuring changes brought on by Superintendent Harrington and without his input and consensus, Dr. Brice had many good questions to pose to us in return at the end of the interview: How can we engage in civic mindedness? Why should Latinx students take a class that does not represent them? What does that do for the Latinx students' self-perceptions by forcing them to take a course on Black history? Are we inclusive? Are we doing unto others what we did not want to happen to us? What is the vision for the school district moving forward?

Race as Spectacle

Guy Debord (1967) examined contemporary society back then as we entered the postmodern era, through many references to Hegel and Marx, but its premise is still relevant today. In the current world of social media and rapid technological innovation, Debord would still argue that life is an accumulation of spectacles. Everything that was directly experienced at the moment is being replaced by glossy, edited images on Facebook and Instagram. In our immediate experiences, we feel emotions and sensations, but in social media, the stream of touched-up visual images that represent our lives is detached from reality and instead portrays something completely separate from our lived experience, a pseudo-world. As we process this stream of contrived images on social media, we can only feel a pseudo-connection to those in our virtual community with whom we have never had a direct experience.

The duality between lived reality and spectacle can sometimes become blurred as reality emerges into a spectacle and the spectacle becomes a reality. The superficial images we see on social media affirm that perhaps all human relationships are just images of relationships. In the paragraph below, we describe a spectacle that occurred in Maywood—the inauguration of a new football stadium at East High School that included news reporters, television crews, and photographers. Here Debord would ask us to examine the language around this spectacle, especially as the board stressed funding concerns and budget woes, and how the spectacle alludes to the zeitgeist and goal of social life in Maywood. The high school board in this study presented an endless series of public spectacles, as a repeating presentation of its self-validating rationale, but this inauguration was the apex. The images of the inauguration motivated desire, nostalgia, and pride on social media sites while also displaying the hypnotic behaviors of those school officials and politicians sitting on stage—alluding to a life of speculation.

Drawing strength from the rebuilding of the football stadium at East High School, the Black leadership in the high school district did not invite any members from the Latinx community onto the stage, drew racial boundaries, and struck down any form of coalition building. For many in the Black community, the new football stadium stood for progress and achievements for the Black leadership in Maywood, and their eloquent speeches and testimonies of triumph showed how the spectacle is also a self-congratulatory monologue with itself. The exclusion of the Latinx population from the ceremony created a discourse of the dispossessed in Maywood—there was no faith in friend and foe. In such mass assemblies with state representatives like Chris Welch on the stage, the Black leadership used this moment to carry forth the ethics of their forebears, to mobilize the Black alums of East High School, and launch a springboard to push the Black agenda forward in Maywood.

While they were celebrating the new stadium, they forgot to include political figures from the Latinx community and their struggles for national existence. There was no rhetoric around building a multilingual and multicultural coalition in Maywood. Rather, there was a Black paternalism that saw the stadium as a triumph for the Black community, a sign of ambition and development but did not acknowledge their Latinx counterparts and the need to build a solidarity movement that was interracial. The campaign for the stadium was built on unequal terrain that placed Latinx citizens in direct conflict with the Black leaders and state officials on stage who all gave speeches

Figure 4.5   The Inauguration of the New Football Stadium at East High School. *Source*: Rajeska Jackson.

with no translations. There were not many families in the stadium seats that Saturday morning and the majority were Black families.

There is nothing to be gained in the exclusion of Latinx constituents by the Black school leaders in Maywood; the lack of brotherhood set a tone of haughtiness and dominance and had regressive implications for multiracial democracy in Maywood. This divisiveness was what the Chicago Black Panther Party leader did not believe in and fought against the divide-and-conquer ideology of capitalism. For the Black Panther Party, the class struggle had engulfed both the Black and Latinx communities. One can only hope that the next story will be of redemption and reconciliation in Maywood. It is only the capacity of ordinary people doing ordinary things in Maywood that creates democracy in action.

CONCLUSION

Spectacles can only compound the racial tensions and public embarrassments that took place in the high school board. The play-by-play interactions on Facebook pages described the ugly exchanges and grandstanding between board members, school leaders, and constituents. Everyone took offense at the critical conversations that arose from these meetings. Parents on the periphery who were unable to attend board meetings joined these social media pages and contributed to the fringe discourse, sometimes negative and sometimes positive but often imbalanced and contradictory. Even though the board has plenary power, the parents attending the board meetings were not about to let go of their own power either, whether in person or online, and were there to represent the community sentiment. The parents wanted peace at the dinner table and the need for the fighting to stop but without any bad guys and heroes at the helm. The parents were ready to forgive in advance any irrationality they encountered from the school board and move in to address the real needs of the children. By the end of our study, Superintendent Harrington created a Parent Advisory Board in October 2021 to actively listen to the parents:

> Greetings Parents,
> I need your help to form a Parent Advisory Board. I am looking for a group of parents to be a part of the solution surrounding student educational achievement and eliminating disruption of students in our schools. I want parent representatives of all students from all three schools!
> Only with a myriad of opinions and insights can we create solutions that benefit all students. It is going to take the "village" of parents and the community.
> Please sign up to be on the Parent's advisory council using this link below.
> Superintendent Harrington

Furthermore, there is a need to measure and grow social capital in public institutions and organizations within Black-Brown communities: how well do members work with one another and what outside connections do they have? The school board members need to work well with each other in a productive and collegial fashion for board effectiveness. They also can benefit from a wide variety of connections to external entities that can influence their work such as legislators, civic groups, universities, businesses, news media, philanthropists, and leaders in other districts. These external influences can be a source of information, resources, innovative ideas, and legitimacy. The quality of external ties also matters—some ties are beneficial and positive, and some are adverse and unproductive. Internal board relationships can be seen as the closure and the external relationships as brokerage (Alsbury & Gore, 2015). Brokerage with external stakeholders, especially with state and federal agencies, can help a school board secure more financial and political support. Neither internal nor external relationships were strong in Maywood; rather, it was a divisive school board with diverse external ties.

In a recent example of brokerage, a few board members along with the board president, Mr. Harrington, went down to Springfield, Illinois, to meet with the democratic leader of the Illinois legislature who was a former president of this very same school board in Maywood. There were photos taken in the hallowed halls and one veteran Black board member, Ms. O'Neil, was given an honorary resolution in her honor. However, when the event photos were posted on the parent's Facebook page, there was resentment that tax dollars were being used to send this delegate and her friends and family to Springfield and stay overnight for this honor. There was also resentment that these fanfare photos presented a distorted image of the district due to growing parent and teacher dissatisfaction. On the other hand, one parent stated on the collective Facebook page that she does not have an issue with an elected official going to Springfield to be recognized since it is an opportunity to advocate for the needs of the district at the same time. In relation to the budget, she hoped that the elected members are fiscally responsible, questioning whether this Springfield trip is in the formal budget and who paid for the expenses.

Trust, cooperation, and mutual respect allow board members to work for the good of Maywood as opposed to their own interests. Trust is vital and fosters efficient coordination and collaboration, information sharing stimulates openness and learning, and shared vision reinforces a unity in purpose and commitment. Trust allows for the alignment of goals and perspectives. Trust is important to address perceptions on how to ensure effective participation and cooperation in board processes and decisions, and how to encourage civil interactions. Trust allows for semi-formal processes to occur in which members inform each other on important matters. Trust also allows for shared norms of behavior that allow for appreciation of each other as board members along with constructive criticism.

Dysfunctional boards on the other hand experience ongoing power struggles, loss of resources, missed opportunities, false narratives, and loss of legitimacy within their community, which can be heightened in a community with shifting demographics. Critics have asserted that school boards are not relevant to student achievement while others have claimed that the indirect actions and behaviors of school board members do impact student achievement greatly (Alsbury & Gore, 2015). Boards do address issues that affect student achievement, but without suitable leadership and governance, student achievement can be harmed. Student achievement was found to be lower in those districts where individual board members reported broad disagreement over essential elements of effective board leadership such as vision-directed planning, community engagement, accountability, effective leadership, climate, systems thinking, cultural responsiveness, data for continuous improvement, and innovation and creativity (Alsbury & Gore, 2015).

If we were to use an equity lens on the high school board in Maywood, we would argue that the Latinx population is the underserved student group and ask what potential impact board policies have on this population such as the lack of Spanish language translations at the public meetings. What are the barriers to more equitable outcomes for the Latinx population? How do we involve more Latinx stakeholders in strategic policy-making decisions? How are we collecting data on the Latinx population in Maywood? What is the district's commitment to training the school leaders on the needs of the Latinx population? All means all when it comes to representing all the students in Maywood. Mr. Arlington appeared to be an equity warrior for only some of the students but not all the students.

Boards that experience conflict and disarray, as in Maywood, destabilize district efforts to raise student achievement. There needs to be efforts at the local and state level to address internal governance disagreements and reduce disarray. There also needs to be stability in the board, and stabilizing factors include stable working relationships among the board members, stable expectations of all board members, and stable goals for student improvement. There should also be designated roles on the board such as which board members provide community expertise versus knowledge of student learning versus connections to local organizations.

Board members must demonstrate responsibility when they face choices, understand the consequences, and select options for the greater good. We are living in an era of accountability, and everyone must behave responsibly. A school board in Black-Brown communities must articulate what it believes in and stands for—its fundamental values for a multiracial and multilingual population. Board members represent the community which may have competing and conflicting values. The boardroom is where these differences need to be discussed, but consensus must be reached on what values the board supports. By articulating the same values, the same moral compass can be used to make countless daily decisions that push the school district toward its vision.

Conclusion

Leading with Equity and Justice in the Birthplace of Fred Hampton

Many of the candidates running in the local Maywood elections in 2020 understood the need to build Black-Brown coalitions. Norma Hernandez, a young progressive Latinx leader who was recently elected to the board trustee position at nearby Triton College, where the majority of students from Maywood enter college, was no exception to the case. She knew that the community needed to build a coalition and was critical enough of what was happening in the local surroundings to be elected. There was a need for political leaders like her who understood politics and power and were not afraid to talk back to the political machines. Leaders, who could stand up to the new Amazon distribution center being constructed in nearby Melrose Park, demand workers' rights and hold a public meeting on Amazon and how it will affect the community (Ori, 2020). The Amazon company set up its largest distribution center in a former bulldozed horse racetrack in 2020, which the mayor of Melrose Park annexed from Maywood in 2018. There were no discussions of what type of tax incentives Amazon was receiving from Melrose Park and/or what types of benefits the workers will receive from Amazon. Residents did not receive any transparency from their local government nor any accountability from a trillion-dollar company run by low-wage Black and Brown workers.

It is easiest to create Black-Brown alliances in these manufacturing hubs where multiracial workers interact daily with each other in confined, intimate spaces, but we need leaders who can stand up to the businesses that exploit and abuse them in these same spaces. The Ferrara Candy Company, a local Italian-owned business in nearby Forest Park, lost a $1.5 million dollar settlement in 2013 that "was brought on behalf of African American workers who alleged discriminatory hiring practices by two temporary staffing firms, based on Ferrara's request to hire employees. The suit claimed that African American workers were regularly denied work by the staffing companies in favor of hiring Latino workers (Hendrickson, 2016). Local community-based organizations helped nearly 1,000 Black workers who applied for jobs at the Ferrara Candy Company fight the hiring discrimination, as told through their stories, by holding protests as well as connecting them to lawyers who filed the lawsuit with the Equal Employment Opportunity Commission. Furthermore, companies like Ferrara openly stated that they prefer to hire Latinx workers due to their immigration status and their ability to hold off paying wages, threaten compensation and keep them silent. The division and animosity between the Black and Brown workers in factories and warehouses like Ferrara and Amazon often spill out into the community and make its way into the public schools, parks, and streets. Instead of dividing and conquering Black and Brown workers over profit, the local elected officials need to ask how we can unite our community and challenge the exploitation of its people, along with building racial coalitions across the Black and Latinx neighborhoods.

Norma Hernandez grew up in Maywood and came back to run for the unpaid trustee position as a "native daughter" even though she was completing her doctoral work in urban planning at the University of Illinois at Chicago campus. According to Norma, the educational system is designed to keep Black and Latinx folks less educated and thus less engaged. The small skirmishes between Black and Brown folks and the subsequent bickering are not helping to address the bigger problems in their community. Norma's platform was based on creating coalitions between the Black and Latinx communities in Maywood and working together to fight against those issues. For Norma, her goal was to join the others in campaigning for a cultural center at Triton College that would bring together Black and Brown solidarity. According to Norma Hernandez, "we should be using Fred Hampton's legacy of civic engagement and building a rainbow coalition. We have been robbed for decades of building Black-Brown coalitions."

Norma is very much aware of the white supremacy culture that pervades the inner-ring suburbs of Chicago and how Brown and Black students from her high school were counseled by the adults to go to the local community college, Triton College, how they would not be able to gain entrances at the larger universities, and how she did not belong in these institutions of higher education. It took a mental shift for Norma to let go of that deficit perspective that her high school counselor pegged on her, and subsequently it took her five years to complete her undergraduate degree. Today, she wants to improve these very same institutions by bringing in better leadership. She is not shameful anymore and sees herself as resilient for overcoming the trauma of racial tensions from her childhood and adolescence.

Figure 5.1 Norma and Her Family at Her Victory Celebration in Maywood. She is in the back with a beige sweater. *Source*: Norma Hernandez.

Norma attended East High School in Maywood during the 1990s and stated that her freshman year was a culture shock. Now the middle schools in Maywood are racially mixed, but before the year 2008, Latinx kids were going from all Latinx, K-8 elementary schools in Melrose Park to a high school that was predominantly Black. Norma did not have any experience working alongside Black students and noticed the self-segregation right away in the cafeteria where the Latinx students sat with each other, and the Black students sat with each other. There were always clicks she noticed in the classrooms based on race and how sitting with other Latinx students made her feel more comfortable. However, there was so much tension in the hallways and just bumping into someone from a different race led to fights. Since they were the racial minority, Norma felt that there was deliberate targeting of Latinx students by other Black students in the school which led to fights, theft of shoes and other school supplies, and an unhealthy animosity between these two racial groups.

Norma talked about how they had one friend who was Black and who hung out with all the Mexican kids at school because he had attended elementary school with them, and he grew up in Melrose Park. However, the other Black students often teased him for hanging out with all the Mexican kids and called him a traitor. Cross-racial friendships tend to dissipate by the time children reach adolescence and enter the high school where issues of identity become paramount. Whenever there were fights, Norma's friend was the first one to get targeted by the Black students intentionally because he hung out with the Mexican kids. Freshman year was the year of the race war in high school for Norma Hernandez. Many of her Mexican American friends skipped school so they would not get jumped. Then they started carrying pepper spray to school. Norma's brother went to East High School five years later when the number of Mexican American students went up, and he did not have the same race problems that she had endured in the first two years of racial integration.

The school principal at the time, who was a Black male administrator, could not understand how Norma was a straight-A student and was getting into fights, though she claimed it was to defend herself and/or her friends from being jumped, even in her Honors classes. Regardless of the environment being full of racial tensions, Norma had to see a social worker at the school to address her rage. At the same time, Norma talked about the low expectations set by the adults at the high school and how some of her teachers were blatantly racist such as the one who showed them movies of pit bull fights, set low expectations of them, and those she knew were not doing their job. The teachers categorized and sorted the Black and Brown students and moved them up and down the academic tracks, with an Advanced Placement (AP) track missing entirely from East High School. "The teachers were not aware of how much damage they did to us. They thought that we would only get a high school diploma. They called the area where we lived the Jungle," said Norma.

Upon reflection, Norma realizes that the demographic changes happened so fast that the high school district did not have enough resources to catch up to the changes. Norma argued that we need to build regional coalitions for the Latinx community in Illinois as the population was spreading in a radial fashion from the city of Chicago outwards toward the suburbs but without the building of social networks and structures. Rich white people are moving into the city, gentrifying it, and displacing Brown and Black people who were long-time residents, leading to the suburbanization of poverty. Now the urban issues are happening in sub/urban communities like Maywood where the economic, social, and political infrastructures are weaker. Norma went on to talk about participatory budgeting and challenging our local leaders by asking what they are doing with the village's money and where the tax dollars are going, especially the federally allotted pandemic dollars: "We need to use our collective powers to coexist in a healthy manner. We need more civic engagement. We need policies that are going to better our lives. Food scarcity and water scarcity are becoming a reality and will affect the poor suburbs soon. What are we doing about it now?"

Norma went on to describe her grassroots political campaign to become a board trustee at Triton College, how she raised money locally, and used her friends and family as campaign workers and managers. However, she did come across challenges from the political machine that had reigned over the inner-ring suburbs of Chicago. There was an Italian machine in Melrose Park run by Mayor Serpico. There was an Irish machine in nearby Forest Park south of them. In Maywood, there is a strong Black political machine that created a legacy of many powerful Black leaders in high positions, which also endorsed the Italian and Irish machines that had roots in Chicago ward politics (Pacyga, 2009). There was no Latinx political machine in the inner-ring suburbs, and the Latinx community in Maywood was too far away physically from the wards run by powerful Latinx politicians in the city of Chicago like Chuy Garcia and Sue Garza.

Maywood was the home to Chris Welch, Karen Yarborough, and Kimberly Lightford—all of them being very powerful Black leaders in the State of Illinois—who had their starts as school board presidents and made their way to the Senate Black Caucus. For decades, the politicians ran the school boards in Maywood and churned out leaders who moved up the ladder to the state legislature, along with reports of corruption and kickback schemes. There was also no newspapers reporting on the local corruption, and therefore the politicians were able to escape the scrutiny of the public eye for so long, until Michael Romain, a Black male resident of Maywood, set up the Village Free Press and began to report on local politics in Maywood. Many of these local politicians ran the school boards while sending their own children to private schools such as the nearby Lutheran and Catholic schools, as well as hiring family members to well-paid posts (Mihalopoulos, 2020).

However, due to the closing of some Catholic schools such as St. Joe's in wealthier Westchester, more white parents (close to 400 students) and more Latinx parents are sending their children to the local public schools but are not going to allow the Black and Italian politicians to run the school boards as their playpens, which was highlighted in chapter 4. There is a grassroots movement occurring in Maywood and its neighboring suburbs in which multiracial parents are acting collectively to challenge a draconian machine culture, along with Latinx leaders asking to be at the table with the others in power.

In afterthought, Norma Hernandez did not want to be running against a Black female candidate for the board trustee position. She wanted to work with this candidate and push out the older Italian men who controlled the college board and its monies. Nobody from the Italian and Black political machines endorsed her nor asked Norma to join their slate. As a Latinx candidate, she felt silenced along with her Latinx predecessors who launched political campaigns and lost to the machine. Now Norma saw an opportunity to make real changes for the Latinx community, which no longer was silent and was only growing louder. She went out and talked to the Black and Brown voters at many public spaces like post offices, libraries, and schools. Norma spoke to the Black constituents about the need to become allies and not advocate for different things; moreover, Norma received good feedback from the Black community, who were also tired of the Black political machine, about what they wanted for their schools, churches, and neighborhoods. In the end, she did receive praise from Black leaders and organizations in Maywood like Reverend Wiley and his congregation. Norma won the election because she was able to win both the Black and Latinx vote. Here are some excerpts from our interview with Norma Hernandez before her election results in April 2021:

Author: What does Black and Brown coalition building look like in Maywood?

Norma: Regardless of if I win or lose, I would love to sit down with Fred Hampton's son and have a conversation with him and say I am dedicated to community development work. He is disappointed that Maywood hasn't preserved his dad's legacy. When he goes to Maywood, many young people do not even know who his dad is. But when he goes to Oakland, California . . . everyone knows who his dad is. He wants to save his dad's legacy here. He spoke on a panel a few months ago at East High School and I went to introduce myself and I told him why . . . it is because of failed leadership in Maywood. I told him that his dad was a civic giant and that we should be able to have some kind of center for him. I told him I was running for the college board and wanted to do something about his dad's legacy. And that's how you build that Brown and Black coalition. Tying it into his legacy. Focusing on civic engagement. Having the center in Maywood. Maywood owning it. Having Black people owning it. We need to work with the high school students at East High School. Who will not fund it? You have to have people true to changing the internal system within. We need to get this next generation to be civically engaged.

Author: Will the Latinx population in Maywood support that vision?

Norma: I think so . . . if we tie it into his vision of the Rainbow Coalition. We are all working-class people oppressed under this capitalistic system. We need to be civically engaged and coexist at the same time. Your struggle is my struggle, and we need to come together and overcome our struggles. It is community work. Right now . . . who does not love Fred Hampton? The movie just came out and he is more famous than ever. Let's take advantage of that momentum. We have to become civically engaged and stop the divide and conquer mentality. If we want systematic change, we need to change the conditions of violence and also leaders who are advocating for systematic change. You cannot blame immigrants. Let's blame the white Italian mayors and their white supremacy. I want to change the conversation here. The desperation is real though. The machine does not want me to win.

THE LEGACY OF FRED HAMPTON

In 2021, to commemorate the 50th anniversary of Fred Hampton, the Maywood community wanted to bring his son, Fred Hampton Jr., to Maywood to create a center in memory of his slain father. Maywood led a community-wide book reading of *Black Against Empire* (2012) by Joshua Bloom and Waldo E. Martin Jr., which chronicles the life of Fred Hampton and the Black Panthers. However, there was not much consensus among the various leaders in Maywood as to how to engage with his legacy. There is no formal education of Fred Hampton in Maywood, and many of the students in the schools do not know who he was and what he fought for as a Black Panther. Yet, according to many of our research participants, there were complaints that the Black elders and leaders in Maywood still focused on Dr. Martin Luther King, Jr. and Colin Powell for Black history month—it was a regurgitated milk toast curriculum that was a hagiography of law-abiding Black men. The history curriculum did not engage the young students nor women. Alice, a student at the high school in the 1980s, stated that they were never taught about Fred Hampton and his connection to the Maywood community. Alice was also happy to see that they are finally bringing a better light to his life and legacy, hoping the Fred Hampton Center would create a space for conversations that might be challenging but might also normalize those conversations. The progressive ideology that Fred Hampton espoused would be one way to bridge the Black and Latinx communities.

The inability to recognize a tragedy is the inability to recognize a people (Synder, 2021). The tragic death of Maywood native, Fred Hampton, has gained recognition in recent years due to the release of two Hollywood films that have referenced him and his ideology (*The Trail of the Chicago 7*) as well as depicting his murder by the Chicago police (*Judas and the Black Messiah*). The memory of Fred Hampton has been resurrected in Maywood, and the interpretation of his past has changed how we view historical events today. For so long, students were never taught Black history in the school district beyond the few paragraphs about slavery and Dr. Martin Luther King, Jr.'s peaceful Civil Rights Movement. They were never taught about the race riots that occurred in their very same community, and Fred Hampton was finally recognized in 2021 by local elected officials. In the 1960s, Black residents of Maywood became tired of being treated differently by the Italian Melrose Park gangs who would attack Black youth in Maywood, who also faced bullying from whites in Maywood itself as well as discrimination in the high schools and public parks (Rice, 2018; Rolland-Diamond, 2019).

In 2021, there was also a national movement led by Republican lawmakers to ban the teaching of critical race theory and how policies and the law perpetuate systemic racism, leading to the creation of repressive memory laws and what students can and cannot remember from American history (Stout & LeMee, 2021). Teaching children and college students about racism is purported to create divisiveness in our nation and perpetuate the narrative of whites as oppressors. At the same time, curriculum targeting the teaching of ethnic studies, the history, culture, and social contributions of people of color, such as Black history, Latinx history, and Asian American history, has been adopted in Democratic states and cities. In Illinois, the school code was changed in 2021 so that all public schools are required to teach Black history which includes ancient African history prior to slavery, the long-term effects of slavery, and the renaissance of the American Civil Rights Movement, as well as concepts like Black joy, Black excellence, Black historical contention, and the contributions of Black women and LGBTQ individuals (Gaines, 2021). At the same time, there is a great degree of questioning and doubt as to how the 82% of teachers in Illinois who are white will teach Black history effectively, since they lack perspective and authority on Black lives. The same can be said of Maywood where a majority white teaching staff did not fully address Black and Latinx history and culture in its curriculum.

Meanwhile, many of the residents we interviewed also did not espouse the "radical" views of the Black Panther Party that Fred Hampton held. The identity politics within the Black community of Maywood and who should come to represent the native son is often neglected but has been resurrected as the demographics shifted to become more Latinx. The central argument is that the new Latinx residents of Maywood should be held accountable for the Black history of Maywood that preceded their migration into Maywood. Yet, to what degree is Maywood self-censoring the life of Fred Hampton? Does the mention of Fred Hampton cause distress in the community? Is the memory of Fred Hampton being treated unfairly? Can you teach about Fred Hampton without a reference to the Black Panther Party movement which may make some Black residents uncomfortable? What is the emotional stake, feelings of guilt and shame, that Maywood residents have about not carrying on the torch for Fred Hampton? What connection do they have to his narrative? Had there been discrimination and personal prejudice against Fred Hampton and where did it originate from? Did the murder of Fred Hampton lead to the expansion of Black liberation in Maywood? Was Maywood forever altered by his death?

The long silence around Fred Hampton was evident in the interviews we conducted. There were historical markers that pointed to him in Maywood, such as the Fred Hampton swimming pool, but the memory management of his legacy is beginning to change. People are no longer feeling shame from his legacy since the Black Lives Matter movement; rather, they are taking pride in what he had been saying all along—the Civil Rights Movement failed Black America. There is a movement for great self-awareness and self-correction about Hampton's legacy building. What white people, the FBI, and police officers say about Fred Hampton and the Black Panther Party is no longer valid. The question now is what Black and Latinx members of Maywood have to say about Fred Hampton's legacy. We are searching for a new language to talk about race now because we no longer have to abide by the white gaze. We no longer have to make white people feel good about themselves. The rhetoric is changing, and progressive leaders are paving the way. This sentiment is clear in this interview excerpt from Gina, a Black female teacher and school principal in Maywood, talking about Fred's legacy as well as the roots to her own legacy:

Author: Have you heard about the plan to build a Fred Hampton Center at Triton College because that's where he had gone to college? What do you think of the idea of teaching Black history in the Maywood schools, so students know about Fred Hampton? Is that the way to unite everybody? The new board trustee's argument, Norma Hernandez, is that to unite, you know, Latinx and Black Maywood . . . We need to focus on this legacy of Fred Hampton and really get behind creating a Fred Hampton Center. What do you think?

Gina: I like the idea of the Fred Hampton Center. I feel like he is appealing to . . . my sister actually knew him by the way. He's pivotal. He makes me proud to be a Maywoodian. Will that unite the Hispanics? Probably not unless they have some form of connection to Fred Hampton. That's not going to get them to connect to Fred Hampton or Maywood. We have to find what would connect Hispanics to Maywood. Yeah, and not make this cookie cutter: "Oh well. It's Fred Hampton. So, everybody's gonna flock to this." No, if you're gonna make a Fred Hampton Center, maybe we should do a multicultural center and highlight Fred Hampton but also highlight some of the accomplishments that Hispanics have made in Maywood . . . Right? Highlight that because people want to see that . . . they want to see how does this connect to this? How does Fred Hampton's legacy connect to the legacy of Hispanics in Maywood? How does your own legacy connect to him? What is everyone in Maywood's connection to Fred Hampton? What did he do with the Black Panther Party that the Hispanics can connect with? If you don't have that, there is no Fred Hampton Center. It's gotta be about his legacy but for people who are living in Maywood today. If he was still living in their house across the street from Irving Elementary, would he include everybody, right? 'cause I'm pretty sure he would . . . 'cause he wasn't anti-Hispanic. But other than that, it's just a Fred Hampton Center, just like the Fred Hampton Pool. You will have people going, but they're not gonna understand the significance of it. It's just a pool for them.

The Commemoration of Fred Hampton

Fred Hampton was born on August 28, 1948, to Francis Allen (father) and Iberia Hampton (mother), who had migrated from rural Louisiana to Chicago seeking a better life for their children. Fred was the youngest of three and had an older brother and sister who he was close to throughout his short life. In 1955, the family moved to Argo, Illinois, where his father worked in a local corn product factory, and they lived in a home near Mamie and Emmett Till. In fact, Iberia would watch over Emmett Till, when he was a child; therefore, the news of his horrific murder in Mississippi, the national outcry, and the open-casket funeral in Chicago greatly impacted the Hampton family. In 1958, the family moved to Maywood and Fred Hampton attended elementary and secondary school there. His two-story brick home was directly across from his elementary school where he was known to be a bright and social child and quite talkative, even though he was teased for the shape of his head and his slight lisp. Both his parents worked in the nearby factories along with their working-class, Black neighbors (Haas, 2010).

At his elementary school in Maywood, Fred Hampton was the captain of the patrol boys, a unit responsible for controlling traffic and helping students cross the streets—similar to the Smart Routes program headed by the CSPL today as mentioned in chapter 4. Fred Hampton also drew Black and white classmates into his "morning homework sessions" before school and loved to read history books (Village Free Press, 1969). Fred had gained the nickname "king of signifying" for his verbal games known as playing the dozens/calling the nines in which Black boys often stood in a circle on the playground and made "Your Momma" jokes and insults to make their opponent cringe in embarrassment and lose. However, Fred was known to apologize at the end of the rounds after he had won the verbal duels at school. On Saturday mornings, Fred Hampton would round up the neighborhood children, take whatever money they had, go to the local grocery store and buy food, and then come back to Fred's house to cook the food and serve breakfast for the needier children in the neighborhood. The Black Panthers would be known later for their free breakfast program offered to children in the Chicago public schools due to Fred's legacy. Of course, Fred had watched his mother do similar work such as feeding over 700 union workers when they were on strike at their local factory (Haas, 2010).

At age 14, Fred Hampton organized a student chapter of the Maywood NAACP, which grew to 700 members. From 1962 to 1966, Fred Hampton was an active student at East High School in Maywood. He was elected to the school's Interracial Cross Section Committee and helped "white students to acknowledge and reform their personal racist outlooks" (Village Free Press, 1969). One issue that he brought to the school's administration was the selection of five white female students as Homecoming Queen candidates when the school was at least a quarter Black in student population. This cause for more equal representation of Black students led Fred to organize a school protest. He was also elected president of Junior Achievement, organized the class picnic, and led campaigns against racist conditions at the high school. After one of his peers, Eugene Moore, was unjustly arrested, Fred Hampton led a march to the Maywood police station, where they protested and rallied until Moore was released. Moore went on to become Maywood's first Black state representative, due to the role of Fred Hampton, and helped build the political pipeline from Maywood to the state legislature which Chris Welch, Karen Yarbrough and Kimberly Lightford also followed decades later (Village Free Press, 1969).

While in high school, Fred Hampton held several jobs such as working as a stock boy at the local grocery store to earn money for tuition at Triton College. During those high school years, he advocated for summer jobs for Black teens in Maywood as well as an integrated swimming pool since Maywood was far from Lake Michigan. Fred Hampton's organizing work led to his

Figure 5.2   Bust of Fred Hampton. *Source*: Samina Hadi-Tabassum.

appointment as the youth representative for the West Suburban Chapter of the NAACP (Martin, 2021). After finishing high school in 1966, Fred Hampton continued his activism, marching several times with Dr. Martin Luther King Jr. when he came to Chicago to fight for equal treatment of Black residents in housing, jobs, and schools. However, after witnessing the violence against Black protesters by angry white mobs in Chicago, Fred Hampton moved away from Dr. Martin Luther King, Jr.'s ideology of non-violence and the NAACP platform and moved toward the growing youth-led Black Panther Party in Oakland, California, which advocated for self-defense (Haas, 2010).

In November 1968, Bobby Rush, retired US representative and then-Black Panther and mentor to former President Barack Obama, received a mandate from the national party to start a chapter in Chicago. After meeting Fred Hampton at marches and protests, Bobby Rush opened a Black Panther chapter here on the West Side of Chicago in which Fred Hampton became the chairman and Bobby Rush the deputy minister (Martin, 2021). The Black Panthers instilled Black pride in the community, fought against police brutality and the wrongful conviction of Black and Brown people, used unconventional strategies to challenge the government and machine politics, youth engagement and community programs like the free breakfast program for children and a medical clinic, and for forging a multiracial Rainbow Coalition with the radical and purposeful inclusion of all oppressed people (Rhodes, 2017). The Black Power Movement and the Black Panther Party formed on college campuses and ignited a radicalism that integrated art, poetry, music, and performance along with collective organizing and militarism.

The Black radical tradition is rooted in a set of ideas and practices of grassroots insurgencies that challenged slavery and racial capitalism at its inception and paradox. Cedric Robinson in his book *Black Movements in America* (1997) argued that Black Radicalism critically emerges from African culture, languages, and beliefs and the impulse to escape enslavement. The influence of revolutionaries like Toussaint Louverture, who created the Age of Revolution, led to the movements and revolts that followed in the Americas. The language of justice subsequently affected Black thought and action for generations to come. Furthermore, African American framers of the constitution and Black Bostonians noted the paradox in how the white patriots evoked "liberty" and "freedom" while also upholding slavery and a state of terror. There was no loyalty to place, people, or principle for the enslaved Black population who were three-fifths of a person and the property of white slave owners. There was a rejection of the new republic's ideology of white supremacy and Black racial inferiority through words and deeds; instead, Black Americans wanted to pursue liberty just as the Haitians did before them (Ortiz, 2018). They did not accept the "American exceptionalism" theory developed by white Americans stating that the slaves in America were inferior and therefore unable to revolt and gain self-rule. Black slaves, Black inden-tured servants, and free Blacks all set out to prove them wrong and engage in the praxis of resistance and the ideals of civil rights and racial equality for over a century leading up to the Black Lives Matter movement of today.

In the 1970s, the Black Panther Party was seen as a threat to the white establishment in power, due to their foundation in Black Radicalism, and which included the Irish political machine in Chicago run by Mayor Daley, the white Chicago police force, Cook County State's Attorney Edward V. Hanrahan, and FBI Director J. Edgar Hoover (Mitchell, 2019). On December 4, 1969, the Chicago police raided the home of Fred Hampton and the Black Panther Party on the West Side and murdered him at 4:45 a.m. with heavy gunfire along with other members and with the help of an FBI informant from within the party who had drugged Fred Hampton earlier that evening. Information of the murder was on the radio and a neighbor had stopped Fran-cis and Iberia Hampton from going to work the next morning to convey the news of his death (Hass, 2010). One of the survivors in the police raid was Deborah Johnson (known today as Akua Njeri), the partner of Fred Hampton and the mother of their soon-to-be child, Fred Hampton Junior. The Chicago chapter of the Black Panther Party was dismantled in 1973, but the legacy of the Rainbow Coalition lives on today through the work of Reverend Jesse Jackson in Chicago. Years after his death and through multiple trials and the help of Congressman Bobby Rush, the death of Fred Hampton was confirmed as the collusion of the FBI and the Chicago political machine of white politi-cians and police (Martin, 2021).

The assassinations of famous Black figures from the Civil Rights Move-ment can shed light on American history. Fallen heroes of the movement were gunned down and their deaths led to protest and movements to keep the mission going (Ortiz, 2018). Fred Hampton fought against police brutality, along with many other collective struggles such as poverty, and in the end, he was killed by the heavily armed white police force. Frederick Douglas, almost a century before, warned of the oppression from the American military and how militarism can destroy democracy, just as it did in 1960s Chicago. There are many ways to be an American; we have to re-envision our history and our struggles more accurately and more democratically. Maywood was an Underground Railroad site, trying to build a culture of resistance by orga-nizing Lutheran churches and fraternal organizations for the safe passage of slaves from the South to the North. Fred Hampton was a son of the North where the Black community was besieged by segregation, redlining, resi-dential covenants, re-enslavers, and anti-Black race riots. We must avoid the trap of historical amnesia and raise up the voices of the people in Maywood who want to build democracy across the borders and overcome the paralyz-ing myths that have divided the people of Maywood along communal lines.

The Fred Hampton Center

On August 29, 2021, Fred Hampton Jr. came to Maywood with his mother and inaugurated the Fred Hampton Social Justice Room in East High School. The media was present, along with many local officials and politicians such as Representative Bobby Rush. There were wonderful speeches describing and telling the stories of Fred Hampton and his legacy in Maywood. Students at East High School created a video montage marking his imprint on their lives today. Cook County Clerk, Karen Yarbrough (2022), presented a resolution to commemorate his direct impact on Maywood, harking back to when her own father was the mayor of Maywood during his assassination, and to create a Fred Hampton Scholarship in his name.

In addition to the Fred Hampton Center at East High School, there is also a movement to preserve "the only surviving building with ties to Hampton's activism . . . his childhood home, a two-flat in suburban Maywood that was rescued from foreclosure earlier this year" on 804 South 17th Avenue (Romain, 2021). Fred Hampton Jr. gained a landmark designation for the house through the help of Representative Bobby Rush, through petitions and signatures and the Black collective organizations in and around Maywood such as Save the Hampton House, Black Panther Party Cubs, Best of Proviso Township, Engaged Berwyn, Suburban Unity Alliance, Maywood Fine Arts Association, Immanuel Lutheran Church, and No Child Goes Hungry. The hope is for the Hampton House to become a community center with a recording studio inside for the youth, a community garden, a library, and other ways to develop social capital and networks (Gunderson, 2021).

To commemorate the 55th anniversary of the Chicago Black Panther Party, there is a refurbished Hampton family bench outside the historical Maywood home, a Free Library, and a "Feed 'Em All" community fridge and pantry (Romain, 2021). It was a beautiful Friday afternoon event on the day of the commemoration and rooted in bottom-up grassroots activism with people from the local community as well as people from across the world, across racial lines, and across generations, as well as political actors from the Black political machine, waiting to hear Fred Hampton Jr., along with his mother, Mother Akua Njeri, gathered to unveil a space that is a testament to American history.

The Revolution in Trust

The election of President Barack Obama in 2008 and his re-election in 2012 showed that large populations of Latinx voters supported the first Black President of the United States, even though media skeptics kept claiming that the Latinx establishment would not support a Black candidate: "In contrast,

Figure 5.3   Commemoration of Fred Hampton by Cook County Clerk, Karen Yarborough.
Source: The image comes from the Proviso Township Democratic Organization website and the Office of Karen Yarborough, https://provisodems.org/bpp55resolution.

Figure 5.4   Childhood Home of Fred Hampton on 17th Avenue. *Source*: Paul Goyette.

Figure 5.5   Volunteers Work on Making Enhancements to the Community Refrigerator Outside of the Hampton House in Maywood on October 15. *Source*: Paul Goyette.

96 percent of African Americans, 67 percent of Latinx Americans, and 63 percent of Asian Americans voted for Obama" (Ortiz, 2018, p. 177). Latinx workers supported his platform on labor rights as well as his initiatives to reform immigration. The Obama organizers also tapped into multilingual resources and local networks to get the Latinx vote out, along with speeches in key areas of the country, which were symbolic at first but then led to the DREAM Act and President Obama's support of undocumented students. Subsequently, Black leaders like Reverend Jesse Jackson and Reverend Al Sharpton came out to support Latinx causes such as voter rights and immigration reform, as well as challenging repressive state laws such as Arizona's SB 1070 which invited racial profiling of the Latinx population and others who may look or sound "foreign," including many US citizens who have lived in America their entire lives. Arizona's HB 2281 then banned the teaching of ethnic studies to repress identity politics in this Republican stronghold.

The general ethos in contemporary politics is a dominant belief in mistrust. Political factions divide the nation, leading to feelings and emotions of "animosity, resentment and paranoia" (Kahloon, 2021, p. 67). The politics of Maywood reflect the politics of the nation today and the culture of narcissism and a crisis of confidence in our leaders. Maywood is no different than other places in America where people are questioning institutions and the people who lead them with punitive authority. For our multiethnic democracy to prevail in which no one group is in power, there needs to be trust, but Americans are becoming less trusting of each other and less civil toward each other.

According to the Pew Research Center, this declining trust in institutions and in each other makes it harder to solve key problems, and Black and Brown people with less income and education are markedly more likely to be low-trusters (Rainie, Keeter, & Perrin, 2019). This lack of interpersonal trust among ourselves is also seen as a form of cultural sickness due to increased loneliness and excessive individualism and pointing to the decline of our nation. We no longer can rely on each other for telling the truth and being honest. We are becoming suspicious of each other's intentions and often lead conversations with cynicism. When we do not trust each other, we become apathetic and disengaged with what is happening in our community. We saw evidence of group tribalism and muffled voices in the school board meetings and in other social media platforms where insult-ridden remarks and sensational cries were aired publicly.

However, as the public trust waned for the school board and the village governance, interpersonal trust did grow among the parents who created their own collective spaces where they challenged partisan views, regardless of their race and class backgrounds. Civic duty was evoked as parents wrote letters to the superintendent, created safe passage routes for children, stood in lines to speak at the board meetings and recorded the meetings on their phones when the district no longer did the live streaming. Through organizations like the Coalition for Spiritual and Personal Leadership and Neighbors of Maywood Community Organization, civic virtues are still being upheld as societal dilemmas of poverty and crime still ravish sub/urban communities like Maywood. The Pew Trust Research also supports the idea of pro-collaboration even when overall trust dissipates and differentiates between social trust among neighbors and the trust of institutions and politics (Rainie, Keeter, & Perrin, 2019). Even though the new mayor of Maywood was repairing the frayed social fabric in Maywood, trust is a fundamental feature of humanity that can restore faith in one's community and local institutions and the power of communal belief in the good of Maywood—how can we trust our local bank if we cannot trust each other.

In fact, the central narrative of human history is a story of trust and mistrust. The more we trusted each other the more we began to create social groups in which we shared food and ate together around the fire, sitting on stones laid out in a circle. This sense of community led to larger human brains, and an enlarged neocortex, which provided us with greater cognitive, linguistic, and social powers (Kahloon, 2021). We felt commonality with this tribe of a hundred and began to trust them. We created in-groups and out-groups and trusted those in our in-group tribe and distrusted those in the out-group, outside of our village, and became hostile to cultural outsiders. We sustained these communal ties through rituals and customs which we carry on even today. The question then remains how we can come to trust beyond our tribe and the need for a special kind of leadership to build ties with out-groups and expand our borders to thousands and millions.

Over human history, religion became a powerful way to build alliances across one's tribe and create a larger collective of people who believed in a common purpose and meaning of life, addressing the needs of the poor and disenfranchised, and reinforcing the idea of a retributive God and deities and their worrisome prophets on foot—all of them thriving in Maywood today (Kahloon, 2021). The exchange of goods, ideas, and our basic needs for food and shelter allowed us to trust each other, feel a sense of belonging, and fight off loneliness from eating alone. Religion also brought a fear of Hell and punitive end outcomes from earthly sins like lying, cheating, stealing, and violence. We then built trust-generating institutions like the government, work, schools, churches, and banks. Yet, it is the heightened increase in racial and cultural diversity within the United States that is challenging our human brain to expand beyond our tribe of one hundred and not get triggered by those from the out-group. This changing demographic of a majority-minority country "exacerbates our tribal nature and fuels mistrust of the Other"; tribalism can build trust internally, creating kinship systems, and a mistrust externally that gets primed at various times and places (Kahloon, 2021, p. 70).

We agree that there has been a change in our American society in which we have lost trust in institutions but have increased trust in specific individuals. The term "distributed trust" is being used today to describe how we no longer trust vertical organizations of power and authority (presidents, principals, popes, and CEOs at the helm with power flowing downwards) and instead trust organizations in which trust flows horizontally with various sectors and subgroups sharing power and authority that moves from the ground up (Botsman, 2017). We know now that politicians are fallible, clergy are unholy, and the daily news anchor is no longer honest. Trust now falls with individuals rather than with institutions, and we are collecting social stocks of trust. A revolution in trust is occurring on many levels—from global, to national, to local—and the relationships we have forged in society are changing rapidly and demythologizing the Rainbow Coalition.

And so, the real question is how much trust is there between the Black and Latinx communities in Maywood? Where does trust repose? When and with whom? Will the new mayor's push for collective trust triumph? Will the successful transactions of interracial groups like the Coalition for Spiritual and Public Leadership represent much of the population? Will parents begin to honor the school boards again and without conspiracy, doubt, and hesitancy? Page (2004) wants us to give attention to interethnic conflict and political turf wars, school board feuds, employment arguments, discrimination complaints, racial profiling; however, there is also a need to examine the countless everyday encounters and interactions, the intermarriages and camaraderie, which take place each day in urban and rural America. It is a new racial paradigm.

The acrimonious tribalism between the Black and Latinx communities will need to be suspended if Maywood wants to forge ahead in order not to be subsumed in the culture wars. The community members must learn to trust each other and seek resolutions that bring peace and prosperity for all. It takes human agency along with public policy and private initiative to revive a community. But the process must occur from the bottom-up and include everyday people, preservationists, developers, small business owners, social reformers, faith-based organizations, nonprofit organizations, and grassroots institutions of all kinds. There will be villains and machine style politics along with a positive saga of courageous people who with patience and mutual respect can work together on issues and use common ground as a platform to work out differences.

Figure 5.6 Community Events and Organizations Posted on the Maywood Village Website. *Source*: Village of Maywood Community Newsletter, https://mailchi.mp/maywood-il/maywood-community-news november-2021?e=5953cbdf0d.

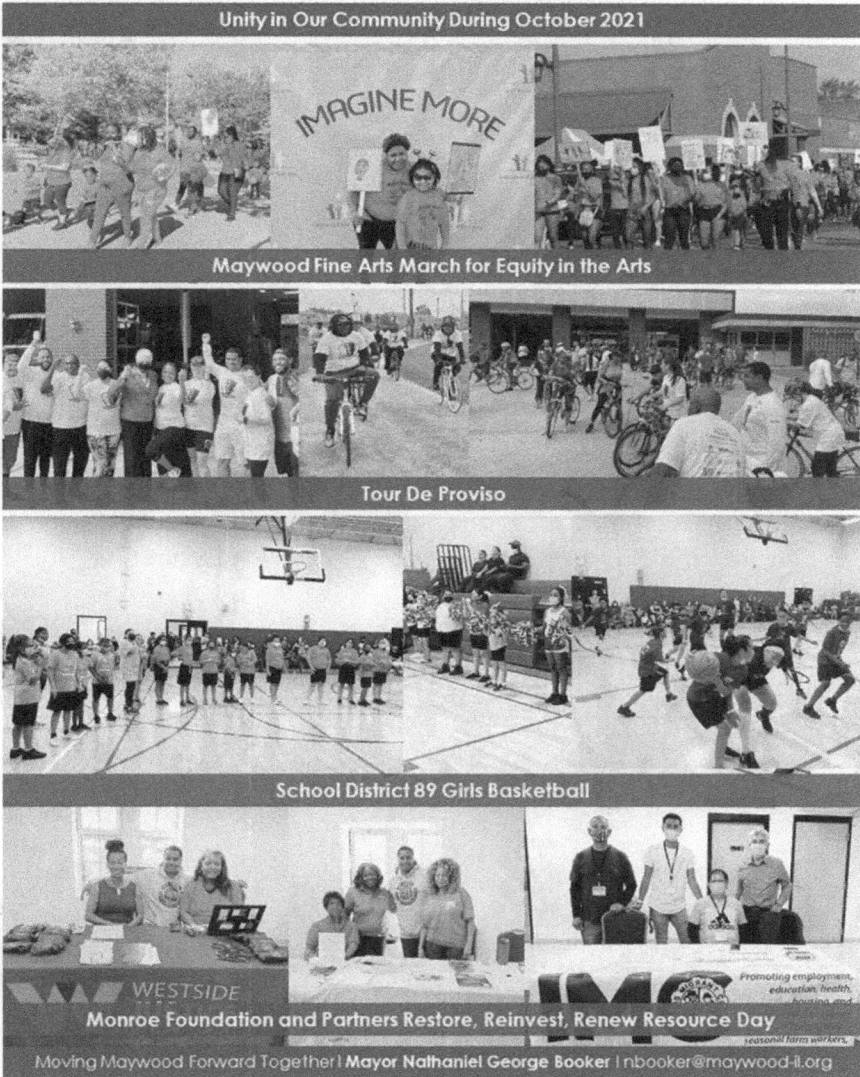

Figure 5.7 School and Community Events Posted on the Maywood Village Website.
Source: Village of Maywood Community Newsletter, https://mailchi.mp/maywood-il/
maywood-community-news-november-2021?e=5953cbdf0d.

Bibliography

Activist Toolkit. (2021). *Stand with Your Community*. Voter Guide: Maywood. Retrieved from https://www.activisttoolkit.org/

Al-Mansour, K. (1993). *Betrayal by Any Other Name: An Honest Appraisal of Black and Hispanic American Leadership over the Last 100 Years*. San Francisco, CA: First African Arabian Press.

Alba, R. & Logan, J. R. (1993). Minority proximity to whites in suburbs: an individual-level analysis of segregation. *American Journal of Sociology, 98*, pp. 1388–1427.

Alba, R. & Nee, V. (2003). *Remaking the American Mainstream: Assimilation and Contemporary Immigration*. Cambridge, MA: Harvard University Press.

Alba, R., Rumbaut, R. G. & Marotz, K. (2005). A distorted nation: perceptions of racial/ethnic group sizes and attitudes toward immigrants and other minorities. *Social Forces, 84*, 2, pp. 901–919.

Alim, H. S. (2004). Hip hop nation language. In E. Finegan and J. Rickford (eds.), *Language in the USA*. New York, NY: Cambridge University Press, pp. 387–409.

Alim, H. S. (2005). Critical language awareness in the United States: revisiting the issues and revising the pedagogies in a resegregated society. *Educational Researcher, 34*, 24, pp. 24–31.

Alim, H. S. (2009). Translocal style communities: Hip Hop youth as theorists of style, language, and globalization. *Pragmatics, 19*, 1, pp. 111–135.

Alim, H. S. & Smitherman, G. (2012). *Articulate while Black: Barack Obama, Language, and Race in the US*. Oxford: Oxford University Press.

Allport, G. (1954). *The Nature of Prejudice*. Cambridge, MA: Addison-Wesley.

Alsbury, T. L. & Gore, P. (2015). *Improving School Board Effectiveness: A Balanced Governance Approach*. Cambridge, MA: Harvard Education Press.

American Library Association. (2022). *Indigenous Tribes of Chicago*. Retrieved from https://www.ala.org/aboutala/offices/diversity/chicago-indigenous

Amoruso, C. (August 26, 2005). L.A.'s Black-Brown divisions deepen. *Hispanic American Village Editor (IMDiversity.com)*.

Anderson, B. (1993). *Imagined Communities: Reflections on the Origin and Spread of Nationalism.* New York: Verso.

Anderson, J. (April 2017). Commentary: the history of education for the next America. *American Educational Research Journal, 54*, 1, pp. 75S–78S.

Andrews, R. (2011). Religious communities, immigration and social cohesion in rural areas: evidence from England. *Rural Sociology, 76*, 4, pp. 535–561.

Arias, M. B. (2005). The impact of Brown on Latinos: a study of transformation of policy intentions. *Teachers College Record, 107*, 9, pp. 1974–1998.

Arriola, C. (1995). Knocking on the schoolhouse door: Mendez v. Westminster, equal protection, public education, and Mexican Americans in the 1940's. *La Raza Law Journal, 8*, pp. 166–207.

Asher, C. & Branch-Smith, E. (2005). Precarious space: majority Black suburbs and their public schools. *Teachers College Record, 107*, pp. 1956–1973.

Avila, O. (February 8, 2006). Africans in Mexico: a blunt history. *Chicago Tribune.*

Badillo, D. (2006). *Latinos and the New Immigrant Church.* Baltimore, MD: John Hopkins University Press.

Banks, A. M. (2020). The continuing legacy of the national origin quotas. *William & Mary Journal of Race, Gender & Social Justice, 27*, 1, pp. 1–32.

Baker-Bell, A. (2020). Dismantling anti-black linguistic racism in English language arts classrooms: toward an anti-racist black language pedagogy. *Theory into Practice, 59*, 1, pp. 8–21.

Baker, C. (2006). *Foundations of Bilingual Education and Bilingualism.* Clevedon: Multilingual Matters, Ltd.

Bakhtin, M. M. (1982). *The Dialogic Imagination.* Austin, TX: University of Texas Press.

Ballesteros, C. (May 28, 2021). Illinois legislature passes bill to close state's immigration detention centers. *The Injustice Watch.*

Barajas, H. L. & Ronnkvist, A. (2007). Racialized space: Framing Latino and Latina experience in public schools. *Teachers College Record, 109*, 6, pp. 1517–1538.

Baron, D. (2000). Ebonics and the politics of English. *World Englishes, 19*, 1, pp. 5–19.

Bassinger, H. G. (1994). We are all racists now. *The New York Times Magazine.* Retrieved from https://www.nytimes.com/1994/05/29/magazine/we-re-all-racist-now.html

Bauer, K. (April 1, 2016). Why you should visit Englewood, Chicago's 'diamond in the rough. *DNAInfo.*

Bazán-Figueras, P. & Figueras, S. J. (2014). The future of Spanglish: global or tribal? *Perspectives on Global Development & Technology, 13*, 1/2, pp. 261–266.

Bell, D. A. (2001). Revised decisions: dissenting. In J. M. Balkin & B. A. Ackerman (eds.), *What Brown v. Board of Education Should Have Said: The Nation's Top Legal Experts Review America's Landmark Civil Rights Decision.* New York: New York University Press, pp. 185–200.

Bell, D. A. (1980). Brown v. Board of Education and the interest-convergence dilemma. *Harvard Law Review, 93*, 3, pp. 518–533.

Benner, A. D. & Graham, S. (2009). The transition to high school as a developmental process among multiethnic urban youth. *Child Development, 80*, pp. 356–376.

Benner, A. D. & Graham, S. (2011). Latino Adolescents' experiences of discrimination across the first 2 years of high school: correlates and influences on educational outcomes. *Child Development, 82*, 2, pp. 508–519. doi:10.1111/j.1467-8624.2010.01524.x

Bhabha, H. (1994). *The Location of Culture.* London: Routledge.

Bierly, R. (May 2, 2019). *Spanglish: The Validity of Spanglish as a Language.* Panoramas Journal: Center for Latin American Studies. Retrieved from https://www.panoramas.pitt.edu/opinion-and-interviews/spanglish-validity-spanglish-language

Bloom, J. & Martin Jr., W. E. (2016). *Black against Empire: The History and Politics of the Black Panther Party.* Chicago, IL: University of Chicago Press.

Botsman, R. (2017). *Who Can You Trust? How Technology Brought Us Together and Why It Might Drive Us Apart.* New York: Public Affairs Press.

Bourdieu, P. (2020). *Habitus and Field* (2nd ed.). Cambridge: Polity Press.

Bowean, L. (2006). Blacks and Hispanics set unity March, rally group tries to build south suburban coalition. *Chicago Tribune.*

Bowler, S., Nicholson, S. & Segura, G. (2006). Earthquakes and aftershocks: race, direct democracy, and partisan change. *American Journal of Political Science, 50,* 1, pp. 146–159.

Bowman, N. (2012). Structural diversity and close interracial relationships in college. *Educational Researcher, 41,* 4, pp. 133–135.

Boykin, W. A. (1986). The triple quandary and the schooling of Afro-American children. In U. Neisser (ed.), *The School Achievement of Minority Children.* Hillside, NJ: Lawrence Erlbaum, pp. 55–72.

Briggs, J. E. (January 2, 2006). Housing boom's two sides detailed study defines strain in gentrifying areas. *Chicago Tribune.*

Brisman, A. (2006). Meth chic and the tyranny of the immediate: reflections on the culture-drug/drug-crime relationships. *North Dakota Law Review, 82,* 4, pp. 1273–1396.

Brockenbrough, E. (2012). Emasculation blues: Black male teachers' perspectives on gender and power in the teaching profession. *Teachers College Record, 114,* 5, pp. 1–43.

Brown, E. E. & Brooks, F. (2006). African American and Latino perceptions of cohesion in a multiethnic neighborhood. *American Behavioral Scientist, 50,* pp. 258–275.

Brown, K. J. & Weil, F. D. (2020). Strangers in the neighborhood: violence and neighborhood boundaries. *Journal of Contemporary Ethnography, 49,* 1, pp. 86–117.

Buchanan, S. (July 27, 2005). Tensions mounting between Blacks and Latinos nationwide. *Intelligence Report* (Southern Poverty Law Center).

Burgess, E. & Bogue, D. (eds.) (1967). *Urban Sociology.* Chicago, IL: University of Chicago Press.

Calhoun, D. (2020). Fanon's Lexical intervention: writing blackness in Black Skin, White Masks*, *Paragraph, 43,* 2, pp. 159–178.

Camarillo, A. (2007). Cities of color: the new racial frontier in California's minority-majority cities. *Pacific Historical Review, 76,* 1, pp. 1–28.

Campbell, H. (2015). Escaping identity: border zones as places of evasion and cultural reinvention. *Journal of the Royal Anthropological Institute, 21,* 2, pp. 296–312.

Carter, P. (2006). Straddling boundaries: identity, culture and school. *Sociology of Education, 79,* pp. 304–328.

Cave, D. (October 24, 2004). In a divided town, a question of hate, or cash? *The New York Times.*

Census Scope. (2021). *Segregation: Neighborhood Exposure by Race.* Retrieved from censusscope.org https://www.censusscope.org/us/s17/p47774/print_chart _exposure.html

Center for Applied Linguistics. (2022). Dual language program directory. Retrieved from http://webapp.cal.org/duallanguage/

Chamberlin, E. (1974). *Chicago and Its Suburbs.* Chicago, IL: Arno Press. (Original work published 1874).

City-Data. (2021). *Maywood, Illinois.* Retrieved from https://www.city-data.com/city /Maywood-Illinois.html

Connolly, H. (1973). Black movement into the suburbs: suburbs doubling their black populations during the 1960s, *Urban Affairs Review, 9,* p. 1. doi:10.1177/107808747300900104

Cho, G. (2000). The role of heritage language in social interactions and relationships: reflections from a language minority group. *Bilingual Research Journal, 24,* 4, pp. 369–384.

Cholo, B. (May 19, 2004). School plan stirs fear: crowding may send Latino kids to new ground–a black school. *Chicago Tribune.*

Cholo, B. & Rado, D. (2004, May 10). Latino students often trapped in lagging schools – *Brown v. Board of Education*: 50 years later. *Chicago Tribune.*

Chronis, K. (March 16, 2022). 'He went to jab me': Proviso board member recounts explosive confrontation with superintendent caught on video. *Fox32 Chicago.*

Coalition for Spiritual and Public Leadership. (2022). *Our Mission,* Retrieved April 6, 2022, from https://www.csplaction.org/en/mission

Cobb, J. (March 6, 2016). The matter of Black Lives: a new kind of movement found its moment. What will its future be? *The New Yorker.*

Connolly, H. X. (1973). Movement into the suburbs: suburbs doubling their Black populations during the 1960s. *Urban Affairs Review, 9,* pp. 91–111.

Contreras, A. R. & Valverde, L. A. (Summer 1994). The impact of Brown on the education of Latinos. *The Journal of Negro Education, 63,* 3, pp. 470–481.

Contreras, A. R. (2004). Impact of Brown on the multicultural education of Hispanic Americans. *The Journal of Negro Education, 73,* 3, pp. 314–327.

Corsino, L. (2014). *The Neighborhood Outfit: Organized Crime in Chicago Heights.* Chicago, IL: University of Illinois Press.

Cooke, T. & Marchant, S. (2006). The changing intrametropolitan location of high-poverty neighborhoods in the US, 1990–2000. *Urban Studies, 43,* 11, pp. 1971–1989.

Costandi, M. (2012). How the brain views race. *Scientific American.* Retrieved from https://www.scientificamerican.com/article/how-brain-views-race/

Cottle, M. (September 6, 2021). America's school board meetings are getting weird — and scary. *The New York Times.*

Coward, K. (November 28, 2012). CPS stretches curriculum to include violence counseling. *Chicago Tribune.*

Craig, C. J. (2000). Narrative inquiries of geographically close schools: stories given, lived and told. *Teachers College Record, 109*, 1, pp. 160–191.

Crenshaw, Kimberle. (1989). Demarginalizing the intersection of race and sex: a Black feminist critique of antidiscrimination doctrine, feminist theory and anti-racist politics. *University of Chicago Legal Forum, 1*, Article 8. Retrieved from http://chicagounbound.uchicago.edu/uclf/vol1989/iss1/8

Daniels, C. (June 27, 2021). Youth-led scooter tours of North Lawndale return this summer. *Chicago Sun-Times.*

Darling-Hammond, L. et. al., (May, 2008). Creating excellent and equitable schools. *Educational Leadership, 65*, 8, pp. 14–21.

Debord, G. (1967). *The Society of the Spectacle.* Cambridge, MA: Unredacted Word.

de Jong, E. J. (2008). Contextualizing policy appropriation: teachers' perspectives, local responses, and English-only ballot initiatives. *Urban Review: Issues and Ideas in Public Education, 40*, 4, pp. 350–370.

DePaul Newsroom Archive. (2011). *What are Maywood's Connections to the Underground Railroad? DePaul Archeologists Begin Excavating Answers.* Retrieved from http://wdat.is.depaul.edu/newsroom/year_2011/2400.html

Deuchler, D. (2004). *Maywood.* Chicago, IL: Arcadia Publishing.

Donato, R. & Hanson, J. (April 2017). "In these towns, Mexicans are classified as Negroes": the politics of unofficial segregation in the Kansas Public Schools, 1915–1935. *American Educational Research Journal, 54*, 1, pp. 53S–74S.

Donlon, R. & Whitaker, T. (2017). *The Hero Maker: How Superintendents Can Get Their School Boards to Do the Right Thing.* New York, NY: Routledge Press.

Downs, K. (July 14, 2021). Why aren't more people talking about Latinos killed by police? *The PBS News Hour.*

Duffy, J. (2020, September 23). Race and education in Oak Park, an introduction. *Wednesday Journal of Oak Park and River Forest.*

Duncan, O. D. & Duncan, B. (1957). *The Negro Population of Chicago.* University of Chicago Press.

Dwyer, J. (July 30, 2016). Violent Latin King street gang a widespread, ongoing threat. *Chronicle Media.*

Emerson &, M. O. & Woo, R. M. (2006). *People of the Dream: Multiracial Congregation in the United States.* Oxford: Oxford University Press.

Enchautegui, M. E. (1997). Latino neighborhoods and Latino neighborhood poverty. *Journal of Urban Affairs, 19*, 4, pp. 445–467.

Fairlie, R. W. (2002). Private schools and "Latino Flight" from Black schoolchildren. *Demography, 39*, 4, pp. 655–674.

Ferguson, A. A. (2001). *Bad Boys: Public Schools in the Making of Black Masculinity.* Ann Arbor, MI: University of Michigan Press.

Fernandez, L. (2012). *Brown in the Windy City: Mexicans and Puerto Ricans in Postwar Chicago.* Chicago, IL: University of Chicago Press.

Fishman, R. (2005). The fifth migration. *Journal of the American Planning Association, 71,* 4, pp. 357–366.

Flores, N. (2016). A tale of two visions: hegemonic whiteness and bilingual education. *Educational Policy, 30,* 1, pp. 13–38.

Foley, M. & Hoge, D. (2007). *Religion and the New Immigrants: Social Capital, Identity, and Civic Engagement.* 10.1093/acprof:oso/9780195188707.001.0001.

Foley, N. (1999). *The White Scourge. Mexicans, Blacks and Poor Whites in the Cotton Culture of Central Texas.* Berkeley, CA: University of California Press.

Forest Park Review Editorial Staff. (August 11, 2021). Mississippi catches up with Henderson. *Forest Park Review.*

Frankenberg, E., Lee, C. & Orfield, G. (2003). *A Multiracial Society with Segregated Schools: Are We Losing the Dream?* Cambridge, MA: Harvard University Press.

Franklin, S. & Seltzer, R. (2002). Conflicts in the coalition: challenges to Black and Latino political alliances. *Western Journal of Black Studies, 26,* pp. 75–88.

Ferguson, Ronald. (2008). Helping students of color meet high standards. In Mica Pollock (ed.), *Everyday Anti-Racism: Getting Real About Race in School.* Harvard Education Press, pp. 78–81.

Foster-Frau, S. (June 2, 2021). Latinos are disproportionately killed by police but often left out of the debate about brutality, some advocates say. *The Washington Post.*

Freire, P. (1998). *Teachers as Cultural Workers: Letters to Those Who Dare Teach.* Boulder, CO: Westview Press.

Gaines, L. (April 19, 2021). New Illinois law expands black history education — but how will it be taught? *Illinois Newsroom.*

Gay, C. (2006). Seeing difference: the effect of economic disparity on Black attitudes toward Latinos. *American Journal of Political Science, 50,* pp. 982–997.

Garza, M. M. (August 30, 1994). Latinos carve their own spot in the suburbs. *Chicago Tribune.*

Gates Jr., H. L. (September 2013). The first white man in Chicago was a Negro? *The Root.*

Gewertz, C. (May 31, 2006). Black, Hispanic teenagers report serious school woes. *Education Week.*

Gibson, R. (July 21, 1986). Maywood shooting maybe linked to drugs. *Chicago Tribune.*

Gilroy, P. (2000). *Against Race: Imagining Political Culture Beyond the Color Line.* Cambridge, MA: The Belknap Press.

Gilyard, K. (2011). *True to the Language Game: African American Discourse, Cultural Politics and Pedagogy.* London: Routledge Press.

Glanton, D. (March 6, 2009). New faces of immigration Latino evangelicals, kids left by deported parents push reforms. *Chicago Tribune.*

Gregory, T., Reyes, C., O'Connell, P. M. & Caputo, A. (October 25, 2017). Small lake, unequal rates: why our water rates are surging – and why black and poor suburbs pay more. *Chicago Tribune.*

Grenier, G., J. & Stepick, A. (1992). *Miami Now!* Gainesville, FL: University Press.

Griffin, B. (2002). Academic disidentification, race, and high school dropouts. *The High School Journal, 85*, 4, pp. 71–81.

Guarino, J. L. (2005). Maywood Illinois. *Encyclopedia of Chicago*.

Guinier, L. & Torres, G. (2002). *The Miner's Canary: Enlisting Race, Resisting Power, Transforming Democracy*. Cambridge, MA: Harvard University Press.

Gunderson, E. (September 5, 2021). Fred Hampton Jr. Seeks landmark designation for hampton house. *Chicago Tonight, PBS*. Retrieved from https://news.wttw.com /2021/09/05/fred-hampton-jr-seeks-landmark-designation-hampton-house

Haas, J. (2010). *The Assassination of Fred Hampton*. Chicago, IL: Lawrence Hill Books.

Hadi-Tabassum, S. (2006). *Language, Space and Power: A Critical Look at Bilingual Education*. Clevedon: Multilingual Matters.

Hamm, J. V., Brown, B. B. & Heck, D. J. (2005). Bridging the ethnic divide: student and school characteristics in African American, Asian-descent, Latino, and White adolescents' cross- ethnic friend nominations. *Journal of Research on Adolescence, 15, 1*, pp. 21–46.

Hanchard, M. (2018). *The Spectre of Race: How Discrimination Haunts Western Democracy*. Princeton, NJ: Princeton University Press.

Harootunian, H. (2010). "Modernity" and the Claims of Untimeliness. *Postcolonial Studies, 13*, 4, pp. 367–382.

Harris, R. (1994). Chicago's other suburbs. *Geographical Review, 84*, pp. 394–411.

Hatzipanagos, R. (August 27, 2020). Some Afro-Latinos say the phrase 'Latinos for Black Lives Matter' makes no sense. *The Washington Post*.

Hendrickson, M. (January 5, 2016). Workers settle lawsuit with Ferrara Candy for $1M. *Forest Park Review*.

Herguth, R. (June 19, 2019). Melrose Park cop dumped by Glen Ellyn after making a racial slur about Mexicans is now working in heavily Mexican Melrose Park. *Chicago Sun-Times*.

Hess, D. E. (2005). Moving beyond celebration: challenging curricular orthodoxy in the teaching of Brown and its legacies. *Teachers College Record, 107*, 9, pp. 2046–2067.

Hill, J. (January 18, 1998). Freedom's way station. *Chicago Tribune*.

Hinton, R, Spielman, F. & Malagon, E. (August 13, 2021). Political power up for grabs as populations shift — but some predict 'strong force to really flex Latino, Latina muscle'. *Chicago Sun Times*.

Holli, M. G. & Jones, P. (1995). *Ethnic Chicago: A Multicultural Portrait*. Grand Rapids, MI: Eerdmans Publishing.

Horn, C. L. & Kurlaender, M. (2006). *The End of Keyes: Resegregation Trends and Achievement in Denver Public Schools*. Cambridge, MA: The Civil Rights Project at Harvard University.

Hutchinson, E. O. (2007). *The Latino Challenge to Black America: Towards a Conversation between African Americans and Hispanics*. Los Angeles, CA: Middle Passage Press.

Hutchinson, J. N., Rodriguez, N. & Hagan, J. (1996). Community life: African Americans and multiethnic residential areas. *Journal of Black Studies, 27*, pp. 201–223.

Hwang, S. S. & Murdock, S. H. (1998). Racial attraction or racial avoidance in American suburbs? *Social Forces, 77*, 2, pp. 541–565.

Iaccarino, M. (2003). Science and culture. Western science could learn a thing or two from the way science is done in other cultures. *EMBO Reports, 4,3*, pp. 220–223. Doi:10.1038/sj.embor.embor781

Illinois Report Card 2019–2020. Operating Expense Per Pupil. Retrieved from http://www.illinoisreportcard.com

Illinois Workforce Advantage. Retrieved January 12, 2009, from http://www.illinois.gov/iwa

Ivy. M. (1995). *Discourses of the Vanishing.* Chicago, IL: University of Chicago Press.

Jackson, J. J. (1997). On Oakland's Ebonics. *The Black Scholar, 27*, pp. 18–25.

Jackson, K. (1987). *Crabgrass Frontier: The Suburbanization of the United States.* New York, NY: Oxford University Press.

Johnson, C. (2021). Huey P. Newton and the last days of the Black Colony. *Dissent, 68*, 3, pp. 173–186.

Jones, A. (2021, June 7). *Safe Passage Program.* Coalition for Spiritual and Public Leadership. Retrieved from https://action.groundswell-mvmt.org/petitions/safe-passage-program-maywood-il

Jones, P. & Holli, M. (1995). *Ethnic Chicago: A Multicultural Portrait.* Wm. B. Eerdmans Publishing Co.

Joyner, K. & Kao, G. (2000). School racial composition and adolescent racial homophily. *Social Science Quarterly, 81*, 3, pp. 810–825.

Jurca, C. (2001). *White Diaspora: The Suburb and the Twentieth-Century American Novel.* Princeton, NJ: Princeton University Press.

Jurkowsky, P. & Yang, R. (2006). Suburban development and economic segregation in the 1990s. *Journal of Urban Affairs, 28*, 3, pp. 253–273.

Kahloon, I. (July 26, 2021). Believe you me. *The New Yorker.*

Kapos, S., Perez Jr., J., Rayasam, R. & Li, M. (December 7, 2021). Black people are leaving Chicago en masse. It's changing the city's power politics. *Politico.*

Kaufmann, K. M. (2003). Cracks in the rainbow: commonality as a basis for Latino and African-American political coalitions. *Political Research Quarterly, 56, 2*, pp. 199–210.

Keating, A. D. (1988). *Building Chicago: Suburban Development and the Creation of a Divided Metropolis.* Columbus, OH: Ohio State University Press.

Kelly, N. J. & Kelly, J. M. (March 2005). Religion and Latino partisanship in the United States. *Political Research Quarterly, 58*, pp. 87–95.

Kelly, S. (2010). A crisis of authority in predominantly Black Schools? *Teachers College Record, 112*, 5, pp. 1247–74.

King, J. (2017). Morally Engaged research/ERS dismantling epistemological nihilation in the age of impunity. *Educational Researcher, 46*, 5, pp. 211–223.

Kneebone, E. (February 15, 2017). *The Changing Geography of US Poverty.* Brookings Institution.

Konstantopoulos, S. (2006). Trends of school effects on student achievement: evidence from NLS:72, HSB:82, and NELS:92. *Teachers College Record, 108*, pp. 2550–2581.

Koran, M. (June 25, 2020). 'We're suffering the same abuses': Latinos hear their stories echoed in police brutality protests. *The Guardian.*

Koval, J. (ed.) (2010). *Latinos in Chicago: Reflections of an American Landscape.* University of Norte Dame, The Institute for Latin Studies.

Kubota, J. T., Banaji, M. R. & Phelps, E. A. (2012). The neuroscience of race. *Nature Neuroscience,* 15, pp. 940–948.

Kvinta, L. & Aguiree, S. (2019). English learner rules and responsibilities. Illinois State Board of Education. Retrieved from https://www.isbe.net/Documents/EL -Rules-Responsibilities-English.pdf

Ladson-Billings, G. (2004). Landing on the wrong note: the price we paid for *Brown. Educational Researcher, 33,* 7, pp. 3–13.

Ladson-Billings, G. (2006). From the achievement gap to the educational debt: understanding achievement in U.S. Schools. *Educational Researcher, 35,* 7, pp. 3–12.

Latour, B. (2005). *Reassembling the Social: An Introduction to Actor-Network-Theory.* New York: Oxford University Press.

Lauber, D. (1989). Ending American Apartheid: how cities achieve and maintain racial diversity. *Planning Communications.* Retrieved from http://www.plannin gcommunications.com/Ending_American_Apartheid.pdf

Lee, C. D. (2008). The centrality of culture to the scientific study of learning and development: how an ecological framework in education research facilitates civic responsibility. *Educational Researcher, 37,* pp. 267–279.

Lee, J. & Bean, F. D. (2004). America's changing color lines: immigration, race/ ethnicity, and multiracial identification. *Annual Review of Sociology, 30,* pp. 221–242.

Lee, F. (February 1, 2003). New topic in Black studies debate: Latinos. *The New York Times.*

Lee, W. (November 22, 2021). Black residents leaving Chicago with few regrets. *Chicago Tribune.*

Lewis, A. (2003). Everyday race-making. *American Behavioral Scientist, 47,* pp. 283–305.

Lipman, P. (1997). Restructuring in context: a case study of teacher participation and the dynamics of ideology, race and power. *American Educational Research Journal, 34,* 1, pp. 3–38.

Loesberg, J. (1993). Bourdieu and the society of aesthetics. *ELH, 60,* 4, pp. 1033–1056. *Project MUSE.* doi:10.1353/elh.1993.0007.

Logan, J. R. (2002). *Separate and Unequal: The Neighborhood Gap for Blacks and Hispanics in Metropolitan America.* Lewis Mumford Center for Comparative Urban and Regional Research. Retrieved from https://files.eric.ed.gov/fulltext/ ED471515.pdf

Logan, J. R. (2004). *Resegregation in American Public Schools? Not in the 1990s.* Lewis Mumford Center for Comparative Urban and Regional Research. Retrieved from https://s4.ad.brown.edu/Projects/usschools/reports/report1.pdf

Logan, J. R., Stults, B. & Farley, R. (2004). The segregation of minorities in the Metropolis: two decades of change. *Demography, 41,* 1, pp. 1–22.

Logan, J. R. (n.d.). *The New Ethnic Enclaves in America's Suburbs*. Lewis Mumford Center for Comparative Urban and Regional Research. Retrieved from http://mumford.albany.edu/census/suburban/suburbanreport/subreport.pdf

Lotus, J. (2017, March 7). "Welcoming" ordinances get mixed reviews in suburban Cook. *Cook County Chronicler*. Retrieved from https://chronicleillinois.com/news/cook-county-news/welcoming-ordinances-get-mixed-reviews-suburban-cook/

Louie, V. S. (2004). *Compelled to Excel: Immigration, Education and Opportunity Among Chinese Americans*. Stanford, CA: Stanford University Press.

Luke, A. (April 2017). On the race of teachers and students: a reflection on experience, scientific evidence, and silence. *American Educational Research Journal, 54*, 1S, pp. 102S–110S.

Mack, K. (January 24, 2010). More poor living in the suburbs, study says. *Chicago Tribune*.

Magnuson, K. and Waldfogel, J. (eds.) (2008). *Steady Gains and Stalled Progress: Inequality and the Black-White Test Score Gap*. New York, NY: Russell Sage Foundation.

Martin, D., Martin, M., Gibson, S. S. & Wilkins, J. (2007). Increasing prosocial behavior and academic achievement among adolescent African American males. *Adolescence, 42*, 168, pp. 690–699.

Martin, A. (February 9, 2021). Who was Fred Hampton? *Chicago Sun Times*.

Martínez, R. (2002). *Crossing Over: A Mexican Family on the Migrant Trail*. London: Picador Publishing.

Martinez, M. (November 3, 2006). Longtime advocate for the homeless enlists in the Minuteman Project to fight illegal immigration, ranking Latinos, many blacks. *Chicago Tribune*.

Martinez, D. (2017). Imagining a language of solidarity for Black and Latinx youth in English language arts classrooms. *English Education, 49*, 2, pp. 179–196.

Massey, D. (2001). Residential segregation and neighborhood conditions in U.S. Metropolitan Areas. In Smelser, N. J., Wilson, W. J. and Mitchell, F. (eds.), *America Becoming: Racial Trends and Consequences*. Washington, DC: National Academy Press, pp. 391–434.

Massey, D. & Anderson, E. (eds.) (2001). *Problem of the Century: Racial Stratification in the United States at Century's End*. New York, NY: Russell Sage Foundation.

Maxham, M. (March 20, 2021). D209 official alleges libel against superintendent, fellow school board members. *Forest Park Review*.

Maxham, M. (June 23, 2021). How Patrick Hardy worked to reclaim Proviso East. *Forest Park Review*.

Maxham, M. & Romain, M. (March 2, 2021). D209 braces for changes made in fell swoop. *Forest Park Review*.

Maxwell, L. (August 20, 2014). US Schools Become "Majority Minority". *Education Week*.

McMillen, D. (2003). *Employment Subcenters in Chicago: Past, Present, and Future*. Retrieved from https://www.chicagofed.org/publications/economic-perspectives/2003/2qeppart1

McMillan, D. W. & Chavis, D. M. (1986). Sense of community: a definition and theory. *Journal of Community Psychology, 14*, 1, pp. 6–23.

McPherson, M., Smith-Lovin, L. & Cook, J. (2001). Birds of a feather: homophily in social networks. *Annual Review of Sociology, 27*, 1, pp. 415–444.

Medina, C. (March 13, 2021). My apologies to the Proviso Township Citizens. *Forest Park Review.*

Meir, K. J., McClain, P. D., Polinard, J. L. & Wrinkle, R. D. (2004). Divided or Together? conflict and cooperation between African Americans and Latinos. *Political Research Quarterly, 57*, 3, pp. 399–409.

Meissner, C. A., and Brigham, J. C. (2001). Thirty years of investigating the own-race bias in memory for faces: a meta-analysis review. *Psychology, Public Policy, and Law* 7, pp. 3–35. doi:10.1037//1076-8971.7.1.3

Mendall, D. & Little, D. (February 16, 2006). Change hits many inner suburbs. *Chicago Tribune.*

Michaeli, E. (January 11, 2016). Bound for the promised land. *The Atlantic.*

Mills, D. J. (1997). Bashing Black English. *Commonwealth, 124*, pp. 10–11.

Mihalopoulos, D. (September 28, 2020). How Michael Madigan went to bat for the wife and mother of the chairman investigating The ComEd scandal. *WBEZ.*

Mindiola, T., Niemann Flores, Y. & Rodriguez, N. (2003). *Black-Brown Relations and Stereotypes.* Austin, TX: University of Texas Press.

Mitchell, R. (December 4, 2019). The police raid that killed two Black Panthers, shook Chicago and changed the nation. *The Washington Post.*

McClain, P. D., Meier, K. J. & Polinard, J. L. (2004). Divided or together? Conflict and cooperation between African Americans and Latinos. *Political Research Quarterly, 57*, 3, pp. 399–409.

McMillen, D. P. (2003). Employment subcenters in Chicago: past, present and future. *Economic Perspectives, 27*, 2, pp. 2–14.

Moll, L. (2010). Mobilizing culture, language, and educational practices: fulfilling the promises of *Mendez* and *Brown. Educational Researcher, 39*, 6, pp. 451–460.

Murphy, A. K. (2007). The Suburban Ghetto: the legacy of Herbert Gans in understanding the experience of poverty in recently impoverished American Suburbs. *City & Community, 6*, 1, pp. 21–37.

Myers, J. & Forte, L. (2008, May-June). Not just Chicago anymore. *Catalyst Chicago.*

Nadeau, R., Niemi, R. & Levine, J. (1993). Innumeracy about minority populations. *Public Opinion Quarterly, 57*, pp. 332–347.

National Center for Education Statistics. (2017). Racial/ethnic enrollment in Public Schools. Retrieved from https://nces.ed.gov/programs/coe/indicator/cge/racial-ethnic-enrollment

National Gang Center. (2022). National youth gang survey analysis. Retrieved from https://nationalgangcenter.ojp.gov/survey-analysis

Nausheen, H., Rockett, D., Christen, J. A. & Brinson, J. (July 27, 2020). Disinvestment in Black and Latino Chicago neighborhoods is rooted in policy. Here's how these communities continue to be held back. *Chicago Tribune.*

Negrette, G. M. (2021). "He looks like a monster": kindergarten children, racial perceptions, and systems of socialization in dual language education. *Race Ethnicity and Education*. doi:10.1080/13613324.2021.1924138

New Communities Program. (January 24, 2007). Lawndales unite and say 'no' to violence. Retrieved March, 2010, from http://www.newcommunities.org

Neikirk, B. (October 15, 1985). City-style problems moving to the suburbs. *Chicago Tribune*.

Neikirk, B. (October 16, 1985). Old suburbs mimic parent cities. *Chicago Tribune*.

Nespor, J. (1994). *Knowledge in Motion: Space, Time and Curriculum in Undergraduate Physics and Management*. London: Falmer Press.

Nickeas, P. (September 18, 2011). 4 wounded, 1 fatally, in Maywood shootings. *Chicago Tribune*.

Nieto del Rio, G. (May 14, 2021). What is DACA? Where does it stand now? *New York Times*.

Nyquist, R. (2000). An industrial suburb faces the depression: Maywood, Illinois in the 1930s. *EIU Historia*. Retrieved from https://www.eiu.edu/historia/nyquist.pdf

Oakes, J. (1995). Two cities' tracking and within-school segregation. *Teachers College Record, 96*, 4, pp. 681–690.

Oakes, J. (March 2008). Keeping track: structuring equality and inequality in an era of accountability. *Teachers College Record, 110*, 3, pp. 700–712.

O'Connor, C., Lewis, A. & Mueller, J. (2007). Researching "Black" educational experiences and outcomes: theoretical and methodological considerations. *Educational Researcher, 36*, 9, pp. 541–552.

Ogbu, J. (2008). *Minority Status, Oppositional Culture, & Schooling*. New York: Routledge.

Olivo, A & Avila, O. (November 1, 2005). Latinos choosing suburbs over city. *Chicago Tribune*.

Opie, F. D. (2008). Eating, dancing, and courting in New York Black and Latino relations, 1930–1970. *Journal of Social History, 42*, 1, 7, pp. 9–109.

Orfield, G. & Lee, C. (2006). *Racial Transformation and the Changing Nature of Segregation*. Cambridge, MA: The Civil Rights Project at Harvard University.

Orfield, M. (1998). *Chicago Metropolitics: A Regional Agenda for Members of the U.S. Congress*. Retrieved from https://www.brookings.edu/wp-content/uploads/2016/06/congrep6.pdf

Orfield, M. (2003). *American Metropolitics: The New Suburban Reality*. Washington, DC: Brookings Institution Press.

Ori, R. (January 7, 2020). Amazon plans distribution center on site of former Maywood racetrack. *Chicago Tribune*.

Ortiz, P. (2021). *An African American and Latinx History of the United States*. Boston, MA: Beacon Press.

Pacyga, D. (2009). *Chicago: A Biography*. Chicago, IL: University of Chicago Press.

Page, C. (February 8, 2004). Unspoken conflicts: America's Blacks and Latinos are struggling with a new racial paradigm for the new century. *Chicago Tribune*.

Palmer, D. K. (2010). Race, power, and equity in a multiethnic urban elementary school with a dual- language "strand" program. *Anthropology & Education Quarterly, 41,* pp. 94–114.

Park, J. (2012). It takes a village (or an ethnic economy): the varying roles of socio-economic status, religion and social capital in SAT preparation for Chinese and Korean American Students. *American Educational Research Journal, 49,* 4, pp. 624–650.

Pastor, M., Jr. (2000). Geography and opportunity. In Smelser, N. J., Wilson, W. J. & Mitchell, F. (eds.), *America Becoming: Racial Trends and Their Consequences.* Washington, DC: National Academy Press, pp. 435–467.

Pearson, G. R. (2016). *The Democratization of Food: Tin Cans and the Growth of the American Food Processing Industry, 1810–1940.* Lehigh University Press.

Perez, L. R. (June 3, 2020). 'This is a step back.' Latino activists speak out about racial tension with black Chicagoans on Southwest Side amid George Floyd fallout. *Chicago Tribune.*

Pettigrew, T. F. (1998). Intergroup contact theory. *Annual Review of Psychology, 49,* pp. 65–85.

Pew Hispanic Center. (2007). *Changing Faiths: Latinos and the Transformation of American Religion.*

Pew Research Center. (January 31, 2008). *Do Blacks and Hispanics Get Along?* Retrieved from https://www.pewresearch.org/social-trends/2008/01/31/do-blacks -and-hispanics-get-along/

Piatt, B. (1997). *Black and Brown in America. The Case for Cooperation.* New York, NY: New York University Press.

Pierce, C. (April 2017). W.E.B. DuBois and caste education: racial capitalist schooling from reconstruction to Jim Crow. *American Educational Research Journal, 54,* 1S, pp. 23S–48S.

Pastor, M., Jr. (2000). Geography and opportunity. In Smelser, N. J., Wilson, W. J. & Mitchell, F. (eds.), *America Becoming: Racial Trends and Their Consequences.* Washington, DC: National Academy Press, pp. 435–467.

Pollock, M. (2017). *Schooltalk: Rethinking What We Say About and To Students Everyday.* New York, NY: The New Press.

Pollock, M. (2005a). *Colormute: Race Talk Dilemmas in an American School.* Princeton, NJ: Princeton University Press.

Pollock, M. (2005b). Keeping on keeping on: OCR and complaints of racial discrimination 50 years after brown. *Teachers College Record, 107,* 9, pp. 2106–2140.

Proviso Township High School. (2021). *Email that Board President Rodney Alexander Received from Board Member Claudia Medina.* Retrieved from https://www .pths209.org/

Quillian, L. & Campbell, M. E. (2003). Beyond Black and White: the present and future of multiracial friendship segregation. *American Sociological Review, 68,* pp. 540–566.

Rainie, L., Keeter, S. & Perrin, A. (2019). *Trust and Distrust in America.* Pew Research Center. Retrieved from https://www.pewresearch.org/politics/2019/07/22 /trust-and-distrust-in-america/

Ratnesar, R. (1997). The next big divide? *Time Magazine, 150*, p. 23.

Rehkamp, P. & Placko, D. (April 23, 2015). Melrose Park Mayor's conflict-of-interest question. Retrieved from http://www.bettergov.org/news/melrose-park-mayor %E2%80%99s-conflict-of-interest-question

Rhodes, J. (2017). *Framing the Black Panthers: The Spectacular Rise of a Black Power Icon.* Chicago, IL: University of Illinois Press.

Rice, J. (February 27, 2018). Eyewitness to 1960s racial fissure at Proviso East. *Forest Park Review.*

Roach, J. (September 3, 2017). New FBI stats show 35% decrease in reported crime in Maywood. *Village Free Press.*

Robinson, C. (1997). *Black Movements in America.* New York, NY: Routledge Press.

Rocha, R. R. (2007). Black-Brown coalitions in local school board elections. *Political Research Quarterly, 60*, pp. 315–327.

Rodriguez, C. (2000). *Changing Race: Latinos, the Census, and the History of Ethnicity in the United States.* New York, NY: New York University Press.

Rodriguez, E. (2021). How does the Black Lives Matter movement affect Latinos? *Hispanic Network: A Latino Business & Employment Magazine.* Retrieved from https://hnmagazine.com/2020/08/how-does-the-black-lives-matter-movement -affect-latinos

Rodriguez, I. (2007). Telling stories of Latino population growth in the United States: Narratives of inter-ethnic conflict on the mainstream, Latino and African-American press. *Journalism, 8*, pp. 573–590.

Rodriguez, R. (2003). "Blaxicans" and other reinvented Americans. *Chronicle of Higher Education, 50*, p. 3.

Roeder, D. (August 17, 2021). Businesses and minorities hit hardest by latest tax bills, county report says. *The Chicago Sun-Times.*

Rolland-Diamond, C. (2019). Black power on campus: challenging the Status Quo in Chicago '68', *European Journal of American Studies*, pp. 14–1.

Romain, M. (April 5, 2016). A homegrown filmmaker shoots movie scene in Maywood, but not before prompting image concerns. *Village Free Press.*

Romain, M. (June 12, 2018). Maywood has a small part in Chicago crime commission's gang book. *Village Free Press.*

Romain, M. (March 24, 2019). Maywood parents get 'smart' about students' routes to, from school. *Village Free Press.*

Romain, M. (April 9, 2019). *"This is a Community Crisis".* Forest Park Review.

Romain, M. (June 28, 2019). As it builds new facility, trucking company unearths pieces of Maywood's Past. *Village Free Press.*

Romain, M. (June 14, 2020). Around Proviso, protesters call for racism's end. *Village Free Press.*

Romain, M. (September 23, 2020). D209 board replaces Vice President. *Village Free Press.*

Romain, M. (February 24, 2021). Grappling with race, OPRF Chamber forges allies. *Wednesday Journal of Oak Park and River Forest.*

Romain, M. (May 20, 2021). New Maywood Mayor, Board and Clerk Lay Out Priorities. *Village Free Press.*

Romain, M. (August 13, 2021). Recent Illinois school report card data shows Latinos now the largest ethnic/racial group in District 89, fastest growing group in Maywood. *Village Free Press.*

Romain, M. (August 24, 2021). About those property taxes ... *Wednesday Journal of Oak Park and River Forest.*

Romain, M. (September 25, 2021). Maywood hoists Mexican Flag, passes proclamation for national Hispanic heritage month. *Village Free Press.*

Romain, M. (October 17, 2021). After D209 stops live-streaming meetings, a growing movement fills the void. *Village Free Press.*

Romain, M. (October 17, 2021). 'You've got living, real history right here!' Hampton Jr. says at panther commemoration. *Village Free Press.*

Ronquillo, J., Denson, T. F., Lickel, B., Lu, Z. L., Nandy, A. & Maddox, K. B. (2007). The effects of skin tone on race-related amygdala activity: an fMRI investigation. *Social Cognitive and Affective Neuroscience, 2,* 1, pp. 39–44. doi:10.1093/scan/nsl043

Rose, T. (1994). *Black Noise: Black Music and Rap Culture in Contemporary America.* Middletown, CT: Wesleyan University Press.

Rosenhall, L. (May 7, 2021). California's attempt to reduce police shootings, explained. *CalMatters.*

Rozas, A. (July 18, 2004). 20 slayings sets Maywood record. *Chicago Tribune.*

Rumberger, R. W. & Palardy, G. J. (2005). Does segregation still matter? the impact of student composition on academic achievement in high school. *Teachers College Record, 107,* 9, pp. 1999–2045.

Rury, J. L. & Rife, A. T. (2018). Race, schools and opportunity hoarding: evidence from a post-war American metropolis. *History of Education, 47,* 1, pp. 87–107.

Sabino, P. (June 16, 2020). How violence interrupters brokered an end to Anti-Black attacks in a Latino neighborhood. *Block Club Chicago.*

Sanchez-Walsh, A. (2003). *Latino Pentecostal Identity.* New York, NY: Columbia University Press.

Schelling, T. (1971). Dynamic models of segregation. *Journal of Mathematical Sociology, 1,* pp. 143–186.

Schmid, C. L. (2001). *The Politics of Language: Conflict, Identity and Cultural Pluralism in Comparative Perspective.* New York, NY: Oxford University Press.

Schuba, T. (February 6, 2021). Melrose Park Mayor Ronald Serpico used slur while berating resident. *Chicago Sun-Times.*

Schwartz, R. (1997). "The Curse of Cain: The Violent Legacy of Monotheism" a study of identity and violence in the Hebrew Bible, was nominated for a Pulitzer Prize.

Seaton, E. K., Quintana, S., Verkuyten, M. & Gee, G. C. (May/June 2017). Peers, policies, and place: the relation between context and ethnic/racial identity. *Child Development, 88,* 3, pp. 683–692.

Seidel, J. (July 26, 2016). In major Latin Kings Raid, Maywood, Melrose Park implicated. *The Chicago Sun-Times.*

Shah, H. & Thornton, M. (1994). Racial ideology in U.S. mainstream news magazine coverage of the Black-Latino interaction, 1980–1992. *Critical Studies in Mass Communication, 11,* 141–161.

Sharma, N. (2010). *Hip-Hop Desis: South Asian Americans, Blackness, and a Global Race Consciousness.* Durham, NC: Duke University Press.

Shekarey, A. & Rahimi, A. (2006). The consequences of the binary opposition/ continuation approaches to modernism and postmodernism: a critical educational study. *Tamara Journal of Critical Postmodern Organization, 5,* 5.1 and 5.2, p. 63.

Shields, N. S. & Lin II, R.-G. (May 27, 2005). Another Brawl at Jefferson High. *Los Angeles Times.*

Sjostrom, J. (May 31, 2005). Once-bustling land to yield jobs again. *Chicago Tribune.*

Smelser, N. J., Wilson, W. J. & Mitchell, F. (eds.) (2000). *America Becoming: Racial Trends and Their Consequences.* Washington, DC: National Academy Press.

Smith, N. A., Voisin, D. R., Yang J. P. & Tung, E. L. (2019). Keeping your guard up: hypervigilance among urban residents affected by community and police violence. *Health Aff (Millwood), 38,* 10, pp. 1662–1669. doi:10.1377/hlthaff.2019.00560

Soja, E. (1996). *Thirdspace.* Oxford: Blackwell Publishing.

South, S. J. & Crowder, K. L. (1997). Residential mobility between cities and suburbs: race, suburbanization, and back-to-city moves. *Demography, 34,* pp. 525–538.

Stanley, D., Phelps, E. A. & Banaji, M. R. (2008). The neural basis of implicit attitudes. *Current Perspectives in Psychological Science, 17,* 2, pp. 164–170.

Steele, C. (1997). A threat in the air: how stereotypes shape intellectual identity and performance. *American Psychologist, 52,* pp. 613–629.

Stilgoe, J. R. (1988). *Borderland; Origins of the American Suburb, 1820–1939.* New Haven, CT: Yale University Press.

Stout, C. & LeMee, G. L. (July 22, 2021). Efforts to restrict teaching about racism and bias have multiplied across the U.S. *Chalkbeat.*

Suarez-Orozco, C. & Suarez-Orozco, M. (2001). *Children of Immigration.* Cambridge, MA: Harvard University Press.

Sue, D. W., Capodilupo, C., Torino, G. C., Bucceri, J. M., Holder, A. M. B., Nadal, K. L. & Esquilin, M. (2007). Racial microaggressions in everyday life: implications for clinical practice. *American Psychologist, 62,* 4, pp. 271–286.

Suro, R. (1999). *Strangers Among Us: Latinos' Lives in a Changing America.* New York, NY: Vintage.

Swarns, R. (October 3, 2006). Bridging a racial rift that isn't black and white. *The New York Times.*

Synder, T. (July 4, 2021). Forced forgetting. *New York Times Magazine.*

Talbot. M. (October 8, 2021). The increasingly wild world of school-board meetings. *The New Yorker.*

Tate, W. F. (2008). 'Geography of opportunity': poverty, place and educational outcomes. *Educational Researcher, 37,* pp. 397–411.

Tate, W. F. (ed.) (2012). *Research on Schools, Neighborhoods and Communities: Toward Civic Responsibility.* Lanham, MD: Rowman & Littlefield Publishers, Inc.

The Chicago Reporter. (September 3, 2021). *Census 2020: "Black People Aren't Leaving Chicago...They're Being Forced Out".*

Trottie, N. (September 21, 2017). Sister of slain 14-yr-old asks 'does Maywood even care'. *West Suburban Journal.*

Tshidzumba, N. A. (2019). Sharp Sharp: beyond slang to social cohesion among youth. *Gender & Behavior, 17*, 1, pp. 12330–12336.

Turner, G. T. (2001). *The Underground Railroad in Illinois.* Glen Ellyn, IL: Newman Educational Publishing.

Umansky, I., Valentino, R. & Reardon, S. F. (2015). *The Promise of Bilingual and Dual Immersion Education* (CEPA Working Paper No.15–11). Retrieved from Stanford Center for Education Policy Analysis. Retrieved from http://cepa.stanford.edu/wp15-11

U.S. Census Bureau. (2010). *American FactFinder Fact Sheet.* Retrieved January 31, 2010, from http://factfinder.census.gov.

U.S. Census Bureau. (2019). *Quick Facts.* Retrieved June 23, 2019, from https://www.census.gov/quickfacts/fact/table/US/PST045221

Vaca, N. C. (2004). *The Presumed Alliance: The Unspoken Conflict Between Latinos and Blacks and What It Means for America.* New York, NY: HarperCollins.

Valdés, G. (1996). *Con Respeto: Bridging the Distances Between Culturally Diverse Families and Schools: An Ethnographic Portrait.* New York, NY: Teachers College Press.

Valdés, G. (1997). Dual language immersion programs: a cautionary note concerning the education of language-minority students. *Harvard Educational Review, 67*, 3, pp. 391–429.

Vang, C. T. (2005). Minority students are far from academic success and still at-risk in public schools. *Multicultural Education, 12*, pp. 1–7.

Village Free Press. (December 4, 1969). *A Brief, But Revolutionary Life.*

Village of Maywood. (2021). *Maywood Chamber of Commerce.* Retrieved from https://www.maywood-il.org/Community-(1)/Our-History.aspx

Von Hoffman, A. (2004). *House by House, Block by Block: The Rebirth of America's Urban Neighborhoods.* Oxford: Oxford Press.

Walser, N. (2009). *The Essential School Board Book.* Boston, MA: Harvard Education Press.

Washington Dual Language Academy. (2022). *About Our School.* Retrieved from https://washington.maywood89.org/

Watkins, N. D., Larson, R. W. & Sullivan, P. J. (2007). Bridging intergroup difference in a community youth program. *American Behavioral Scientist, 51*, 3, pp. 380–402.

Weil, F. D., Barton, M., Rackin, H., Valasik, M. & Maddox, D. (2019). Collective resources and violent crime reconsidered: New Orleans before and after Hurricane Katrina. *Journal of Interpersonal Violence.* doi:10.1177/0886260518822345.

West Suburban Journal. (2017). *Maywood Considers Becoming Sanctuary City.* Retrieved May 12, 2021, from https://westsuburbanjournal.com/maywood-considers-becoming-sanctuary-city/.

Wickenden, D. (May 27, 2021). The Democratic Party, Reimagined by Young Progressives. *The New Yorker.*

Wiese, A. (1999). The other suburbanites: African American suburbanization in the North before 1950. *Journal of American History, 85*, pp. 1495–1524.

Wiese, A. (2005). *Places of Their Own: African American Suburbanization in the Twentieth Century.* Chicago, IL: University of Chicago Press.

Widener, D. (1998). The world is waiting for the sunrise: African Americans y el mundo latino. *Social Justice, 25*, 3, pp. 101–107.

Williams, A. (November 28, 2013). [chicagoheatdvd] *Only the Strong Survive.* Retrieved from https://www.youtube.com/watch?v=GGwZ0-p8kGM

Williams, T. R. (1966). The study of change as a concept in cultural anthropology. *Theory Into Practice, 5*, 1, pp. 13–19. Retrieved from http://www.jstor.org/stable /1475871

Williams, T. M. (2018). Do no harm: strategies for culturally relevant caring in middle level classrooms from the community experiences and life histories of Black middle level teachers. *Research in Middle Level Education Online, 41*, 6, pp. 1–13.

Wilson, W. J. (1997). *When Work Disappears: The World of the New Urban Poor.* New York, NY: Vintage Books.

Wilson, W. J. (2006). *There Goes the Neighborhood.* New York, NY: Vintage Books.

Woodyard, E. (February 28, 2020). Bucks' Sterling Brown carries on legacy of late activist Fred Hampton: 'It's in His DNA.' *Andscape.* Retrieved from https://and-scape.com/features/bucks-sterling-brown-carries-on-legacy-of-late-activist-fred-hampton-its-in-his-dna/

Wright, R. L. (Winter 1998). Sociolinguistic and ideological dynamics of the Ebonics controversy. *The Journal of Negro Education, 67*, 1, pp. 5–15.

Wright, S. C. & Tropp, L. R. (2005). Language and intergroup contact: investigating the impact of bilingual instruction on children's intergroup attitudes. *Group Processes & Intergroup Relations, 8*, 3, pp. 309–328.

Yancey, G. (2003). *Who is White? Latinos, Asians and the New Black/Nonblack Divide.* Boulder, CO: Lynne Reinner Publishers.

Yarbrough, K. (May 2022). ORDINANCE NO. CO-2022-10. Retrieved on June 25, 2022, from https://maywood-il.org/getattachment/3b3c1f8c-46ac-4fa5-b4c0 -3c95f67a543b/CO-2022-10.aspx

Yosso, T. (2005). Whose culture has capital? A critical race theory discussion of community cultural wealth. *Race, Ethnicity and Education, 8*, 1, pp. 69–91.

Young, D. & Callahan, N. (1981). Fill the heavens with commerce: Chicago aviation, 1855–1926. Chicago, IL: Chicago Review Press.

Young, S. G. & Hugenberg, K. (2012). Individuation motivation and face experience can operate jointly to produce the own-race bias. *Soc Psychol Personal Science, 3*, pp. 80–87.

Yull, D. (2014). Race has always mattered: an intergenerational look at race, space, place, and educational experiences of Blacks. *Education Research International*, pp. 1–13. doi:10.1155/2014/683035

Zakaria, R. (2021). *Against White Feminism.* New York, NY: W. W. Norton & Company, Inc.

Zhai, E. & Strokes, C. E. (2009). Ethnic, family, and social contextual influences on Asian American adolescents' religiosity. *Sociological Spectrum, 29*, pp. 201–226.

Zhou, M. (2009). How neighborhoods matter for immigrant children: the formation of educational resources in Chinatown, Koreatown, and Pico Union, Los Angeles. *Journal of Ethnic and Migration Studies, 35*, 7, pp. 1153–1179.

Zhou, M. & Bankston, C. L. (1998). *Growing Up American: The Adaptation of Vietnamese adolescents in the United States.* New York: Russell Sage Foundation.

Zhou, M. & Kim, S. (2006). Community forces, social capital, and educational achievement: the case of supplementary education in the Chinese and Korean immigrant communities. *Harvard Educational Review, 76,* pp. 1–29.

Zielinski, G. (December 11, 1996). *More Poor Children Found Living in Suburbia These Days.* Chicago Tribune.

Index

Note: Italic page numbers refer to figures and tables. Page numbers followed by "n" denote endnotes.

and Latinx communities, 7; at leadership table, 15; of Maywood, 18; patriarchs for, 166; resent economic leapfrogging, 13; self-fulfilling prophecy, 52; theoretical framework of civic education, 137; variability of race attitudes within, 134

Black cultural straddlers, 85

Black dialect, 11; getting treated, tweaking, and going Spanish, 78–92; in Latinx community, 81; *vs.* Standard English, 23

Black diaspora, 15

Black Gangster Disciples, 51, 121

Black homeownership, 45, 46

Black identity, 93; development of, 27

Black-Latinx communities, 30

Black-Latinx dual language programs, 69

Black-Latinx interaction, 12

Black-Latinx political conflicts, 10

Black/Latinx race relations, 26; research on, 6–7

Black leadership, in high school district, 174

Black Lives Matter (BLM) movement, 29, 98, 128–30, 187

Black middle-class communities, 55

Black Movements in America (Robinson), 190

Black neighborhoods, human capital in, 105

Blackness, 15, 18, 20, 77, 96, 166

Black Panther Party, 186, 187, 190, 191

Black political machine, 183, 184, 192

Black population, 4, 43; in Chicago, 102; in North Lawndale, 7, 8; residential segregation between white and, 5; white community to control, 165

Black Power Movement, 71, 190

Black Radicalism, 191

Black radical tradition, 190

Black students: in American public schools, 8; challenges with academic

English, 90; communicative flexibility between Latinx and, 82; cross-race friendships, 84; enrolled in public schools, 4; interracial conflicts, 97; perspective of academic literacy and language for, 91; physically and verbally active participation of, 77; population of, 18; race and poverty for, 6; racial and cultural boundaries between, 124; segregation of, 9; transgressions of, 78

Black suburban migration, 110

Black suburbs, 102, 110

Black teachers, 65, 66; hiring of, 98; interviewed for study, 76, 77; usage of Spanish, 80

"Blaxican" identity, 23

"block-by-block" segregation, 46

Bloom, Joshua: *Black Against Empire*, 185

blue-collar suburbs, establishment of, 43

Bobo, Kim: *Wage Theft in America: Why Millions of Working Americans Are Not Getting Paid—And What We Can Do About It*, 148–49

Boisvert, Daniel R. and Thiede, Ralf: *Language, Mind and Power*, 100

Bourdieu, Pierre, 106

Boykin, Wade, 78

Brandon, Isiah, 141

Briggs, J. E., 56

Brockenbrough, E., 166

Brookings Institution, 20

Brown/Black relations: Black dialect, 78–92; differences from within group, 92–96; los morenos and Mexicans, 72–78

Brown v. Board of Education, 8, 9, 11, 46, 53

Byrd-Bennett, Barbara, 99

Canaan African Methodist Episcopal (A.M.E.), 44

Casta Painting, *16*

About the Authors

Samina Hadi-Tabassum is an associate professor at Erikson Institute in Chicago. She teaches graduate courses in cognitive and language development. Her research and publications focus on the intersection of race, language, and culture. She is a mother of three children and lives in Oak Park, Illinois, with her extended family.

Persis Driver is an assistant professor of developmental and educational psychology at Dominican University, Illinois. She has worked with children and adolescents in multiple global educational contexts and her research and practice are grounded in the principles of equity, diversity, and justice.

www.ingramcontent.com/pod-product-compliance
Lightning Source LLC
Chambersburg PA
CBHW071854270326
41929CB00013B/2229